This Is Not A Game

A Guide to Alternate Reality Gaming

By Dave Szulborski

ISBN: 1-4116-2595-1

Published by New-Fiction Publishing

www.new-fiction.com

Dedication

This Is Not A Game is dedicated first and foremost to my family, for always believing in me and for encouraging and reminding me to enjoy life. For my parents, who taught me that success lies in doing what you love, not in what pays the best. For my brothers and sister, who taught me that family bonds can grow stronger through the years, despite miles between us and different lives to lead. For my children and grandchildren, who gave me the strength to carry on through the darkest of times. For my late wife Rose, who passed away much too young, but will live on in our hearts forever. And finally, for Brittany and Cole, who proved to me that miracles do happen, and that strength, hope, and courage sometimes come in the smallest of packages.

Secondly, This Is Not A Game is dedicated to the **Urban Hunt** Puppetmaster team – Dee, Becca, Diandra, Rick, and Paul – who made my latest excursion into the land of Alternate Reality Gaming enjoyable and memorable. I miss our Tuesday night meetings.

Dave Szulborski

January 1, 2005

Acknowledgements

This Is Not A Game would not have been possible without the work and contributions of many people including:

· Joseph Matheny, who edited, encouraged, organized, and marketed the book. He also contributed the Appendix relating to cooperative writing projects.

· Steve Peters, the owner of ARGN.com, who contributed a section in Chapter 15 looking ahead at the future of ARGs.

· Ben Mack, award winning magician and advertising guru, who wrote Appendix E, "The Structure of Magic."

· Dee Cook, one of my fellow Puppetmasters from my latest game **Urban Hunt**. She contributed a personal reflection on the game creation experience in Appendix C.

· Paul Melamud, another of my fellow Puppetmasters from **Urban Hunt**. Paul contributed a detailed analysis of one of the puzzles he created for the game in Appendix D.

Thank you to each and every one of the above people who made This Is Not A Game possible. I hope the book inspires many new Alternate Reality Gaming fans and Puppetmasters long into the future.

Table of Contents

Introduction

Imagine an event so powerful, so pervasive, that years after the initial exposure people who participated in it still gather to talk about it and long for the days when it actually took place. An event that participants willingly gave months of their lives to, without any thought of reward or recognition, in a collective effort to help others. How would you classify such an event, what would you call it, and how would you go about understanding it? Would you think it was something religious or spiritual, or perhaps even cultish?

What if the event itself never took place but was entirely fictional? A carefully constructed and deliberate attempt to deceive people while promoting a secret agenda. And, to make it even more difficult to comprehend, the participants came to know that they were indeed being misled, and still reminisce about the event as one of the most enjoyable things in their lives. Maybe now you would think it was some sort of mind control or conspiracy on a grand scale. And you wouldn't be too far wrong.

In April 2001, observant people attending the Steven Spielberg movie **A.I.: Artificial Intelligence** noticed a curious listing in the movie's credits that seemed strangely out of place amidst the listings for Best Boy, Stunt Man, and the other familiar positions required to make a feature film. The listing read "Jeanine Salla, Sentient Machine Therapist." Many people who saw it passed it off as a playful inside joke, a tongue-in-cheek nod at the artificial intelligence themes of the movie itself, until some other small and intriguing clues were also discovered. This time, the clues were small letters on the back of the movie's promotional posters, some circled in silver spelling out the phrase, "Evan Chan was murdered," and others, outlined in gold squares, yielding the message, "Jeanine is the key." Googling the name "Jeanine Salla" led to a series of intricately detailed and highly realistic websites and eventually led thousands of people to get involved, trying to figure out who killed the fictional character Evan Chan.

When it was all said and done three months later, somewhere between seven and ten thousand people had joined the collective effort to solve the mystery, while hundreds of thousands (perhaps millions) more were exposed to **the Beast**, as it retrospectively came to be known, through the massive media coverage and Internet buzz it generated. Afterwards, almost universally, the dedicated core of approximately eight thousand participants, who named themselves "the Cloudmakers" early in their quest, declared it one of the most unique, exciting, and enjoyable things they had ever been a part of. And this was in spite of the fact that they had learned that the whole thing had been a promotional vehicle, a marketing campaign to publicize the **A.I.** movie itself. Judging from the lack of success of the movie, it would be hard to classify the marketing aspect of **the Beast** as overwhelmingly effective, but that would be missing the bigger picture. And it certainly wouldn't explain how, years later, the Cloudmakers are still talking about and wishing for ways to relive the experience.

Fast forward three years later to the summer of 2004. In a movie trailer for the highly anticipated upcoming video game **Halo 2**, people in the audience think they see something strange happen to the tagline that gives the website address for X-Box, the system for which the game is being developed. It looks like, momentarily, the address changes to http://www.ilovebees.com. Simultaneously, the creators of certain key gaming sites on the Internet receive mysterious packages via FedEx – honey jars with letters placed inside the honey. The letters spell out the same odd message that was hidden in the **Halo 2** trailer, "i love bees."

Their curiosity aroused, people who had either seen the message in the trailer or received the mysterious packages went to the website they were being directed to and discovered a web page as odd as the messages themselves. The hidden messages they discovered on the website led them down a three month long trail of e-mail messages, puzzle solving, and actually venturing forth for weeks on end to answer hundreds and hundreds of payphone calls across the country. During the course of the game, thousands and thousands of people participated both online and in real life, with an estimated one million people in total having been exposed to the project in one way or another. And even though it has only recently concluded, the campaign is already being hailed as one of the most innovative and successful promotional efforts of the year.

So what accounts for the tremendous success of both these efforts? What is powerful enough to motivate thousands of people to devote hours and hours of their time online and in the real world participating in what they all know is essentially an advertising campaign?

Welcome to the world of Alternate Reality Gaming.

Notes from the Author

I want to take a moment to set forth my goals in writing This Is Not A Game, and also to explain some of the decisions I made about structure and content while writing it.

First and foremost, this book is intended to be an introduction to the exciting world of alternate reality gaming, and an attempt to explain just exactly what an alternate reality game (ARG) is. It was inspired partially by the recent huge influx of new fans to the genre as a result of the widely successful campaign called **I Love Bees**, but also out of the sheer frustration of trying to explain to anyone who asked me what I had been spending my time on for the last few years. To those who have never heard of them, alternate reality or immersive games aren't an easy concept to put into words. So, from now on, I can just hand them a copy of this book, instead of trying to even explain it.

Some common questions I always receive when I do try and introduce people to ARGs are: Is it just a video game? Isn't it just an online story? Is it only a series of puzzles? Because alternate reality games combine aspects of all three of these forms of entertainment in a unique way, it's only natural that those are the things people would turn to in trying to understand this new concept. Consequently, the first part of the book is a comparison between ARGs and what we normally think of when we say games, stories, and puzzles, to see exactly how they fit in each of these categories.

Next, <u>This Is Not A Game</u> approaches alternate reality games from a historical perspective, to see how they have been constructed and used in the past, as well as how they have been received by the people who played them. Examining completed games will help illustrate the many different forms an ARG can take and highlight how they use the various features of games, stories, and puzzles to create powerfully immersive and entertaining experiences.

Finally, the third section of the book is a "How to Guide" for aspiring ARG developers based on my experience creating and running five alternate reality games in the last four years, including some of the most successful independent projects ever produced. Not unusual for a genre still defining itself, there are hardly any comprehensive and practical resources available to anyone wishing to learn how to get involved in making ARGs. <u>This Is Not A Game</u> presents a hands-on, detailed plan for constructing an alternate reality game from start to finish, with concrete examples from games I have conducted in the past. With the information contained in this section, anyone will be able to begin crafting the next game to captivate the world.

Part One:

Alternate Reality Games

in Theory

Chapter 1: Game or Not a Game?

Alternate Reality Gaming. Immersive Gaming. Viral Marketing. Interactive Fiction. If we can't decide what to call it, how can anyone hope to explain it? And does whatever it is even fit into any of these labels anyway?

Regardless of which name we ultimately choose to apply, Alternate Reality Gaming is a rapidly emerging game genre and is one of the first true art and entertainment forms developed from and exclusively for the Internet. So what exactly is an alternate reality game and why are they suddenly so popular?

First of all, as the name implies, an alternate reality game, or ARG for short, is a game of sorts, that takes place on the Internet, although it's nothing at all like most Internet or video games you may have played in the past. In fact, one of the main goals of an ARG is to deny and disguise the fact that it is even a game at all. This is what the community of immersive gaming fans and creators embrace as the main principle of Alternate Reality Gaming and what has come to be called the *TINAG* philosophy, for ***This Is Not A Game.***

So how does a game pretend or appear *not* to be a game?

An alternate reality game achieves this goal by ignoring the paradigms most people have about games in general and video games in particular, and then by transcending the media used to present it. That may sound impressive but it's probably not very helpful at this point. What are the "paradigms" of games and video games?

Think about all the games you played growing up - board games, card games, even video games - and what elements they all have in common. The similarities can be divided into four basic categories. They all have defined rules for playing the game, a defined playing space where the game takes place, a given set of components and / or game pieces through which the game is conducted, and a set of win / loss scenarios which define the end of the game and the objectives for the players involved. Alternate reality games have none of those elements and so, on face value, they do not appear to be games at all. In order to resolve this conflict, let's take a closer look at the things that define a game as a game and how they relate to alternate reality games.

There is actually an academic field of study involving games that has produced many competing if not conflicting attempted definitions of a game. We'll start by looking at some of these existing definitions and see how they can be applied to the genre of alternate reality games.

Definitions of a Game

There have been many attempted academic definitions of games but none that have ever been accepted as definitive and all encompassing. In fact, there is quite an active community of game theorists among whom the debate of exactly how to define a game goes on continuously. Although the field of the serious study of games in general and electronic games in particular is still very young, philosophers and social scientists have been studying and writing about the related concept of play for many years. And like most disciplines of academia, the people working to create and standardize the language of the field of game study today often refer to previously published definitions in their work. Here are a few examples of some of the more popular definitions.

1938 – Johan Huizinga – <u>Homo Ludens: A Study of the Play Element in Culture</u>

"Summing up the formal characteristics of play we might call it a free activity standing quite consciously outside 'ordinary' life as being 'not serious,' but at the same time absorbing the player intensely and utterly. It is an activity connected with no material interest, and no profit can be gained by it. It proceeds within its own proper boundaries of time and space according to fixed rules and in an orderly manner. It promotes the formation of social groupings which tend to surround themselves with secrecy and to stress their difference from the common world by disguise or other means."

Dave Szulborski

1961 - Roger Caillois – <u>Man, Play, and Games</u>

"Play is … an activity which is essentially: Free (voluntary), separate [in time and space], uncertain, unproductive, governed by rules, make-believe."

1978 – Bernard Suits – <u>What Is a Game?</u>

"To play a game is to engage in activity directed towards bringing about a specific state of affairs, using only means permitted by rules, where the rules prohibit more efficient in favor of less efficient means, and where such rules are accepted just because they make possible such activity."

1981 – Elliot Avedon & Brian Sutton-Smith – <u>The Study of Games</u>

"We can define game as an exercise of voluntary control systems in which there is an opposition between forces, confined by a procedure and rules in order to produce a disequilibrial outcome."

1981 – Chris Crawford – <u>The Art of Computer Game Design</u>

"A closed formal system that subjectively represents a subset of reality."

1993 - Jesper Juul - <u>The Game, the Player, the World: Looking for a Heart of Gameness</u>

"A game is a rule-based formal system with a variable and quantifiable outcome, where different outcomes are assigned different values, the player exerts effort in order to influence the outcome, the player feels

4

attached to the outcome, and the consequences of the activity are optional and negotiable."

2003 – Katie Salen & Eric Zimmerman – <u>Rules of Play</u>

"A game is a system in which players engage in an artificial conflict, defined by rules, that results in a quantifiable outcome."

Despite their differences, there are many common elements in most of the definitions quoted above. They all include the concept of rules, either explicitly or in their mention of a *formal* system. These rules are what govern the way in which the game is interactive, a feature which is also implied from almost all of the definitions' inclusion of the idea that the players influence both the game play and outcome.

For simplicity's sake, I am going to start with Jonathan Steuer's definition of interactivity as "the extent to which users can participate in modifying the form and content of a mediated environment in real time," from his 1993 paper "<u>Defining Virtual Reality: Dimensions Determining Telepresence</u>," although we will have to modify it somewhat when we begin applying it to alternate reality games. For now, let's reword it slightly to apply it to games generically, by saying *interaction in games can be defined as the player's choices or decisions, as expressed through his manipulation of some element of the game interface, changing something in the virtual world of the game.*

Defining a game as a system also characterizes it as something separate and apart from ordinary life or the everyday world. John

Huizinga's definition perhaps sums it up best by saying play is something "consciously outside 'ordinary' life." In other words, the person at play realizes at all times that he is just playing and that it is artificial; i.e., not a part of his everyday world.

Almost all of the above definitions also include the idea of an *outcome* or a fixed end to the game, based on the rules established for the game. A few of the definitions add the important word "quantifiable" as well, meaning that there exists a specific way of measuring and determining the outcome, and implying that this method is part of the defined rules of the game.

All these definitions therefore address three of the elements of a game mentioned when I asked you to reflect back on games you've played – defined rules, a defined playing space or system, and a defined outcome or win / loss scenario based on the rules. None of them, however, include an important fourth element that I believe is especially critical when trying to fit alternate reality games into any definition of a game. That is the category of game pieces or components, the mechanical elements of the game that facilitate the play but also mark it immediately as a game. Examples could be a game interface that looks like a console on the screen, the digital representation of a gun being held in front of you in a first person shooting game, or just an image with "clickable hotspots" in game such as **Myst**.

In all of these cases, the very presence of a symbolic interface of any kind has a significant impact on how the game is both perceived and played. In earlier game definitions it may have sufficed to include

6

this element under the category of rules, but that doesn't work when discussing alternate reality games, as I'll explain below. So we'll treat game pieces or components as a separate element in our quest to define a game and look at how all of these standard game components relate to ARGs.

Rules and Winning Conditions

Unlike standard games, as reflected in the academic definitions already quoted, alternate reality games have no defined or implicit rules for playing them (or creating them for that matter, but we'll get to that shortly), and generally no pre-known objectives or winning conditions. That's because ARGs try to pass themselves off as real, as not being games at all. Defining the rules of play and how the game might possibly end would totally destroy that illusion of reality right from the start. Interestingly, a recent online discussion of the aforementioned **I Love Bees** marketing effort centered around exactly whether or not such a game does or does not have rules, and if that defines it as a game or not.

David Thomas, on his website devoted to game theory http://www.buzzcut.com, writes, "I'll step out and say that **I Love Bees** is nothing more complex than a good old mystery story . . . . I don't think it is a game or a puzzle . . . . there is nothing to play with. There is no rule system to enjoy. The collection of sites drizzles clues and hints at cryptic possibilities. But there is nothing to do but follow along. People have created a game out of 'trying to figure it out'. But the site, the mystery itself, is not a game in any respect."

Another online game theorist, Cody Brown, argues the exact opposite in direct response to Thomas' buzzcut.com article. Writing on his http://www.avantgaming.com site, Brown claims, "I couldn't disagree more . . . . I feel secure in stating that all experiences that follow this general form are most definitely games." He goes on to explain his assertion, "Now to say that **I Love Bees** is not a game is to say that **the Beast** is not a game. As for the rationale that it is not a game because there is no rule system to enjoy falls short based on our definitions because the activity takes place in a digital environment where rule systems are omnipresent . . . . The rules of **the Beast** were such a part of the players' everyday lives that if one were to write out the rules for **the Beast**, one might as well include the Law of Gravity or the mandate of the U.S. Postal Service."

I would take exception to both of these arguments, starting with Brown's declaration that both **I Love Bees** and **the Beast** (and other alternate reality games by implication) have "omnipresent rules" just because they are presented in a digital environment. While I understand his point that technology has become so commonplace that many people inherently know how to operate in various software and computing environments, to say that one automatically knows the rules of an ARG just because it is primarily based on the Internet is an oversimplification of the very idea of rules. We've already unofficially defined rules as the formal system or underlying logic of the game, the outline, if you will, of cause and effect actions that take into account all the possibilities in the game and defines the flow of action accordingly. If player A does *this*, while the conditions of the game are like *this*, *that* happens. To think that all forms of games share the same pattern of cause and effect just because they are digital is just silly. Where does Brown go wrong?

Brown is implying two things with his claim. First, that because the game is digital and distributed via the Internet, the computer savvy audience it is intended for already knows how to play it. That's equivalent to saying that, just because someone knows how to roll a pair of dice, they automatically know how to play **Monopoly**. Brown's idea confuses the mechanics of the game – knowing how to press keyboard buttons or click on items on a computer screen – with the logic of the game, the rules that define how and why things happen. Next, Brown also uses the fact that ARGs attempt to mimic real life in their interactions to support his claim, implying that players, since they obviously already exist and function in the real world, intuitively understand the underlying principles and rules of the game, by comparing them to such things as the Law of Gravity. Again though, he misses a critical point about the very nature of ARGs.

By definition, ARGs are supposed to be about *alternate realities*, implying that everything in these digital worlds may not function exactly as it does in real life. Also, most ARGs, the successful ones at least, are

9

really about relationships, between characters, between characters and entities in the game, and even between characters and players. Saying that players will automatically recognize and understand how the relationships in a game are supposed to work reflects an unrealistic conception of human nature and ignorance of the interactive nature of ARGs. So I find Brown's claim of implicit rules in an alternate reality game due to its digitized format simply incorrect.

But David Thomas' assertion that the absence of apparent rules automatically disqualifies **I Love Bees** or similar projects from being considered games is equally lacking. His statement, "there is nothing to do but follow along" is the basis of his misconception and also shows he, like Cody Brown, probably hasn't spent much time playing ARGs. While it is certainly true that someone can just "follow along" while an immersive game plays out, that is definitely not the way most fans of the genre participate, or what most alternate reality game creators intend when they develop a game.

ARGs are sometimes compared to digital novels (more on whether ARGs are really only stories in a different format in the next chapter), where the actions and discoveries of the player or players as a whole drive the plot forward. The content of the game is not merely handed out to the players, as Thomas seems to believe; only a small percentage of in-game material is actually "given away" like that. A great deal of the post-launch content is only seen by the players after they have solved a puzzle or interacted with some character who has shared information with them. The process of figuring out the mystery of the game in this way is the process by which the rule system or underlying logic of the game and the world it is representing is learned. So, while there are no apparent rules, at least in the beginning, there are indeed rules governing what happens in the game world and what players must do to progress, but they are discovered and learned, not merely given.

Apparently then, the paradigm of pre-established rules associated with most definitions of a game does not apply to alternate reality games, at least in a way understood by even most modern game theorists. Without an understanding of the rules and with deliberate efforts by the game's creators to disguise that it is even a game at all, it is impossible for a player to know what the objectives or winning conditions are in advance. In fact, figuring out the ultimate goal of the game is one of the parts of ARGs that fans find most fun.

A good deal of the early speculation about a new game involves trying to guess what the purpose of the game is and who might be behind it. If the game is a promotional vehicle for a company or product, it normally becomes apparent fairly quickly. For that reason, games done by major companies as marketing tools, such as the recent **I Love Bees** game, tend to be less immersive and inherently less believable than grassroots or amateur games done by fans of the genre. That's not to say these games can't be successful and enjoyable experiences in their own right, just that the need to tie the game into a known fictional world or real life product goes a long way in destroying the illusion of reality and the principle of *TINAG*.

Game Mechanics and Components

Almost all traditional forms of games use pieces or assets that are dedicated to that type of game and immediately identify the activity as a game. For example, card games require the use of specific tools - the cards themselves - which very rarely have any non-game uses in a person's life. Sure, playing cards are often used for doing magic, or building card houses, or even for collecting in some cases, but even these are *entertainment-based* uses and could arguably be including under the category of gaming or play anyway. The point is, the physical implements used in other kinds of games, whether they are playing boards, dice, or the computer-generated graphics of a traditional video game, generally have no application in a person's real world.

These pieces carry with them what Gregory Bateson calls "metacommunications," in his 1972 work <u>Mind and Nature: A Neces-sary Unity</u>, meaning they not only serve their purpose in the game but also implicitly carry the message that the activity they are being used for is a game. Whenever you roll the dice or draw a card or click on that digitized enemy in a video game, you are automatically reminded on some level that you are playing a game.

Alternate reality games, however, ignore that paradigm, by using tools and methods that are already integrated parts of the player's everyday life. The pieces or components of alternate reality games are websites, e-mail messages, videos, Internet blogs, phone calls, and even real world interactions. Thanks to the advent of *ubiquitous computing*, a term first coined by Jay David Bolter and Richard Grusin in <u>Remediation: Understanding New Media</u>, the constructed elements that make up an ARG – primarily the Internet delivered content – have become such integrated parts of the gamer's everyday world that they no longer contain the *metacommunication* that defines them as part of a game.

In a well-designed and produced ARG, the interactions and in-game events mimic real life and don't announce themselves as elements of a game at all. There is no simulation of a virtual world through a symbolic interface. By integrating technology and devices that players already have and use on a regular basis, it becomes much easier for the player to suppress or ignore the knowledge that he is really just playing a game. As Jane McGonigal wrote in "'This Is Not a Game': Immersive Aesthetics and Collective Play" in 2003, the first serious academic examination of the genre of alternate reality games, "In this sense, it is reasonable to argue that *nothing about this virtual play was simulated.* The computer-driven alternate reality **the Beast** created was make-believe, but every aspect of the player's experience was, phenomenologically speaking, real."

So, unlike almost every other type of game, ARGs do not have a set of pieces or components that constantly remind the player that he is indeed playing a game. The only *interfaces* in alternate reality games appear to be the same ones regularly used to communicate with the real world. Perhaps the words of Friedrich Kittler summarize it best, for if an alternate reality game is done right, "there is no software."

Game Space

Finally, alternate reality games, unlike every other game genre, have no defined playing field or game space. They do originate and take place predominantly online, but by employing such things as phone calls, instant messaging, and real world encounters, immersive games transcend the limitations of the Internet and reach into the everyday world of the player. In describing the methods used and intent of the creators in the original ARG game, **the Beast**, Jane McGonigal writes, "For them, 'immersion' meant integrating the virtual play fully into the online *and* offline lives of its players." In other words, the creators of **the Beast** made the game space the players' own lives and everyday world.

Unfortunately, this seems to contradict one of the other important elements of most games, as stressed in some of the academic attempts at a definition above, the idea that play is separate in time and space and "consciously 'outside' ordinary life." This is all part of the illusion of reality within alternate reality games. So, while traditionally most ARGs employ a multitude of websites made especially for the game, an entire game could be developed around a single website, by using multiple and various other methods of contacting and interacting with the players, and by making the game even more interactive with the real world.

A recent promotional game for the video game **Halo 2** that came to be known as **I Love Bees** did just that, by having only one main website but using hundreds of phone calls to public payphones, requiring players to go out into the real world and answer them in order to advance the story. The "alternate reality" of **I Love Bees** existed entirely in one website, hundreds of payphone lines, and in the minds of the players. In doing so, it has become one of the most overwhelmingly successful ARGs ever produced.

If an alternate reality game doesn't even appear to be a game, and has no rules, no game boards, no playing pieces, and no winning conditions, just what does it have, and how do you even know you are playing it? And, if it has none of the common elements that commonly define a game as a game, is it even a game at all? Perhaps by looking at the other part of the common names for the genre – the idea of immersion into an alternate reality – we can come to a little better understanding of exactly what we are dealing with in alternate reality games.

Chapter 2: Immersion in an Alternate Reality

Immersion is a word often associated with alternate reality games; in fact, two other common names for the entire genre are immersive gaming and immersive marketing. But, just like trying to define a game itself, trying to explain exactly what immersion is and how it relates to gaming in general and alternate reality gaming specifically, is not an easy task. Again, let's start by looking at some existing academic definitions of immersion in relation to various media and entertainment forms.

Definitions of Immersion

1997 - Coomans and Timmermanns - Towards a Taxonomy of Virtual Reality User Interfaces

"the feeling of being deeply engaged where participants enter a make-believe world as if it is real."

1997 – Janet Murray – Hamlet on the Holodeck

"Immersion is a metaphorical term derived from the physical experience of being submerged in water. We seek the same feeling from a psychologically immersive experience that we do from a plunge in the ocean or swimming pool – the sensation of being surrounded by a completely other reality, as different as water is from air, that takes over all of our attention, our whole perceptual apparatus."

2002 – Marie-Laure Ryan – <u>Narrative as Virtual Reality: Immersion and Interactivity in Literature and Electronic Media</u>

" . . . immersion is the experience through which a fictional world acquires the presence of an autonomous, language-independent reality populated with live human beings."

2002 – Steve Poynter – <u>Immersed in the News</u>

"What's immersive? It can be roughly defined as story presentation that allows the Internet user to interact with story elements or data. Instead of "reading" a story online, the user gets to "do" something -- and in the process learn, and better understand the topic."

2003 – Katie Salen & Eric Zimmerman – <u>Rules of Play</u>

"The immersive fallacy is the idea that the pleasure of media experience lies in its ability to sensually transport the participant into an illusory, simulated reality. According to the immersive fallacy, this reality is so complete that ideally the frame falls away so that the player truly believes that he or she is part of an imaginary world."

As you can see, immersion has a myriad of concepts and subtleties in each of these definitions, although there are some similarities in most of them as well. One of them, the quote from Steve Poynter, is just plain wrong, as it defines immersion, at least from a journalistic perspective, as being nothing more than interactivity. As explained previously, interaction in games, or in this case a digitally-presented news piece, can be stated in the simplest terms as the player's (or reader's) choices or decisions, as expressed through his manipulation of some element of the game interface, changing something in the virtual world of the game. While interactivity is certainly one of the first steps a creator can use to try and induce a feeling of immersion, it is certainly not the only element necessary.

Unfortunately, Poynter's misconception betrays a lack of understanding common to other newly digitized fields, like journalism and marketing, of what immersion really is. The practitioners in these fields obviously grasp, to some extent, the power that true immersion can bring as evidenced by their forays into the ideas of immersive journalism and marketing in ever-increasing numbers. Unless they come to understand the difference between immersion and simple interaction, however, most of their efforts have very little chance of being truly immersive.

First, it is entirely possible for a game to be interactive and not immersive in the least. Games like **Tetris** are entirely symbolic and make no attempt to present any kind of virtual world for the player to

19

be immersed in, yet they are undeniably interactive, in that the player obviously manipulates elements on the game screen through the mechanical interface of the game system. There is no logical frame of reference for the player to even try and imagine a world where these oddly shaped falling pieces make sense or have some plot attached to their descent. So interaction does not automatically generate true immersion. There are some arguments for the idea that games like **Tetris** can indeed be immersive, but not in a way easily understandable from the definitions above.

It's also possible, though not as likely, for a game or electronic presentation to be immersive and not really interactive. The most obvious example, although not a game per se but still illustrative by comparison, is film. A well-done movie can pull the observer into the storyline, action, and even fictional world of the film, similar to the previously described feeling of being lost in a book, with absolutely no interaction between the watcher and the medium (the movie). Perhaps a better example more akin to video games is a simple virtual reality environment a player can walk through, totally immersed in the artificial world via the virtual reality devices he is wearing. Although he can look around and move through the environment, he doesn't really interact with it in a meaningful way. Yes, the image on the monitor within the virtual reality headset changes as the player moves his head, but there is no actual change to the world reflected in that, merely a change in the symbolic representation he is presented with. The result could be defined as immersion, at least sensory immersion, without interaction.

Some game theorists have used equivalences from the world of literature, such as Victor Nell's idea of being "lost in a book," and Samuel Coleridge's concept of the willing suspension of disbelief, to try and define and explain immersion in games. Before we decide on the definition that bests fits our purpose, let's examine how immersion has influenced other forms of art, entertainment, and even philosophy throughout history, in hopes of understanding why it is so powerful and just exactly how it fits into the world of alternate reality gaming.

The History of Immersion

If we accept the simple premise that seems to be common to all of the definitions above that immersion, in the very least, involves the feeling of being actually present in another world or reality, it becomes fairly easy to find examples of immersion, or at least attempts at immersion, in other areas of humanity's past. Perhaps the earliest example cited by many scholars dates back to pre-history in the form of the cave paintings made by our earliest ancestors. The caves at Lascaux, France are thought to have originated around15,000 BC and are often cited as some of the finest examples yet found of this form of immersive prehistoric art. Buried deep within the Lascaux cave system, at the most remote and secluded areas, primitive man etched a variety of images, including symbols of animal, plants, the sun, the moon, and the stars, as well as markings best described as "shamanistic scrawls."

Some archeologists argue that cave paintings such as these were the "storytelling medium" of the time, a means of cultural transference and even entertainment among the primitive people. Others argue that their private and almost inaccessible locations mark these rooms and the images they contain as something much more than mere stone-age storybooks. Joseph Campbell, the pre-eminent researcher and author on mythology and its purpose in man's life, said of these very caves, "these magical spots occur far from the natural entrances of the grottos, deep within the dark, wandering chill corridors and vast chambers, so that before reaching them one has to experience the full force of the mystery of the cave itself."

Whether these early artistic endeavors were attempts to entertain, transfer knowledge, or just pass the time is obviously debatable, but there is little doubt they were an attempt by early man to create an artificial environment, removed from his daily activities, in which he could immerse himself.

Another historical example of man's quest for immersion through artwork can be found in the frescoes of Dionysian rituals hanging on the walls of the Villa dei Misteri in Pompeii, Italy. Oliver Grau, in his book Virtual Art: From Illusion to Immersion, cites these early attempts at a 360° panorama as the beginnings of immersive art, a tradition carried on ever since, and exemplified by such works as Baldassare <u>Peruzzi's Sala delle Prospettive</u> in Rome and the religious dioramas and panoramas popularized in Europe in the 19th century.

Attempts at immersion are not restricted to art, however, and examples can be found in literature, the stage, and film as well, leading up to the current exploration using computers of what we now call *virtual reality*. That's right, virtual reality is both our latest and perhaps most successful attempt at true immersion yet, at least on a sensory level. In fact, one of the famous game theorists from whom we quoted a definition of immersion, Janet Murray, has suggested that the holodeck from the <u>Star Trek</u> television series is an example of the quintessential immersive experience. This brings us quite nicely to immersion in video games and the ongoing quest to constantly deliver better and more lifelike graphics and realistic simulations.

Before the advent of multimedia digital technology in the average home computer, traditional games could hardly be described as immersive at all. Traditional board, card, and dice games have very few elements that deliver any kind of true immersive experience. Even early electronic games, limited by the still-developing technology of the time, had no degree of immersion into another world. Interestingly though, accordingly to many serious academic researchers, immersion is one of the psychological motivations and benefits of *play* in the first place. Russian psychologist Lev Vygotsk, often called the "Mozart" of Psychology, stressed the importance and value of a child's ability to create a "pretend play" situation. Focusing on the emotional nature of play, Vygotsk claimed that the origin of man's fascination with and drive to play is an instinctual human need to realize desires that cannot be fulfilled in real activity. In other words, the immersive aspect of a play is a necessary part of the development of imagination and psychological wellness in a person. So it appears that many forms of popular games, though entertaining, do not actually fulfill the psychological need of true play activities.

Today, however, the truly incredible exponential increase of raw computing power available to the average gamer has at least opened up the possibilities of video games being truly immersive experiences. Again, in the context of games, we're using immersion to mean the feeling of being totally absorbed and participatory in the fictional world of the game. Obviously not all video games deliver or even attempt to deliver such an experience. How do the ones that achieve it actually accomplish it? And, more importantly, is there something beyond the need for play that makes an immersive experience so meaningful and desirable to us as humans?

The Power of Immersion

Although we've already touched briefly upon Vygotsk's theory of the beneficial effects of pure play as exemplified in the playing of truly immersive games, there seems to be something deeper, an almost primal desire of man to experience realities or states of consciousness outside of his normal existence. In fact, many anthropologists believe the Lascaux cave paintings already cited as prehistoric examples of immersive art were actually sacred or mystic in nature, and designed to pass on spiritual knowledge and beliefs. Victor Nell, in his seminal work Lost in a Book: The Psychology of Reading for Pleasure, states that the immersive feeling of being "lost in a book" has "the power to change consciousness."

Again we turn to Janet Murray and her ideas about immersion. She believes that immersion is but the first of a possible three-step process of immersion, agency, and transformation, three items that she calls the "aesthetic properties of narrative." We'll define agency in a moment, but it's in her concept of transformation that Murray raises the possibility for real personal transformation and metamorphosis through the immersive power of digital media. Like the psychological and literary examples already cited, the true immersive power possible through electronic gaming may go far beyond just the enjoyment derived from playing the game.

Techniques of Immersion

Since our specific goal is to look at how immersion works in alternate reality gaming, we're going to restrict the remaining discussion of immersion to video games first of all, and then narrow it down to the sub-genre of ARGs. The point is to show how the concept of immersion in games, at least as we traditionally define and think of it, does not apply really at all to alternate reality games, despite having the name of "immersive gaming" as one of the genre's aliases. Actually, the traditional techniques used to create immersion in regular video games work against the immersive effect that alternate reality games try to achieve.

Although the heading of video games encompasses an almost endless variety of sub-categories and genres, I am going to lump all of the rest together and single out ARGs, declaring them unique when it comes to the concept of immersion and the techniques required to achieve it. The justification for that claim is the fact that, in every other form of video game, the world the designers are trying to get you immersed in is obviously and blatantly artificial, and portrayed through a symbolic representation on the computer screen. Even the most realistic looking graphics in a video game are still exactly that – symbols, tools for viewing, understanding and interacting with the virtual world being presented. This includes games that are based entirely in reality and perhaps even factual history; they still attempt to present a virtual recreation of that reality or history, precisely the opposite of what alternate reality games attempt to do. Instead of trying to create a realistic experience in an artificial setting of a video game, alternate reality games use real life settings to try and create a realistic yet fictional experience.

So what techniques do regular video games use to try and create an immersive experience for the players? For one thing, most of them place the player at the center of the main story or plot. He is not just an observer, but also an actor, a participant in the in-game world. Another method is to use highly photorealistic graphics and a first person perspective within the game. When augmented with carefully produced sounds reflecting spatial orientation, video games can deliver an immersive experience, at least on the sensory level. Most importantly, however, the player must feel as if he engaged in and able to affect the action in the game. This goes beyond mere interactivity, as defined earlier, into what Janet Murray calls "agency", which she labels a necessary part of any immersive experience.

To better understand the difference between interaction and agency, we'll turn to the work of another influential game theorist, Michael Mateas, who wrote in an August 2003 Internet piece, "By 'interaction' I mean the act of physically manipulating an input device (e.g. wiggling a mouse, moving in front of a camera, etc.) and eliciting a response (e.g. an image changes on a screen, motors turn on and off, etc.). Interaction is an abstract concept, saying nothing about the character of the relationship between input and elicited response, just that there is some relationship between them. Agency is a phenomenal category, describing what it feels like as a player/interactor to be empowered to take whatever actions you want and get a sensible response."

All of the above immersive techniques can basically be summarized as the game creators trying to create as realistic a world as possible within the artificial framework of the computer screen, a world in which the player can take symbolic actions that somehow modify the world of the game, creating the feeling of agency. If successful, the game then becomes an immersive experience for the player. Or does it?

The Illusion of Immersion

Let's return to one of the definitions of immersion from the experts quoted above, the one from Katie Salen and Eric Zimmerman, in which they mention "the fallacy of immersion." Salen and Zimmerman claim that true engagement or immersion in a fictional world has nothing to do with realistic graphics, three-dimensional perspectives, or any of the other techniques of immersion carefully laid out above. Instead, it is the very act of play itself, losing one's self in that "free activity standing quite consciously outside 'ordinary' life," that evokes the feeling of engagement or immersion. This is how games like **Tetris** can arguably be seen as immersive, since it is theoretically possible to have the feeling of being lost in the game, as reflected by the player moving his physical body to mimic the actions on the screen. Salen and Zimmerman's concept ties back into the idea of metacommunications and the inescapable fact that any kind of symbolic diegetic interface automatically destroys the effect of true immersion in a game. Play after all, as defined by Huizinga and quoted above, requires a conscious awareness that the play activity is occurring outside of ordinary life and therefore, by implication, an ongoing awareness that it isn't real.

Jay David Bolter and Richard Grusin's theories of new media also delve into why immersion isn't quite as simple as some previous definitions have made it out to be. Bolter and Grusin are two media theorists whose 1998 book Remediation: Understanding New Media posits the ideas of immediacy and hypermediacy as the two possible states that any form of digital media achieves. The things we have described as the techniques of immersion - virtual reality programs, photo realistic computer graphics, first person involvement in the storyline and so on – are all attempts to achieve transparency by eliminating any signs of a symbolic interface from the game, the condition Bolter and Grusin term immediacy. This would constitute immersion by the common definitions we have used above. Bolter and Grusin differentiate immediacy from hypermediacy, which is their name for digital media that becomes the opposite of transparent by focusing attention in some way on the technology used to present it. The authors cite medieval illuminated manuscripts, video games, the Internet, most software programs, and even television, as examples of hypermediacy because they all regularly use some form of digital interface or exaggerated graphics as part of their presentations.

The most interesting part of Bolter and Grusin's theories for our purposes is the apparent contradiction between the two concepts of immediacy and hypermediacy. Still, the authors claim that it is possible to experience both states simultaneously and, in fact, that our new digital age almost demands it. They conclude, quite in parallel with the definitions of play and Salen and Zimmerman's immersive fallacy, that there is indeed a dual consciousness in which the viewer can both be immersed in a game and still aware on some level of the technology being used.

Which leads us back quite nicely to how immersion and all the related concepts apply to alternate reality gaming.

<u>Immersion in Alternate Reality Gaming</u>

To repeat what I said earlier, the concept of immersion in games, at least as we traditionally define and think of it, does not apply really at all to alternate reality games. Yes, that's right. First I claimed alternate reality or immersive games were not really games. Now I'm claiming they may not really be immersive. Can that possibly be right?

All of the above definitions and explanations, even Salen and Zimmerman's idea of the fallacy of immersion, are based on the assumed goal of trying to evoke the feeling in the player of immersion in an artificial world, a fictional world created expressly for the purposes of the game. While that may be true for other forms of video games and all other earlier attempts at immersive media of any type, that is not the goal of an alternate reality game.

As Jane McGonigal wrote when she was describing the motivations and methods of the creators of **the Beast**, "For them, 'immersion' meant integrating the virtual play fully into the online *and* offline lives of its players." That begins to describe the subtle yet significant difference of the idea of immersion in alternate reality games and regular gaming, but I'd like to take it one step further.

In an alternate reality game, the goal is not to immerse the player in the artificial world of the game; instead, a successful game immerses the world of the game into the everyday existence and life of the player. Once again, this implies that the very name - alternate reality game – is misleading, because you don't really want the player to think of the game world as an *alternate* reality at all. The ultimate goal is to have the player believe that the events take place and characters of the game exist in his world, not an alternate reality. In a strange but very real way, the ARG creator is trying, not to create an alternate reality, but to change the player's existing world into the alternate reality.

That is why the game pieces and components in an alternate reality game are the things and technology we use already in our everyday life. Things like e-mail, web sites, telephone calls, and instant messaging, are so integrated into the player's world that using them as game elements allows for a truly unmediated interface into the world of the game. If done right, interactions done using these game elements can be as real as the player's interactions with the ordinary world. Because these are the same methods the player already uses to gather and comprehend information from the real world, using them in the game eliminates the level of metacommunication that game elements normally carry. In other words, they don't scream at the player, "Hey, this is a game!"

Furthermore, anything presented in game using these methods has the potential to seem as real to the player as events in the real world. For example, for most people, the only knowledge of and real experience they have with major news stories are the audio and video presentations they see of the events either on television, radio, or increasingly on the Internet. If an alternate reality game uses well-done, simulated newscasts to portray important in-game happenings, they are, in a very genuine sense, as real to the player as occurrences reported to him on the evening news.

And this, of course, is the real beauty and power of alternate reality games and why players rave about them years after they have concluded. The characters they meet when they play the games and the things that happen to those characters are real to the players, in a very significant way. I'm not saying that ARG players are delusion in any sense, because like any form of true play activity, there always seems to be the dual consciousness of the activity being separate and removed from ordinary life. But alternate reality games do seem to offer possibilities for levels of true immersion and engagement that other forms of electronic media and games have no chance of achieving. As Jane McGonigal said in her pioneering work on ARGs, "This close identity in design and function enables an immersive aesthetic in games like **the Beast** that is much more powerful and persuasive than the immersive efforts of the so many other arts that have previously attempted the interfaceless interface."

Chapter 3: Game or Interactive Story?

So far we've taken two of the primary names for this rapidly emerging game genre – alternate reality games and immersive games – and proven that they don't adequately or accurately define exactly what an ARG is. Despite their name, alternate reality games don't seem to fit into the category of games easily. So, is there another possibility as to what they might be?

A third name for ARGs is *interactive fiction* and, as I mentioned before, they are sometimes compared to online, interactive novels in which the actions of the players drive the advancement of the plot. Perhaps ARGs are just a form of digital literature then, stories that take advantage of the ubiquitous computer technology of the times to find new ways to tell a tale. This is not to confuse alternate reality games with other forms commonly classified as interactive fiction, such things as hypertext fiction, text adventures (**Zork**, anyone?), and even multiplayer online real-time gaming environments like **Everquest**. Many of these other formats have already been written about somewhat extensively in terms of their potential as interactive forms of storytelling, but

I believe there are enough significant differences in alternate reality games to look at them from a different perspective.

For help with this we can again turn to the academic world, where there is an ongoing debate over whether or not games can and should be classified and studied as stories. Although the study of games is still a fairly new academic field, there is a wealth of material already written about the conflict between *ludology* - the practice of focusing on the mechanics and form of the game over the story – and *narratology* – the idea that games are stories or narrative devices first, irregardless of the mechanisms used to present them. There are many outspoken advocates of each philosophy and the ideas and definitions they have set forth will help us determine how alternate reality games fit into the discussion, and if ARGs are indeed a form of interactive fiction.

Defining a Story

This should be easy. Everyone knows what a story is, right? Well, yes and no. All of us have an idea of what a story is, although many would have trouble putting the concept into a concise and workable definition. And, not surprisingly, serious academicians also have trouble agreeing on exactly which words best explain what a story is. Actually, most participants in this ongoing discussion prefer the word narrative (hence the term narratology) to story, explaining that a story is really only one example of a narrative form. In either case, I'd like to begin with a common sense explanation from John Kim, in his paper "Immersive Story: A View of Role-played Drama," in which he explains a critical concept that we will use to understand how alternate reality games might act as narrative devices.

Kim writes, "The author creates the work in relative isolation from the reader, and the reader views it without direct contact with the author. In the formalist view of theorists like Tzvetan Todorov and Gérard Genette, there are two parts to this work: *story* and *discourse*. Story is the imaginary sequence of events involving characters and setting. It is a mental construct within the imagination of a person, i.e. a picture in the mind's eye of what is happening. Discourse is the expression of that story: words and / or images that attempt to represent the events. The story begins in the mind of the author, and is then expressed into a discourse which is contained in media. By viewing this media, the reader then forms a mental construct of that story within her own mind.

Although there are some key differences when it comes to applying this concept to ARGs, the main point is that there are two elements to every narrative experience – the *what*, which is the content of the narrative itself, and the *how*, which is simply the methods and technologies used to present the narrative. This concept of two distinct components to stories, which has existed and been widely accepted among narrative theorists for years, is the origin of the current debate already described between ludology and narratology, with ludology focused on the *how* and narratology focused on the *what*. Since our purpose is to discover if an alternate reality game is perhaps just a new form of story, let's examine what each side says about games and stories, and how they relate.

A Ludologist's Point of View

It's a bit of a misconception to state that most ludologists don't believe that any form of narrative can exist within games. Instead, their primary contention is that focusing on what narrative elements there may be within a game is an inadequate method for understanding what a game is and how it does what it does. One notable exception is Markku Eskelinen, one of the earliest and foremost proponents of ludology, who seems to believe a story is a story and a game is a game and never the twain shall meet. He writes, "It should be self-evident that we can't apply print narratology, hypertext theory, film or theater and drama studies directly to computer games, but it isn't . . . . If you actually know your narrative theory (instead of resorting to outdated notions of Aristotle, Propp, or Victorian novels) you won't argue that games are (interactive or procedural) narratives or anything even remotely similar." Eskelinen follows this backhanded slap at the narratologists with several reasons why, despite some games admittedly having narrative elements such as characters and plot, they are fundamentally different from true narrative forms.

His argument proceeds through three basic points of contention involving how the elements of narrative actually function in a game as opposed to a story, the relationship of the player to the game versus the reader to the narrative, and how time is treated differently in games and narratives. Returning to the story / discourse dichotomy of a narrative, Eskelinen defines these elements as "a temporal sequence of events (a plot if you want to water down the concept) and a narrative situation (with both narrators and narrates for starters)." The sequence of events is, of course, the story and the "narrative situation" the discourse. He goes on to argue that there is a critical difference between a sequence of events being recounted as in a narrative, and a sequence of events being produced by actions of the player through interaction in a game. Also, the discourse occurs differently in a game than in a narrative he insists, since characters in a game don't truly act like narrators or even characters in a narrative. So to summarize, even though both story and discourse can and obviously do exist in games, they function entirely differently in Eskelinen's opinion than they do in narratives.

Eskelinen also makes a key distinction in how a player relates to a game as opposed to how a reader or observer experiences a narrative. Specifically, he asserts that, "the dominant user function in literature, theater and film is interpretative, but in games it is the configurative one. Consequently, gaming is seen here as configurative practice, and the gaming situation as a combination of ends, means, rules, equipment, and manipulative action." Finally, Eskelinen relates how time is handled differently in games and narratives, by citing the presence of two distinct time frames in a narrative piece - the time when the events of the story take place, and the time when they are being related to the reader (the discourse). Games, he says, have only one primary time frame, which occurs as the player progresses through the game. Even games that use flashbacks and cut scenes to present narrative content still present them within the context of the primary timeline of the game. In other words, a player's actions to arrive at a certain point in the game trigger the delivery of the cut scene or flashback, so within the context of the game it is still occurring in relation to the primary timeline.

I don't mean to slight the ideas and writings of other ludologists; I've chosen to use this piece by Eskelinen because it addresses many of the issues necessary to try and fit alternate reality games into the game versus story debate. One other recurring theme found in ludology and important for our discussion is the idea of the inherent conflict between interactivity and narrative as another reason why interactive games cannot be considered true narratives. Andy Cameron addresses this issue in his work, <u>D I S S I M U L A T I O N S: illusions of interactivity</u>, where he writes, "There is a contradiction at the heart of the idea of the interactive narrative - that narrative form appears fundamentally non-interactive." The main point of Cameron's theory is the belief that interactivity in a game changes the very way the game is experienced by the player to something entirely different than the experience of reading or other forms of narrative. "It is here that we find the apparent disjuncture between the nature of interactivity and that of narrative. The moment the reader intervenes to change the story (at the nodes of multi-linear narrative or at every moment in a spatio-temporal simulator) is the moment when the story changes from being an account of events which have already taken place to the experience of events which are taking place in the present. Story time becomes real time, an account becomes an experience, the spectator or reader becomes a participant or player, and the narrative begins to look like a game."

Before we look at how the concepts of ludology fit into the question of whether or not ARGs can be classified as interactive stories, let's examine the other side of the ludology versus narratology debate for relevant points about the unique genre of Alternate Reality Gaming.

The Narratologist's Story

Perhaps the most frequently quoted of the narratologists is Janet Murray, who penned one of the definitions of immersion used in Chapter 2, as well as contributing the idea of the process of immersion / agency / transformation discussed in the same chapter. Murray is a firm believer and advocate of the importance of the narrative quality of games, both to their understanding by the academic community and to their potential as truly immersive and transformative environments. In her various writings she cites many examples of the common elements in both narratives and games, one of which being the fact that both narratives and games commonly share the similar structure of being contests or "opposition between forces," referring back to one of definitions of a game found in Chapter 1. Games and stories can also take on the structure of a puzzle, according to Murray, meaning that, at some level, both endeavors require the participant, be they reader or player, to solve things throughout the process. She cites a mystery novel as an example of a narrative incorporating a puzzle structure, encouraging the reader to solve the mystery as he reads, although the puzzles don't become gateway points like they often do in games.

Like many narratologists, Murray fundamentally believes narratives, stories, are the way we as humans perceive everything in our world, and therefore cannot be eliminated from consideration when analyzing games. "The human brain, the map of the earth, the protocols of human relationships, are all elements in an improvised collective story-game, an aggregation of overlapping, conflicting, constantly morphing structures that make up the rules by which we act and interpret our experiences." This belief is echoed in an essay by Hayden White entitled "Critical Responses: The Narrativization of Real Events," in which he states, "Narrative is a form of human comprehension that is productive of meaning by its imposition of certain formal components on a virtual chaos of events, which in themselves cannot be said to possess any particular form at all, much less the kind we associate with stories."

One of the problems with narratology is that almost all of the arguments for interactive fiction or games being considered as true narrative experiences are based on hypothetical imaginings of what the "story-game" would actually be like, since no one seems to believe that anyone has actually achieved this new narrative form yet. Consequently, much of the narratologists' writings begin by summarizing the shortcomings of the current batch of experiences commonly labeled as interactive fiction, and detailing how they all fall short of being both truly interactive and engaging, or truly a narrative experience. Nevertheless, a few of the concepts and possibilities they raise can help us finally determine exactly where alternate reality games belong in this whole mix.

Two of the areas continuously mentioned as places where existing attempts at interactive fiction fall short are interactivity and character development. Not coincidentally, these same two items are common arguing points for the ludologists. Why not, if the narratologists are willing to admit they are problem areas? To their credit, however, many of the narratologists do suggest possible solutions to both of these issues in their hypothetical ponderings about how an interactive narrative might truly take shape.

Michael Mateas, in his work entitled <u>A Preliminary Poetics for Interactive Drama and Games</u>, invokes Aristotle's dramatic theory, which establishes a structure for a narrative experience, as the ludological perspective and Janet Murray's three aesthetic categories of immersion, agency, and transformation, as the narratological perspective for the same structure. In doing so, he focuses on how Murray's idea of agency, which is the ultimate goal of interactivity, can be integrated into the Aristotelian narrative structure. While many other narratologists claim the problem with interactivity is that the creator can never envision and include enough choices or chances for interactivity to ever make a fictional world really believable, Mateas argues that the problem isn't in the number of choices, but the type of choices given and the underlying logic provided to the player for making those choices. He writes, " . . . adding more material opportunities for action would not help the matter. The problem is not a lack of options of things to do, the problem is having insufficient formal constraint to decide between the choices." In other words, the concept of interactivity in and of itself is not the problem; the problem lies in how the interaction is presented. If the game can somehow achieve a believable, internally consistent world in which the player has the information necessary to make choices that affect the game in predictable or at least understandable ways, then interaction in the form of agency can indeed be combined with the narrative form.

The final aspect of interactive fiction that will help us place ARGs at their proper spot on the game versus story dialectic is the area of character development. Again, this is one of the most often cited problems with the whole concept of interactive fiction and one area that even narratologists point to as a shortcoming in their theories. Ken

Perlin, who's aptly titled "Can There Be a Form between a Game and a Story?" admits, "There has been some movement in the computer gaming world toward something that one would call 'character.' But these attempts have been hindered by the fact that characters in games can't act within an interactive scene in any compelling way." Perlin continues by suggesting that a willing suspension of disbelief in a character requires three elements: writing, directing and acting, of which acting is the one where games always end up inadequate. Finally, Perlin posits new and improved forms of artificial intelligence as possible solutions to the dilemma of creating believable characters in games. Unfortunately, as has already been explained, even the best artificial intelligence programs carry with them the metacommunications that identify them as artificial, if they are still presented in a symbolic interface as is present in almost every kind of game, so Perlin's suggestions don't seem to me to be the right solution to the problem. Instead, this is another area where the unique properties of an alternate reality game may be able to overcome this much-debated obstacle. The next chapter takes a look at what features an alternate reality game might actually contain and how its unique features make things like believable interactive characters actually possible.

Chapter 4: If It's Not a Game or an Alternate Reality, What Is It?

Now that we have a general conception of the basic components of both games and stories, we need to have some understanding of what an ARG actually is before we can decide if an alternate reality game really fits into either category at all. The previous chapters pretty much defined what an alternate reality game is not, in terms of common regular game elements, but didn't try and explain what elements or components it might actually have.

What follows is a capsule summary of what an alternate reality game might include, although, like just about everything else involving ARGs, don't expect it to be definitive or all-inclusive. As was stated before, there really are no hard and fast rules for creating an immersive game, but this summary will serve as a starting point.

Rabbit Holes

An alternate reality game normally begins with a *rabbit hole*, so named because it presents an opening into another world, much like the rabbit hole in Lewis Carroll's <u>Alice in Wonderland</u>. To be completely faithful to the *TINAG* philosophy, a game's beginning (or *launch*, as they are commonly referred to) should be unannounced, although not all ARGs have followed this procedure and have still been successful. Quite often, the rabbit hole takes the form of a plea for help on an Internet message board or in an e-mail someone receives. At the very least it will be a description of some strange or dangerous situation someone has found himself or herself in. For example, in the ARG developed to promote the Steven Spielberg movie **A.I.: Artificial Intelligence**, tiny clues were placed on the promotional movie posters and in the credits of the movie itself that led players to ultimately discover the fictional world that came to be known as **the Beast**. These clues - circled letters on the back of the posters and a strange, non-sequitur listing for Jeanine Salla, "Sentient Machine Therapist" in the movies' credits - eventually caused thousands of people to get involved and try and help figure out who killed a fictional character within the game.

Another example of a well-executed, unannounced rabbit hole took place in the summer of 2004 when members of the ARG community, who also happened to be fans of reality television programs, noticed an announcement for an upcoming show called **Urban Hunt** on websites that regularly promoted any and all upcoming reality TV programs. It appeared innocent enough, until people contacted the informational e-mail address for the show and received an auto-responder reply that contained a hidden message. What seemed to be a totally legitimate new reality TV show announcement turned out to be a rabbit hole into a new game and players found an entire alternate reality of eight websites waiting for them at the launch, which expanded to close to twenty sites by game's end. The key to the successful rabbit hole was the fact that the announcement showed up on legitimate, out of game websites, who were tricked into thinking the press release they received was real.

A good rabbit hole needs to appear realistic and intriguing, and will hopefully motivate whoever finds it to proceed further into the fictional world they have unwittingly discovered. If done right, the player doesn't even know that a game has begun and that he is already playing it, the perfect example of the *TINAG* philosophy in action. Instead, the player is drawn to keep investigating because of the clues and pieces he has begun to uncover, signs that there may be much more to this strange little website or message he has found while browsing the Internet.

Most often, the initial clues will lead the players to a series of *in-game* websites, that is, websites with fictional content and characters made specifically for the game. Most ARG creators try to make these sites look as realistic as possible, and not just in terms of appearance. If a website is supposed to be for a functional business, then the website will have (or should have) functional contact methods, such as e-mail addresses and even phone numbers. These initial websites should set the stage for the unfolding storyline of the game, and introduce some

A promotional post card recruiting contestants for the upcoming fictional show **Urban Hunt**. Actual postcards were distributed at a gathering of reality television fans in Las Vegas, Nevada to help launch the game.

of the main characters and / or entities. They should also leave the new player with a sense of mystery and intrigue, encouraging them to look a little closer and dig a little deeper. And so the game begins.

As it progresses, the game eventually reveals more and more of its "reality" through web page updates, player / character interaction, and puzzles. Puzzles have been an integral part of almost every ARG that has been created to date, and are often used as a means of both challenging and rewarding players during the course of the game. Sometimes these puzzles are obvious and direct, such as a web page with a piece of encrypted text on it, making it clear what the player must do to solve it. More often than not, ARG games use fairly well known encryption schemes, such as ROT or Vignere encryption, although game creators are constantly finding new and novel ways to integrate these existing coding methods. Other times the puzzles can take the form of anything the creators of the game can imagine, and the variety of puzzles types employed in games so far has been truly amazing. Much like alternate reality games themselves, sometimes the puzzles are so well done that they don't even appear to be puzzles at all.

Sometimes the in-game updates and changes that drive the plot in an ARG occur on a predictable schedule, while other games use a more realistic approach of having updates, interactions, and website changes happen any and all times of the day and days of the week. The hugely successful game **the Beast** maintained a strict schedule of all in-game changes and events happening once a week, on Tuesdays. While such a concrete schedule definitely hurts the reality and immersion levels of the game, it has the advantage of allowing players to plan their schedules around the game and keeping them from getting overwhelmed with too much information. It also obviously allows the game creators to pace the game and spread out the material and content. On the down side, it slaps the players in the face with the knowledge that it is indeed a game and violates the ARG philosophy of *TINAG* by definition.

Puppetmasters

The creators of alternate reality games are commonly referred to as *Puppetmasters*, because they control the puppets on the stage, that is, the characters in the game. Most successful ARGs have had teams of Puppetmasters creating and running them, as the skills required to pull off an alternate reality game are quite diverse and hard to find in any one person. Additionally, a well-done ARG requires an enormous amount of man-hours in planning and development and having a team obviously reduces the overall length of time in the development cycle. There have been games produced by single Puppetmasters in the past (more on them in the History chapters), but they have been the exceptions to the rule for sure.

Interactions

The interactions in an alternate reality game can take many forms and are generally designed to imitate the kinds of interactions a player might have in his everyday life. In the best games the characters will use real communication methods, such as e-mail messages or telephone calls, to talk to and sometimes guide the players in their adventure. Many ARGs also integrate different forms of Internet instant messaging as well, and it is not unusual for in-game characters to appear online and chat with the players. If done properly, real-time interactions like this go a long way in helping to establish the believability of the characters.

A large percentage of ARG players are already familiar with and actively use instant messaging in real life anyway, so many of the real people they regularly interact with through their *Buddy Lists* are only known to them through the various web messaging programs. In other words, the text chats they have with their friends (as represented by their online *screen names*) are the only reality to many of their real life friends anyway. Because of this, well written character interaction using instant messaging can make the game characters as real to the players as many of their out of game, everyday friends. That is one of the elements that help make ARGs realistic and powerfully immersive.

Some games, such as the ill-fated **Majestic** from Electronics Arts, use online *chatbots* to automate the player / character instant messaging communication, with scripted programs attempting to imitate real people and portray the different characters. Unfortunately, most of the time, it quickly becomes clear that it is a chatbot talking rather than a real person, which ultimately hurts the overall believability and immersion factor of the game.

Real World Events

A few ARGs have successfully made real world events and items part of the game, further transcending the limitations of the Internet and making the games even more immersive. The aforementioned **I Love Bees** game not only used pay phone calls that players had to go out and answer, but also had four actual player meetings at the end of the game, where the dedicated players were allowed to play **Halo 2** five days before it was released to the public. Other games, such as the **Matrix**-inspired and independently produced **MetaCortechs** and another independent game called **Chasing The Wish**, actually hid real items representing their *in-game* counterparts for players to find and recover.

In **MetaCortechs**, the items were computer discs that contained information important to the game. Perhaps the most ambitious integration of real world items so far, however, has been by **Chasing The Wish**, which had many real items and artifacts included as part of the game, and made finding and collecting them critical to solving the mystery of the plot. These items included nine "magic" stones, an ancient hieroglyphic message disc, antique manuscript pages, and several paintings, all created especially for the game. Only after players had found and collected these real world items were they able to solve the mysteries and finish the game.

But honestly, an ARG game doesn't need to include any real world items or even real time interaction between players and characters, to be popular or successful. As long as the game has well planned and well presented concepts and content, it can take on whatever form and methods the Puppetmasters can imagine. The ultimate goal is the illusion of the reality of the game's fictional world, and the PMs of different games have found many different ways to accomplish this.

NOTE: For a more thorough understanding of some of the elements and techniques commonly found in alternate reality games and how to go about actually playing one, please refer to the complete sample ARG especially created for this book entitled **Errant Memories** *and located in Appendix G.*

Chapter 5: Interactive Authoring

Fitting ARGs into the Game versus Story Dialectic

In the previous four chapters we've looked at different definitions and elements of both games and stories in an effort to figure out where alternate reality games might fit in. We've identified the features of both categories that ARGs share, as well as the parts of the definitions that didn't seem to apply at all. In summary, it appears we have two choices: either the definitions we are using are too limiting and don't accurately reflect all the possible variations of stories or games, or alternate reality games really are a new form of entertainment altogether, a hybrid that combines many of the best features of both stories and games.

Game Elements in Alternate Reality Games

Of the four critical game components we have identified as part of our definition of a game, alternate reality games don't necessarily have any of them, at least under the restrictive definitions game theorists have traditionally applied to games. But, upon a little closer examination and analysis, we determined that ARGs can be said to have them all, just not in the traditional ways associated with games. For example, an alternate reality game can be said to have rules but they aren't defined and written out anywhere. Instead, the player learns these rules through his observation of and interaction with the game. In this way, alternate reality games are a very special form of game, shedding the restrictive concept of defined rules and taking on more of the appearance of true play. This is why I have not made a real distinction between play and games in terms of ARGs; because of the very nature of alternate reality games, the normal distinction between the two is virtually irrelevant.

This is unique to alternate reality games, because most forms of games would collapse into chaos right at the beginning if the players didn't have any idea how to proceed. This doesn't happen in ARGs because the mechanics of the game, or the pieces if you will, are things the players already know how to use, so they at least have a starting point, a frame of reference to initially guide them. After that, the ARG depends on the scripted events and interactions of the game to guide the players down the path to learning the logic of the fictional world, which, for all intents and purposes, serves as the rule set for the game. The unique features of constant PM monitoring and real-time interaction also allow the Puppetmasters to serve as the rulebook, in the sense that they reward correct actions and discourage incorrect ones through their responses.

As we've already explained, the game space and components of an alternate reality game also appear non-existent at first but again, that's not entirely true. Alternate reality games have both of these things, but are different from other games because the game space and components in ARGs are the real world and communication methods and devices a person uses everyday in his life, respectively.

Story Elements in Alternate Reality Games

We've seen that ARGs do have many similarities to traditional narrative forms of entertainment like stories, but the inclusion of interaction with the audience raises problems under the strict definitions of stories used by many theorists. These issues are magnified if the goal of the game developer is to create an immersive experience, because immersion requires the player having a feeling of agency in the game and not just opportunities for mechanical and meaningless interaction. Agency implies that the player has a both the understanding necessary to make meaningful decisions in the game and also the belief that his actions affect the experience in a significant way. Normally, any interaction in a traditional narrative piece ultimately feels artificial and fails because the choices and responses need to be pre-written, and it is impossible for the writer to envision and account for every possible option at any given moment. Consequently, the pre-written responses are always limited, allowing for only one or a few "correct" player choices.

The same problem arises when a specialized form of interaction is attempted in narrative works - creating a believable fictional character in an interactive setting. Even with the most advanced artificial intelligence programs, it is virtually impossible to create a simulated character that sounds real and can respond to any and all questions in a logical and consistently in-game manner. So standard digital games, which by necessity have to rely on some form of pre-written programming to portray characters in the game, have little chance of achieving the level of reality in their characters required to allow a game to become effectively immersive.

The Power of Interactive Authoring

Alternate reality games are unique among both different forms of narratives and games in many aspects, but perhaps none as significant as the fact that they allow for *interactive authoring*. In other words, ARG creators are able to watch the players virtually in real time, as they experience the game, and react to what the players are doing and feeling, immediately if necessary. No other entertainment or art form has this level of immediate and direct interaction between author and audience, and it is an unimaginably powerful tool for helping ARG writers create truly responsive, realistic, and immersive environments. All of the unique applications I described above involve this concept, and this is what makes it possible for an ARG to be an actual game-story hybrid. While some other forms of episodic entertainment, television shows for example, can do this to some extent, because of the great length of time between the airing of the first episode and the last of any particular season or story arc, there is nowhere near the immediacy or responsiveness that ARGs allow. ARG creators can change their content overnight if necessary, whereas TV shows and most other media require a much greater reaction and production time.

I'm not suggesting that Puppetmasters change their story in major ways in most cases, only in minor ways that reflect and enhance the players' overall experience. It is the small things, the details, which tend to make fictional stories more believable and psychologically powerful anyway. Interactive authoring allows the ARG writer to see which elements of his story or mechanics of the game aren't working as intended and, in fact, may be disrupting the all-important illusion of reality. In many cases, the things pointed out to him by constantly monitoring the players' actions and statements are things that he can't readily see, because of his depth of involvement with the game and knowledge of upcoming events. This constant cycle of author / audience interaction gives the ARG creator a truly unique perspective on his work and allows him to create a powerful and responsive fictional world.

This feature of interactive authoring also offers unique potential solutions to many of the problems raised in the game versus story debates covered in this first section of the book. Two of the main problems with the concept of interactive fiction commonly cited by theorists are interaction and the creation of believable fictional charac-

61

ters, as discussed in detail in Chapter 3. The genre of Alternate Reality Gaming and its inherent interactive authoring process promise solutions to both of these problem areas.

Depending on whose theories you read and subscribe to, the problem with interaction and interactive fiction is either that the designer can never build in enough choices for his fictional world to ever become real, or that the reader often doesn't have enough knowledge of and insight into the logic of the fictional world to make meaningful decisions. Believing that he has made correct choices that influence the events in the game is a necessary element of creating a sense of agency within the reader. On the one hand, some writers argue that an interactive fictional scene can never be realistic if the author cannot account for and build-in every possible choice a person would have in the same scenario in real life. This is, of course, impossible for an author to do, so their claim is that interactive fiction is at best a myth, something that cannot ever really be achieved. Something is either narrative fiction or interactive but not both.

The other side of the argument is that the number of choices in an interactive scenario is meaningless unless the reader has some logical basis for understanding his choices and their implications and for making the right choice. Without this logical underpinning, the reader's choices become truly random, and therefore can have no real meaning or impact to the context of the story. Instead of engendering a feeling of agency, they actually remind the reader of the artificiality of the fictional world and disrupt any sense of immersion there may have been.

The interactive authoring aspect of ARGs can potentially address both sides of the dilemma of interactivity. The crux of the first argument is that the virtually unlimited number of possible interactive options inherent in any real world scenario can never be written into a fictional interactive encounter. If the number of potential choices were infinite, then a narrative anticipating and including them all would also have to be infinitely long. In an alternate reality game, an interactive encounter, while pre-written, doesn't have to anticipate every possible choice a player might make, because each encounter is being managed in real time by one or more of the creators of the work. In the same manner that a skilled author directs readers to certain discoveries and understandings throughout the course of his novel, an experienced PM can do the same thing in an interactive portion of the game. If the interaction is in the form of an instant messaging conversation and the PM is playing the role of a character, his communication of the character's understanding of the fictional world becomes the basis for the player's future decisions. He doesn't need to provide an infinite number of choices and their subsequent consequences, only a contextual basis for understanding why certain choices are appropriate and others aren't. Interestingly, this same approach also solves the reverse side of the interactivity debate, by providing the knowledge necessary for a player to feel as if they are making informed and correct decisions, and impacting the fictional world in a meaningful way. These, of course, are the necessary components of agency, one of the most important steps to providing a truly immersive experience.

Another major obstacle cited by many experts to ever achieving a real form of interactive fiction is the extreme difficulty in creating believable interactive characters. While powerfully realistic characters can and certainly have been created by skilled authors in traditional works of narrative fiction; i.e., novels and short stories, it is only their careful and deliberate use of established literary techniques that enable the writers to achieve this effect. More importantly, narrative writers control both sides of any fictional interaction within the work, choosing what both characters in the interaction do and say. In interactive fiction and alternate reality games, the reader (or player) assumes the role of one of the characters in the interaction and, as such, the author totally loses control over one side of the interaction. Previous concepts and incarnations of interactive fiction traditionally fail when it comes to creating believable characters in these situations because they have all attempted to use some form of automated program or mechanism to simulate human response. Even the more optimistic proponents of the chance of anyone ever being able to create a form of truly interactive fiction tend to look to the future possibilities of artificial intelligence as the one thing that might eventually make simulated yet realistic characters possible. Realistically however, experts in the fields of artificial intelligence will admit that such technology is years and years away.

The potential for interactive authoring in alternate reality games yields a different and, I believe, much better solution to the problem, by eliminating the need for simulating human response altogether. Although the personality of the character is obviously fictional and the things he says written by an author, there is nothing artificial or simulated about the interaction itself. The methods the player is using to interact with the character are the same ones he uses in his everyday existence, and the responses he receives come from a real albeit role-playing person. Since it is generally in how a simulated character responds to input where the *interactive* in interactive fiction falls apart, ARGs remove the simulation and allow for realistic player / character interaction, eliminating yet another obstacle traditionally working against creating immersive fictional environments.

Finally, interactive authoring has one more important and potentially very powerful implication as well. In some cases, the players of an ARG can actually be allowed to influence, or at least feel as if they have influenced, key segments of the story because of the interactive authoring capabilities inherent in the genre. By presenting the players a choice and monitoring their discussion and actions towards selecting an option, the Puppetmasters can guide the plot accordingly, making the players believe that they have indeed influenced the game in a significant way. This level of interaction adds to the immersive nature of the ARG, as well as making the players feel even more invested in the game.

This concept is perfectly illustrated in an incident from the ARG **the Beast**, as related by one of the game's creator's, Elan Lee, to author Mark Stephen Meadows in his book, <u>Pause and Effect: The Art of Interactive Narrative</u>.

"Meadows: What was the interaction between the authors – you guys – and the readers, or players? Was there an instance when you didn't know what the outcome would be but had to keep writing anyway?

Lee: Oh, definitely. There was one puzzle where there was no answer. We had no idea how it was going to resolve. There was an artificial character that thrived on nightmares and was born in a psychological institute that had become so addicted to nightmares, it was looking for what scared people the most. See, it had to generate more nightmares to feed itself. We opened up the doors to the players and wrote out a distress call: "Help me" came from a character that the players liked who Loki had overwhelmed, but we didn't know what the response would be. We wanted to leave it to the players to come up with something creative. They wanted to find a way to trap Loki and put out bait and destroy him, so they all got together – thousands of people – and they made a dream database and put all of their own nightmares into this database (it was beautiful to see them all work together like that), so we directed Loki toward the site and there he died. We created the animation sequence of Loki living through one line of everyone's nightmare and phrased it in a way that read from everyone's paragraph, but it was a single series of a total, truly nightmarish experience.

Meadows: That's a pretty unique form of authorship that gives a lot of control to readers.

Lee: Oh yeah. The players felt totally in control and totally powerful, so the game was changing the story based on their specific writing."

Dave Szulborski

Part Two:

Alternate Reality Games

in History

Dave Szulborski

Chapter 6: ARG Pre-History

Looking at alternate reality games from an academic and theoretical level has helped us partially define what they are, and allowed us to begin understanding their unique features and abilities. By examining ARGs from a historical perspective, studying early alternate reality games and their predecessors, we can hopefully get a better understanding of what forms they have taken in the past and for what purposes they have been used. Because of its unusually diverse nature, the alternate reality game has roots in many different entertainment forms and cultural traditions, and we can find early elements of the ARG in many examples in these fields. In particular, we'll look at works that used dramatic or narrative techniques in an attempt to create a fictional yet immersive environment. By definition, this implies the creator's attempt to use illusion and interactivity to create a sense of engagement or agency in between the audience and whatever media the creator is working in.

Immersive Art

I've already described some early attempts at immersive art-work, including prehistoric cave paintings and the panoramic paintings done by 19th century artists, although none of these were interactive in any way. A more recent example of using art to create an immersive and interactive environment is the work of artist Char Davies, whose groundbreaking projects Osmose and Ephémère are the first experiments in which an interactive virtual reality environment has been conceived and created as a piece of art. Hiding Spaces, created by Cynthia Beth Rubin and Daniel F. Keefe, is another virtual reality based piece of immersive art that is of particular interest because it is a deliberate attempt to recreate the effect of the immersive environments present in the very cave paintings cited as the beginnings of immersive art. Other recent examples of attempts to integrate interactivity and immersive art are the multitude of software programs available in the last few years that allow users to create 360° interactive panoramas from digital photographs. Of course, none of these forms of interactive art attempt to create entire immersive fictional worlds, only brief interactive encounters.

Immersion in Literature

As we've already discussed, immersion, or the feeling of getting lost in a book, is common in the field of literature, with innumerable examples of skilled authors with the abilities to draw their readers emotionally into the imaginary worlds they create. Additionally, some literature has addressed the idea of artificially created immersive environments thematically, beginning with Ray Bradbury's story "The Veldt" back in 1951, which included an interactive nursery able to generate multiple virtual environments. William Gibson has taken the idea even further in his conceptions of cyberspace in many of his works including Neuromancer, and Neal Stephenson has done likewise in The Diamond Age. It would also appear that Mr. Gibson has been paying attention to the ARG phenomena, because in January, 2003 he published Pattern Recognition. The plot of Pattern Recognition involves a cult-like group of Internet obsessives that strives to find meaning and patterns within a mysterious collection of video moments, merely called "the footage," let loose onto the Internet by an unknown source. If that doesn't sound like an ARG, then I don't know what does.

An overview of immersive fiction in contemporary literature wouldn't be complete without at least mentioning House of Leaves by Mark Z. Danielewski. Briefly, the work was a print / digital crossover success, starting out as a curious website before getting picked up by a print publisher. House of Leaves spilled over between web page and print page, using footnotes, appendices, and text placement in the print book, as well as a soundtrack ('Haunted' by Poe) and interactive web elements to further deepen the interactive and immersive experience. An in-depth look at House of Leaves can be found in Wes Unruh's excellent review at http://www.loudwire.net/~wesunruh/9149.html.

Although there is a strong tradition of interaction in oral story-telling in most cultures, it is much more difficult to find examples of authors attempting to translate that interactivity into the written or printed form. Some experts consider early steganographic works, as exemplified by the writings of Johannes Trithemius, interactive because they require the reader to do something with the text in order to uncover the hidden writing concealed within. The same would have to be said for authors who used various forms of cryptography to conceal secret messages in their works, such as Sir Francis Bacon, and even of such pieces as the Voynich Manuscript, thought to contain hidden meaning in its seemingly nonsensical drawings and text.

The early days of the personal computer saw the rise of a new form of interactive literature, the computer text adventure, although many would question its status as literature at all. Still, these adventures, such as the legendary **Zork**, brought new levels of interactivity to a narrative-based entertainment form. Almost simultaneously with their computer-based counterparts, printed versions of this form of story also came into being in the form of "Choose Your Own Adventure" books. Although they could hardly be considered realistic or immersive, they were early attempts at creating a sense of agency in readers by allowing them to significantly affect the events of the story. These types of adventures were popular enough for a brief while to spawn video-tapes and computer games in the same mold, in an effort to also try and create a visual sense of immersion by integrating visual components into the experience. In fact, these early "Choose Your Own Adventure"

74

video games can be seen as the beginnings of the "point and click" or graphical puzzle adventure genre of video gaming that reached is highpoint in the game **Myst**.

The concept of branching narratives that forms the basis of these kinds of fictional adventures can actually be traced back to earlier and more serious literary works, with Jorge Luis Borges' 1941 story "The Garden of Forking Paths" perhaps being the most famous and oft-cited example. Other examples of literature incorporating elements of interactivity through non-linear narratives include Laurence Sterne's Tristram Shandy and James Joyce's Finnegans Wake, both of which encourage the reader to experience the text in different ways, reflecting the author's intent to redefine the relationship of the audience and the work. This form of literature is sometimes called *ergodic* literature, a name coined by Espen J. Aarseth in his book, Cybertext: Perspectives on Ergodic Literature, in which he writes, "In ergodic literature, nontrivial effort is required to allow the reader to traverse the text."

Aarseth lists several early forms of ergodic writing, starting with the I-Ching, the very structure of which forces the reader to experience the text in non-linear and non-traditional ways. He follows with several more recent and more radical examples, such as Guillaume Apollinaire's Calligrammes, a collection of poems published in 1918, employing unusual layout and typography techniques to encourage the reader to explore them in various ways, and Marc Saporta's 1962 experiment called Composition no 1, a novel published as individual pages which the author suggested the reader shuffle and then read in a whatever order resulted. Another radical example of the same concept can be found in Raymond Queneau's "Cent mille millards de poemes," a 1961 work consisting of ten pages, each with fourteen lines. Each page of the work is cut into strips, so that by interacting with the work, the reader creates his own verse by mixing and matching any combination of the fourteen lines.

Interactivity in a printed narrative probably reached its height with a book called <u>Masquerade</u> written and illustrated by Kit Williams and published originally in 1979. On one level, <u>Masquerade</u> was a simple children's book about the moon falling in love with the sun, but the painted illustrations of the book contained clues and hidden messages that led to a real life treasure hunt. Magician David Blaine copied this idea in his 2002 book <u>Mysterious Stranger</u>, which contained clues for finding a $100,000 treasure. Coincidentally, a fan of alternate reality gaming, a person who had worked behind the scenes with me on one of my games, **Chasing The Wish**, actually solved Blaine's puzzle and won the prize.

Another form of narrative worth noting for containing some elements similar to alternate reality games is known as *epistolary* literature. According to 1990 edition of the Oxford Illustrated Encyclopedia of the Arts, epistolary literature is writing that takes "the form of a series of letters exchanged among the characters of the story with extracts from their journals sometimes included." Works of epistolary fiction can be compared to ARGs in two aspects. Epistolary works often take on the form of fictional letters or diary entries that present themselves as real. Readers are forced to try and ascertain the truth from the various subjective accounts included in the works, implying at least some interaction between the reader and the work. Many ARG games even imitate this format by using the modern day equivalent of diaries – Internet blogs – to present fictional serialized content portraying the inner thoughts or experiences of a character. The ARG player must then construct the imaginary world of the character and game from the inherently subjective blog entries, much like the reader of an epistolary novel is forced to do. The fact that many epistolary novels attempt to disguise the fact that they are indeed works of fiction is another obvious similarity to the techniques employed by the Puppetmasters of today's alternate reality games.

On the Stage

There have been a few attempts to create interactive and immersive environments in the field of live theater. Shows like "Tony and Tina's Wedding" and the murder mysteries that employ audience participation are but a couple of examples. Experiences like this do not evoke any real sense of agency in the participants because there is no feeling that their actions change the story in anyway, but they can offer some insight for the ARG creator into methods used to create the illusion of immersion into a fictional world. The same is true for "dress up" events like Renaissance Fairs and Civil War and other historical reenactments, where at least a sensory level of immersion is possible, although there exists no real narrative to interact with. In some ways, IMAX theater productions mimic this form of sensory immersion too, although they are blatantly artificial in the sense of being a reproduction of reality and not presented as reality itself. One notable exception was a 1936 play by Ayn Rand entitled "Night of January 16th," during which people in the audience were chosen to be members of an onstage jury that actually determined the ending of the play.

The Internet

While all of these ARG precursors included some elements found commonly in alternate reality games, it wasn't until the Internet was developed and became commonplace that the potential to create ARGs in their current form existed. Almost as soon as people discovered the connective and communicative potential of the web, they began to use it to entertain or fool other people in ways very much like alternate reality games.

Early explorers in the use of the Internet for gaming purposes include Flying Buffalo, a company that began by conducting play-by-mail (snail mail) game campaigns in the 1970s, and soon realized that computers could help them run their games and began using the power of personal computers and the early Internet to do so. Although none of Flying Buffalo's games attempted to be immersive or even narrative in anyway, instead being primarily straightforward translations of turn-based strategy board games, they were probably the first to use an Internet form of communication, e-mail, for game related activities.

Another important pioneer in Internet gaming efforts was Steve Jackson and his company Steve Jackson Games (SJG). Founded in 1980 as a developer of traditional board games, SJG launched perhaps the first games-related BBS system in 1986 called *Illuminati Online*. At the same time, SJG had released the first version of their new *GURPS*, or Generic Universal Role Playing System, a system designed to overcome the scenario-specific limitations found in the other role-playing game systems available at the time. Instead if being applicable only to one specific game or setting (fantasy, science fiction, etc.), the GURPS concept could be used in any setting or timeline imaginable, opening up whole new realms of subject matter for potential role-playing games. While the BBS system was primarily a discussion forum and news system for the board and role-playing game products of the company, interestingly it became one of the first examples of the gaming world "crossing over" into the real world with amazing results.

In 1990, Steve Jackson Games was raided by the US Secret Service, primarily because of one specific product the company had been offering. Called GURPS Cyberpunk, the item was a rulebook for a "cyberpunk" role-playing game set in the near future, based loosely on the William Gibson novel Neuromancer. Simultaneously, the home of the author of the GURPS Cyberpunk sourcebook, Loyd Blankenship, was also raided. Among the materials seized were the computers running the Illuminati Online BBS and the source materials for the GURPS Cyberpunk games system. It was believed at the time that, because the rulebook contained information on how to hack into sensitive computer systems within the context of the fictional role-playing system, the Secret Service considered it to be a "handbook for computer crime," failing to take into account its fictional nature. It was later revealed that the raid had really been aimed at Blankenship himself and not SJG directly, because of his association with "the hacker underground" who openly discussed hacking and cracking on BBS systems. While the raid and subsequent legal proceedings nearly shut-down Steve Jackson Games, they were eventually awarded over $50,000 in damages, plus over $250,000 in attorney's fees, and went on to re-establish Illuminati Online in 1993 on the Internet instead of just as a BBS, where it became one of the largest Internet information services, before being sold to PrismNet.

It wasn't long before a new form of online gaming developed that came even closer to the potential of what ARGs would eventually become. In 1978 Roy Trubshaw and Richard Bartle created the first MUD (multi-user dungeon) and deployed it online, allowing multiple players to participate simultaneously in a computer-managed text adventure. Actually, Trubshaw and Bartle's creation predated the rise of popularity of the home versions of the already mentioned computer text adventure, as the game commonly credited for starting the genre, **Zork**, wasn't released until 1979. That year also saw the launch of many more MUD games, as the idea of participating in a fictional reality through the home computer began to take hold, although the narrative aspect of these games was either absent or sadly lacking. It wouldn't be until the early 1980s that a new narrative form came into existence on the Internet that would attempt to combine the concepts of interactivity and storytelling in this newly defined entity of cyberspace.

Ted Nelson first used the word "hypertext" in 1965 and the concept it defined became the technological platform for the World Wide Web. In the early 1980s, the Internet was still predominantly text based, so it seemed only natural that other text based forms of entertainment would find their way online eventually. Since the graphic, video, and audio capabilities of the Internet were either non-existent or extremely limited at the time, the only true art form for which the web could serve as an outlet was literature. And in the early 1980s, the idea of *hypertext fiction* was born.

While there were short experiments in hypertext fiction in the early and mid-1980s, it was Michael Joyce's *"Afternoon. A Story."* published by Eastgate Systems in 1987 that broke the idea of hypertext fiction to the world. Like alternate reality games, *"Afternoon. A Story."* took readers by surprise, as there was no explicit navigation system or explanatory text describing how the viewer was supposed to make their way through the piece. In other words, it didn't present itself as what it was – a non-linear narrative fiction – but instead forced readers to discover that underlying truth on their own. The work was taken seriously enough to be reviewed by both the New York Review of

Books and The Washington Post, and has since come to be recognized as both the starting point and the high-water mark of the genre. Sadly, fans and students of hypertext fiction are still debating to this day, seventeen years after *"Afternoon. A Story."* was published, if anything better or different than it can ever really be done. The only significant changes to the genre since then have been the integration of various new forms of media as they have become available on the Internet.

You can see the various building blocks and ideas of alternate reality games taking shape in the pioneering and experimental works mentioned above. It is all of these components and concepts that the creators of **the Beast** would so skillfully weave together to create what most people call the first ARG over a dozen years later. Often overlooked however, are two intermediate steps from the 1990s, two online projects that were much closer to being alternate reality games than they are commonly given credit for. In fact, I believe that if either of these projects were done today, using basically the same methods as they did then (allowing for new technology, of course), they would indeed be called alternate reality games. Unfortunately, they were done at a time when the Internet was not as user friendly and ubiquitous as it is now, so it was much more difficult for players to find out about, communicate with each other about, or work collectively on to solve these online mysteries. One of these games, Pink Floyd's **Publius Enigma**, actually has been pointed to by some unofficial ARG historians as being the first true alternate reality game, since it began in 1994, seven years before **the Beast** debuted. The other project, however, began even before **Publius Enigma**, and could arguably be called the first ARG ever.

Ong's Hat: Incunabula

It's hard to say exactly when the interactive online mystery that has come to be known as **Ong's Hat: Incunabula** actually began. Do an online search for the terms and you'll be rewarded with an endless repetition of the claim "The delightful legend of the Ong's Hat travel cult has been posted in the form of the 'Incunabula Papers' since the earliest days of BBS and Internet communications." Dig a little deeper and you can find traces of online activity that, in retrospect, can only be considered the *in-game* telling of the story, throughout the 1990s, and real world evidence reaching back as far as 1988, when small pieces appeared in cyber-science fiction magazines, like the old Boing-Boing print magazine, Xerox 'zines' and catalogs, mail-art networks, and photocopied newsletters. As already defined for ARGs, the story was delivered through various media and methods and, at many points, required some form of action or interaction from the "player" to proceed further into the mysteries of the tale. The well-researched and intricately detailed plot, much too long and twisted to do justice to with a brief summary here, took years to unfold and represents, in my opinion, the first real attempt to create a believable and interactive fictional world using the tools of the Internet.

Like any good narrative, the Ong's Hat story actually intertwined two distinct plots or sequences of events: the events in the Ong's Hat Ashram in the 1970s that the "Incunabula Papers" allegedly detail, which served as the *story* level of the narrative, and the discovery and distribution of the documents sometime later, which served as the *discourse* level of the narrative. So, undeniably, the Ong's Hat experience had the aesthetic elements of a story required to make an ARG an immersive experience. Additionally, **Ong's Hat: Incunabula**, by using the various real world communication methods available on the Internet at the time to tell its story, and by requiring players to interact at critical point of the discourse, also incorporated the game elements that traditionally make up and define an alternate reality game. At the very least, like House of Leaves, referenced earlier in this book, it was a literary / digital crossover, utilizing Xerox, BBS and later Internet technology, CD ROM technology, and even traditional print publishing as it's various mediums. In fact, one of the creators of the original CD ROM has said that it included 23 intricate puzzles, most of which were never solved!

Perhaps most telling are the following comments by an Internet researcher named Denny Unger, who spent years unraveling the Ong's Hat mystery and so became one of the foremost authorities on the subject. Writing retrospectively about the experience after it had wound down and most of its secrets had been revealed, Unger writes, "Ong's Hat / Incunabula has always been about levels of understanding. As you research each aspect of the story you are presented with a challenge

84

. . . You find a piece of compelling info that takes you down one path only to find that its a invalid path but wait . . it turns out that the path you thought was a false path is actually the correct path and so on, and so forth." Sounds suspiciously like an ARG, doesn't it?

Unger continues, "A portion of the population just won't 'get' the Incunabula and will pass it off as 'that weird web thing' but some are captured by it, obsessed by its mystery. This obsession generally lasts until that person has extracted whatever meaning is vital to them from the story. There is also another class of Incunabula explorer. This person extends beyond the initial obsession and begins to see a larger picture by piecing together seemingly unrelated bits of information. What this person also sees is a series of carefully constructed tests designed to filter out certain personality types and draw in successful 'candidates'."

Finally, Unger tries to summarize the process of the game as "steps," based on his intimate knowledge of the content, presentation methods, and personal effects of the experience.

"I can break the apparent process down in five simple steps:

1. *Create an interactive medium that immerses the public in an addictive, tantalizing story but keep the content restricted to certain personality types. Reveal concepts and ideas that generally represent your beliefs.*
2. *Along the way, feed this portion of the public information which may or may not be true about the story. (Filtration of the idiots)*

Dave Szulborski

The cover from the book <u>Ong's Hat: The Beginning</u>, part of the mythos that became
Ong's Hat: Incunabula.

3. *Those that breach the truths and untruths may pass to the next level of information. Introduce more directed and personal information. Once again reveal accurate and inaccurate information. (Further idiot filtration)*
4. *As this select group narrows, inject information that more specifically reveals their personal belief systems, ideals, and goals.*
5. *If the users ideals, beliefs and goals have been properly modified by the process or the user already fits the mold, those persons are then accepted into the 'fold'."*

Unger wrote these words in August 2001, after years of involvement with the Ong's Hat material and before anyone was seriously analyzing **the Beast** in these terms. The evidence for this being at least some form of early if not full-fledged alternate reality game is hard to ignore.

Pink Floyd's **Publius Enigma**

In June of 1994 somebody using the name "Publius" began posting enigmatic messages on a Pink Floyd Usenet newsgroup. The initial entry was posted with the simple subject line "The Message" and consisted of the following:

My friends,

You have heard the message Pink Floyd has delivered,
but have you listened?

Perhaps I can be your guide, but I will not solve the enigma for you.

All of you must open your minds and communicate with each other,
as this is the only way the answers can be revealed.

I may help you, but only if obstacles arise.

Listen.

Read.

Think.

Communicate.

If I don't promise you the answers would you go.

Publius

Pink Floyd was touring at the time, promoting their most recent album **The Division Bell**, and many fans passed off the message as either a hoax or some kind of promotional stunt for the album and tour. As the posts continued, however, each one more mysterious and puzzling then the last, Pink Floyd fans began to wonder if there wasn't something more to the whole affair. Publius' messages challenged the fans to solve the mystery presented by both his messages and the **Division Bell** album, and even promised a reward of some sort for the person who did. The members of the Pink Floyd newsgroup reacted with a mixture of messages, half of which angrily decried Publius as a fraud and demanded he present proof of any form to support his claims. The other half of the newsgroup members seemed intrigued by Publius' messages, however, and the possibility of there being a hidden puzzle somewhere inside the latest Pink Floyd album. Many of them had already begun trying to find the clues and solve the puzzles they believed Publius' posts contained.

On July 16, 1994 Publius made a newsgroup post intended, some believe, to answer the challenge of those who doubted him. In it, he told the newsgroup members to watch for a sign in two days in East Rutherford, New Jersey. Coincidentally, Pink Floyd was playing in East Rutherford that night, and precisely at the time Publius had predicted the lights of the show spelled out the words "Enigma Publius" for all to see. The newsgroup doubters quickly became believers and joined in the search for the clues supposedly hidden in the album's content and the artwork found in the booklet included with the album, a search that continues unsuccessfully to this day.

Publius did make additional posts, some of which contained predictions of more real world signs which did take place, including the word "enigma" being projected on the back of the stage at a concert in London in October 1994. More clues have also turned up in other Pink Floyd artwork, specifically in a booklet included in the late 1994 release of **A Momentary Lapse of Reason** in a new format. In 1997 Publius made one final post, the authenticity and implications of which are still being argued.

Many months ago we embarked upon a magical journey. Although most of you displayed truSt at the start---only a haNdful remained faithful. So much has been revealed on thIs newsgroup as to the true nature of modern man (and Woman). Disappointments are heavy upon my hEart. I believe one of you has discovered the truth---and has placed the answer here on this nEwsgroup. I now call for an end to this eniGma. It appears that only one has been foCused on my first message so long ago.

Listen

Read

Think

Communicate

The disbelief on this forum forces me to reveal details in another manner that will be undisputed. This will be forthcoMing. The prize received will be unique as promised. It will be the decision of the winner to discuss it with the rest.

IT IS FINISHED

This message was followed by a post from someone claiming to be the person who solved the mystery, although this individual has never been able to prove it to the satisfaction of most followers of the **Publius Enigma** story. Even in subsequent postings the self-proclaimed winner never provided a detailed explanation of the clues that had been found and universally agreed upon, or convincing evidence of ever having received a prize. Instead, he has said things like, "The reward was in solving the puzzle," despite that fact that several of Publius' messages promised a tangible prize. Whether or not the mystery ever was truly solved, there's no denying that whoever created

Publius Enigma used the very same devices and techniques as found in current alternate reality games.

One of the objections raised by devoted fans of **the Beast** over classifying **Publius Enigma** as an ARG has been the fact that it didn't even use one fictional website, let alone the dozens that the **A.I.** game included. It may be, however, just that any website(s) created for the game have never been discovered, for at least one clue has led people to believe there is indeed a related site. Part of one of Publius' messages was the assertion, "There is great significance in the page numbers," and some clever investigators found a correlation between the twenty four page songbook that came with the **Division Bell** album and Publius' initial message, enabling them to extract an anagrammed hidden message saying "site moniker." This, they believe, is proof that there is a website out there waiting to be found.

More importantly, the recent success of the **I Love Bees** promotional game for **Halo 2** proved that an alternate reality game doesn't need to have dozens of websites to create its illusion of an engaging fictional world, pretty much negating the earlier argument. Just like **ILB, Publius Enigma** used a clever mixture of Internet based communications and real world messages and encounters to convey its story. It could also be argued that the lack of any fictional websites and the plan of relying only on a real world newsgroup message board for communication actually enhances the believability of the project, by removing one more potential layer of artificiality.

If alternate reality games can be defined by the methods and components commonly used to produce them, then it is hard not to classify both **Ong's Hat: Incunabula** and **Publius Enigma** as ARGs. In any case, all that was needed for alternate reality games to reach at least a small level of mainstream consciousness was time - time for the technology of the Internet to become even more pervasive and powerful in terms of multimedia capabilities, and time for the Puppetmasters behind **the Beast** to start creating their paradigm-changing experience.

Chapter 7: A Vision of the Future - the Beast

Whether you consider **the Beast** the first alternate reality game or not, there is no denying that the promotional campaign developed by Microsoft and DreamWorks for Steven Spielberg's movie **Artificial Intelligence (A.I.)** combined the powerfully interactive nature of the Internet with a masterfully written story and unparalleled execution to become the defining moment of the ARG genre for years to come.

Birthing **the Beast**

According to Sean Stewart, the lead writer of **the Beast**, the original idea for creating this new form of online game belonged to Jordan Weisman, who called Sean in the summer of 2000 and asked him to work with a Microsoft employee named Elan Lee on an innovative project, as part of the promotional effort for an upcoming film by Steven Spielberg. Although the project discussed at this original meeting fell through, the foundation had been laid for the team that eventually became the Puppetmasters of **the Beast**. They came together again in early January 2001, once more after a call from Weisman, and began conceiving what they ambitiously termed a "world-changing new art form."

In his "Introduction to the A.I. Web Game" on his website, Stewart lays out the assumptions or tentative goals of the game that were embodied in Weisman's vision of what the game should become.

1. The narrative would be broken into fragments, which the players would be required to reassemble.

2. The game would--of necessity--be fundamentally cooperative and collective, because of the nature of the internet.

3. The game would be cooler if nobody knew who was doing it, or why.

4. The game would be cooler if it came at you, through as many different conduits as possible.

Their charge from Microsoft and the film's creator Steven Spielberg was to create a virtual world exploring the various themes about artificial intelligence that ran through the movie. The world they were to make was not intended to be a simulation or recreation of the events and characters of the actual film, but instead an investigation into the backdrop of the **A.I.** story, the world of 2142. Armed only with that mission statement and the vision of Jordan Weisman's new type of game, they set off to change the world.

Early on they added one more "principle" to Weisman's list of assumptions – the game should never admit it was a game. This idea seems like a natural extension of the third assumption listed above, but it had a particularly personal meaning to writer Stewart. "The mantra--this is not a game--had another meaning particularly important to me. I didn't want this to be a strictly intellectual experience. I didn't want you to be able to view the characters as...game tokens." It is fascinating that Stewart mentions game tokens, the fourth category of defining elements of a game that I added to the three taken from other sources in our original attempts to define a game. If you'll recall, I mentioned having game tokens, and the metacommunications they inherently carry with them in a game, as an almost certain way to *prevent* an immersive environment. Which is, of course, what Stewart is referring to when he says the "strictly intellectual experience" that a non-immersive environment tends to create. Stewart continues with his description of what he wanted the game to be.

"I wanted it to work like art. I wanted people to care, to laugh, to cry--to be engaged the way a novel engages. To put all this ingenuity into the storytelling *method*, and then to tell a stupid story--that would be an unbearable waste. If the game was claiming to be real, the characters in it had to be real too." Stewart's words clearly reflect his deliberate intent to marry the two realms of the story and the game. They also confirm that the purpose of the unique and ingenious storytelling method of using everyday communication methods was an attempt to create an immersive and engaging alternate reality, not just to find a new way to tell a story.

Just two months later, on March 8th, 2001, the first in-game sites were launched in preparation for the release approximately one month later of the **A.I.** movie trailer and billboard ads. The trailer and the movie posters contained the hidden clues that really began the online game. There were actually two separate clues in the trailer, each offering a separate rabbit hole into the fictional world of **the Beast**. The first was an unusual line in the credits of the trailer, easily overlooked among the legitimate names and tasks of people who had worked on the film. The credit read, "Jeanine Salla, Sentient Machine Therapist" and Googling that name provided a link to Bangalore World University, the first in-game website. A news story on the front page of that site mentioned a professor at the university named Dr. Jeanine Salla, and hidden a little deeper into the website were her e-mail address and phone number. The answering machine message at Jeanine's phone number provided the first mention of the recently deceased character Evan Chan and hinted that something just wasn't right with his death.

The second set of clues was in the form of curious notches in the words "Summer 2001" in the trailer and, before long, the notches had been decoded into a phone number. Calling the phone number yielded an intriguing phone message:

"Welcome my child. Once upon a time there was a forest, that teemed with life love, sex and violence. Things that humans did naturally. And their robots copied -- flawlessly. This forest is vast and surprising. It is full of grass, and trees, and databanks, and drowned apartment buildings, filled with fish. It can be a frightening forest, and some of its paths are dark, and difficult. I was lost their once -- a long

time ago. Now I try to help others who have gone astray. If you ever feel lost, my child, write me at thevisionary.net. And I will leave you a trail of crumbs..."

Eventually this path led to a mention of Evan Chan and his murder as well, as the two rabbit holes converged. Players were off and running, searching for that mysterious trail of crumbs leading ever deeper into the world of **the Beast**..

The Interactive Trail

The trail turned out to be a huge and incredibly complex story told across thirty different websites and incorporating hundreds of other in-game assets of various types, from e-mail messages, to video clips, to insanely difficult puzzles. Again, we turn to Sean Stewart's summarized description of their method, as told in his "Introduction to the A.I. Web Game," for insight into how the trail was supposed to work.

"So there was the project: create an entire self-contained world on the web, say a thousand pages deep, and then tell a story through it, advancing the plot with weekly updates, concealing each new piece of narrative in such a way that it would take clever teamwork to dig it out. Create a vast array of assets--custom photos, movies, audio recordings, scripts, corporate blurbage, logos, graphic treatments, web sites, flash movies--and deploy them through a net of (untraceable) web sites, phone calls, fax systems, leaks, press releases, phony newspaper ads, and so on ad infinitum."

Some important things to glean from Stewart's informal analysis of the methodology of **the Beast** include the fact that the story of the game was written and then deliberately broken up and hidden in such a way as to require action from the players to uncover and understand it. More importantly though, is the understanding that what they were doing was *forcing* players to work cooperatively, an essential component of creating the immersive world they intended. By their very nature, ARGs bring groups of players together into communities that work collectively to solve the mysteries of the game. This is evident in the pre-cursor games I mentioned, **Ong's Hat** and **Publius Enigma**, in which almost all the activity of the games revolved around online newsgroups, chat rooms, and discussion groups, but nowhere clearer than in the community of 10,000 plus players that came together to try and solve **the Beast**. These fans came to be known collectively as "the Cloudmakers," and together they posted close to 43,000 online messages in their four month effort to uncover the truth.

Besides the sheer amount of various skills and collective knowledge an alternate reality game brings together, the social nature of the experience and the existence of the online community play important *in-game* roles as well. In a very real way, the other players of the game become *characters in the game* for the individual player, and his interaction with them provides one level of believable human interaction and response within the fictional world of the game. While not the main characters of the game, the other players become the living and breathing backdrop of the alternate reality, against which the story involving the central characters plays out. This technique eliminates the need for a game designer to try and create a simulated and quite often transparently artificial backdrop for the game. When supplemented with carefully scripted and executed interaction with the main characters, the fictional world of the ARG becomes a completely believable and immersive reality.

Even the most well crafted story cannot anticipate and account for the interaction or choices of the players using this method of segmented and scheduled storytelling. This is where the unique *interactive authoring* possibilities of ARGs are so important, because they allow the PM team to monitor the players' progress and actions, and react to them accordingly, based on the pre-defined framework of the story. In their post-game answers to players' questions published as an FAQ on the main Cloudmakers' fan site, **the Beast** PMs acknowledged that this was an inherent part of their strategy. "One of the things we were very excited about was the blurring between fiction and reality. This was best achieved by putting material out there and reacting (as best we could) to whatever method you [the players] decided to use for a solution." In addition in their "Message From the Puppetmasters" they write, "You compelled us to make new sites and fix inconsistencies; when we accidentally used stock photos of the same woman in two different places, you noticed it immediately and spurred us to write one of our favorite storylines to 'explain' the mystery. You drove us to literally double the amount of content we had meant to provide. In short, you were our Puppetmasters . . ."

The World Takes Notice

As word spread of this strange new form of story or game (or marketing campaign or whatever it was), the international press began to take notice. Understandably it started with online sources first, as sites like Ain't It Cool News, BBC News Online, E! Online, and MacSlash began reporting about the strange trail of websites as early as April 2001. By June, however, the story was everywhere, with coverage by ABC News, CNN, Entertainment Weekly, The Guardian, The LA Times, The NY Times, Time magazine, USA Today, and literally hundreds more major news sources. The enormous amount of interest brought a welcome positive spin to the discussion of the **A.I.** movie, which was already surrounded by rumors of major difficulties and potential disastrous reviews, even before it was released. In fact, retrospectively, many serious entertainment writers and critics claimed the web game was a better piece of art than the movie itself.

Much of the media coverage was split between claims of **the Beast** being a brilliant new form of marketing and questions as to whether or not there was any way it could yield results worth the alleged $1,000,000 spent to produce it. That same debate still rages today, although the fact that Microsoft chose to invest the same amount of money, if not more, into another huge ARG, **I Love Bees**, in 2004 pretty clearly states that they believe **the Beast** was indeed a good investment. While the **A.I.** movie was unarguably a disappointment at the box office, there's no sure way of telling how many of the people who did show up were there because of **the Beast**. That's one of the main obstacles to validating the ARG as an effective marketing tool, the fact that their need for stealth and deception make collecting accurate statistics as to their effectiveness extremely difficult. The recent success of **I Love Bees** is certain to add some much needed validation to the ARG as a potential vehicle for future major marketing efforts.

The Legacy of **the Beast**

Perhaps one of the most telling testimonies to the power and uniqueness of the alternate reality game is the entire community of amateur ARG creators that have dedicated years of their time and thousands of dollars of their personal money to create their own versions of **the Beast**. While many different forms of entertainment spawn multitudes of imitators and fan fiction creations, the amount of work and dedication that goes into creating an ARG is way beyond writing a short piece of fiction that includes characters from your favorite television show.

Interestingly, if you talk to Puppetmasters who have created or participated in creating an ARG, many of them cannot verbalize why they did it and what made the endless hours of volunteer work worthwhile. I place myself in that same category. I have tried for years to explain to people unfamiliar with alternate reality games why I literally spend every waking moment, for months at a time, thinking about and working on a game for which I am not being compensated in any way. It is almost as if, once you experience the incredible power of a truly immersive and interactive narrative experience, you are compelled to recreate it in some manner. And not just in the form of other games – witness the amazingly long and detailed guides that players take it upon themselves to create for these games, the poems, stories, and other pieces of art that they create in appreciation of what they have experienced, and the endless hours they personally devote immersing themselves in the world of the game. Looking at this behavior analytically, it appears strikingly similar to the actions of the prehistoric cavemen, who crawled into the darkest and most inaccessible areas of the caves below France to scratch miles and miles of sacred symbols and artwork on the stone walls. Many sociologists and anthropologists explain this behavior as primitive's man almost primal urge to recreate some mystical or exceptionally meaningful experience he had. Would they say the same thing about the actions of the ARG community?

The most obvious legacy of **the Beast** is the list of offspring it has spawned in the form of other games. In the three short years since the game concluded, there have been over a dozen successfully concluded ARGs and more that have ended prematurely for various reasons. While a few of these games have been marketing campaigns or stand alone games created by major corporations, the large majority of them have been independent or grassroots productions. A few of these amateur games have even reached artistic and creative levels comparable to the professional projects, despite having PM teams in the single digits and budgets in the hundreds or thousands of dollars, as compared to the professional teams of hundreds of people and millions of dollars that major corporate projects like **the Beast** enjoy. The last year or so has seen an ever increasing awareness of and willingness to experiment with the genre of alternate reality games by companies and corporations looking for new ways to use the Internet to market their products, with more ongoing promotional ARGs now than ever before.

The Beast can also be credited with opening new avenues for addressing the debate about games and stories, and preliminary analysis of the game on an academic level has already found its way into many published papers on the subjects of ludology and narratology. Additionally, many theorists have begun looking at ARGs as a potential social tool, beginning with Jane McGonigal's analysis of **the Beast** as a cultural phenomenon that can "generate a new sense of social agency in game players, and how collaborative play techniques can instruct real-world problem-solving." Consideration as a serious field of study has long eluded games in general and digital games in particular, but the genre of ARGs has helped changed that and elevated their study to a whole new level.

Chapter 8: A Majestic Failure?

In one of the many strange synchronicities that permeate the world of alternate reality games, another online game was being designed simultaneously as the top secret **A.I.** web game project, with the similar intent to go beyond the boundaries of both traditional storytelling and online gaming. In fact this other game, Electronic Arts' **Majestic**, had actually been announced to the world in November of 2000, as part of a new online game subscription program EA was heavily pre-selling. Described as "the first Internet-based suspense thriller," **Majestic**'s tagline ambitiously boasted it was "the game that plays you!" The creative force behind the game, an EA executive named Neil Young, spoke freely in early interviews and press releases about the game's intent to blur the lines of fiction and reality, and to redefine the boundaries of online gaming. "It extends past the traditional boundaries of a game," said Young in an interview timed to support the initial press release, "It doesn't ask you to step into its world so much as it will step into your world." Young was suggesting the game would be immersive, but not in a traditional sense. Instead, his statement reflects an understanding of immersion specific to alternate reality games, as explained in the theories included in Part One of this book. The game was scheduled to launch in February of 2001 and, although a few online voices decried the potentially invasive aspects of the game's concept, most of the online gaming community waited anxiously for the fun to begin.

Pre-Game Hype

Majestic is unique in ARG history in that it was the first game to publicly announce itself as a game in advance of its launch, and still be considered as an alternate reality game. The very idea of press releases about a game that is supposed to make the players wonder what is real and what is not seems hopelessly contradictory, but EA saw it as necessary for several reasons. First, unlike **the Beast,** their intent was to create a profitable product, not a marketing campaign that could be experienced for free. It's hard to sell something nobody knows about, so EA was forced to promote the game in advance, in hopes of building a player base that would support the expenses of the game.

EA was also worried about the legal implications of **Majestic** and the possibility that the deceptive nature of the game might make some players believe some or all of the fictitious content was real. To eliminate this perceived risk, they made players sign an application to play the game, which included an End User License Agreement (EULA) with the following disclaimers, "The **Majestic** characters are fictional. No Game character will ask to meet you in person. No

Majestic character will make physical contact with you or any other person. If children use your phone, we strongly recommend that you not receive **Majestic** phone calls." EA would not have been able to institute this procedure if they had employed the same stealth launch method as **the Beast**, necessitating the pre-game announcements and admission that **Majestic** was indeed a game.

First Signs of Problems

Although I'm certain EA saw no alternative to marketing **Majestic** as a game, their advance notice soon turned into a problem, as they failed to meet their projected start date of February 2001. In fact, it would be almost five months later, July 2001, before the game would launch officially. While this was close to disastrous in and of itself because it endangered the momentum and excitement they had built for the game with all the pre-game promotion, it had another subtle but possibly more powerful negative impact on the overall game as well.

The long delay meant that **Majestic** didn't launch until after **the Beast** had already concluded to rave reviews. Ironically, the huge player base for **the Beast** should have meant an almost automatic guaranteed audience for EA's new game, but there were two readily apparent and highly significant differences between the two games that fans of the **A.I.** game were quick to point at and complain about. First, **Majestic** announced that it was a game, both in its pre-game promotion and in its method of delivering the in-game content through the "Majestic

107

Alliance" application. The Alliance application also notified the players of changes to the Majestic meta site and delivered a mix of real and fictional links and news stories. By requiring a special software application to be involved in its fictional world, the game separated itself from the "interfaceless" design of **the Beast**, a point many **Beast** fans just couldn't get past. And then there was the matter of the cost.

Despite experiments with a few subscription-based entertainment ventures, the Internet was still predominantly a culture in which everything was free at the time EA was trying to launch **Majestic** as a pay-per-play experience. This mind set was reinforced by the just concluded experience of the **A.I.** web game, which provided its players months of challenging, entertaining, and rewarding game play for free. It was into this environment that **Majestic** was launched with the naively ambitious plans of EA to have a player base of hundreds of thousands of players, each paying $10 per month to play the game. According to a Dec. 19th, 2001 article by Chris Morris on the CNNMoney website, 800,000 people started the registration process for the free introductory episode but only a little over 70,000 actually completed it and were eligible to try the game. It's unclear how many of those who did finish registering actually went on to play even the free episode however, as only an estimated 10,000 to 15,000 ultimately paid anything for any of the subsequent episodes. Altogether, the Morris' article suggests that EA lost between $5 and $7 million of the $10 million they invested to create the game.

Majestic Game Play

   Majestic officially launched in July 2001, but before the in-game story began, the framework had been laid with the concept that EA had contracted a software company, Anim-X, to develop the platform for the game. Anim-X was, of course, a fictional creation and was really EA's clever way of addressing in an in-game way the fact that **Majestic** had been announced as a game. The first official communication from the game was in the form of an instant message received by players shortly after they first ran the **Majestic** client application. The players experienced problems trying to complete the Tutorials included in the software to show players how to use the interface, and the instant message was from a system administrator at Anim-X saying something was wrong, but he's wasn't sure exactly what. He was obviously not at the main Anim-X location, because he stated he couldn't contact anyone there. Within minutes, the Anim-X website was updated to include a news story about an undefined incident at the Anim-X studios in Oregon and not long after that players received their first e-mail of the game:

Date: Tue, 31 Jul 2001 20:07:54 ∂0000 (GMT∂00:00)

From: mailto:mmajesticrep@majestic.ea.com

To: user@hostname.com

Subject: AUTOMATED MESSAGE: Technical difficulties

*****This is an automatically generated message*****

Player account: Username

We are experiencing technical difficulties with the server hosting the game:
MAJESTIC

We are working to determine the cause of the disruption and hope to have service restored

soon. We will keep you updated on our progress.

Thank you for your patience.

Sincerely,

Electronic Arts Operations Group

With that, the game began its ill-fated run.

The actual game play of **Majestic** was limited to brief periods of activity every day when the game would "come to life" and begin interacting with the players. The fact that the game changed the paradigm of the player deciding when he wants to play to the game deciding when he *could* play, was one of the unique selling points of the game ("it invades your life"), but also turned out to be one of the major sources of player complaints about the game. Another one of the jarringly unrealistic aspects of the game, the game used a system of three different "modes" – standby, act, and acquire - to regulate the flow of content and game play. Unfortunately when the game was in standby, which seemed to be about 23 ½ hours per day, the player couldn't interact with the world of **Majestic**, making for a very non-immersive experience.

This problem was magnified by the episodic format of the storyline. The game was written and presented in episodes with additional periods of inactivity between each episode. And even structured like that, the **Majestic** development team again failed to deliver as promised. The first "season" of the game was originally announced to be eight episodes long, each lasting about a month. Once the game had begun, the plans changed to five episodes per season and each episode was now estimated to take twelve to fourteen days to complete. By the time it wrapped up prematurely, **Majestic** ended up consisting of four episodes plus the introductory episode, and at least one of the episodes was only nine days long.

The game itself included some well-produced assets and intriguing plot twists, although some players experienced problems watching the video clips and missed key clues hidden within them. There were also a few enjoyable hacking scenario simulations and interesting puzzles, even though many of the beta testers thought the puzzles in the introductory and first episodes were too simple overall. EA actually added in additional content in the form of "Revelations" part way through the game. While not part of the central storyline, "Revelations" was a series of difficult puzzles introduced by the character Solitaire 1957, who supposedly had inside government contacts and information. "Revelations" was intended to occupy the standby time players had been complaining about. Interesting in retrospect though is the fact that the payoffs of Solitaire's puzzles were audio files delivered by telephone that collectively told a story, a technique used as the main method of delivering content in the highly successful recent ARG, **I Love Bees**. Even this new content and additional challenge failed to spark new interest in the game, however, and it was evident by the second episode that the game was not living up to expectations in terms of sales and player reaction.

Game Interrupted

In what was perhaps a fatal blow from which it never recovered, the Puppetmasters of **Majestic** decided to temporarily suspend the game after the terrorist attacks on the World Trade Center on Sept. 11, 2001. Originally shut down to eliminate any unnecessary burden on the nation's phone system immediately following the attack, EA later announced "some of the fictional elements in the game may not be appropriate at this time," and extended the suspension for one week, resuming the game on Sept. 18, 2001. Many players were already convinced that the game was on its last legs and wouldn't last much longer though, even as it resumed.

Their suspicions were confirmed somewhat when EA, just a week later, announced it would be offering a retail CD-ROM version of the game in November 2001, containing the introduction and the first four episodes for $39.99. Many players and industry experts took this as the first proof that the game would indeed end prematurely after the four episodes included in the boxed version. They turned out to be right, as EA announced on December 19 that they were shutting down the game.

Majestic in Retrospect

Looking back at **Majestic**, it's apparent that the EA development team did a few things right and very many things wrong. It's interesting to note that, according to game creator Neil Young in a Aug. 10, 2001 interview with Salon.com, the PM team set out with three ideas or objectives very similar to the assumptions set forth by Jordan Weisman when he laid out his ideas for **the Beast** to Sean Stewart and Elan Lee. Young said that the ideas that inspired the creation of **Majestic** began when he was, "struggling to find 30 minutes to an hour a night to invest in any type of entertainment, and wanted to create something that didn't require you to spend hours with it each night in order to feel successful at it." After searching for but not finding any truly interactive entertainment on the Internet he realized, "It didn't feel like there was anything created specifically for the medium . . . . So that ended up defining a canvas for us that we then started to paint a picture on." And finally, the third idea that brought it all together was, "the concept of blurring the lines between fact and fiction, specifically around conspiracies."

One of the things **Majestic** did well at times was the blurring of fiction and reality, despite the mechanical elements built into it that constantly reminded the players that it was a game. This blurring began with the storyline, which admittedly contained almost every clichéd conspiracy theory you can think of, but still managed to blend factual elements of real history (well, conspiracy theory history at least) with the fictional world of the game. In particular, the manner in which the Majestic Alliance website would display both real and in-game links and news articles whenever it was updated made it difficult, at times, for many players to know which websites were real and which were not. I remember many players trying to get in contact with an actual government facility that conducted classified research, Sandia National Labs, because the name appeared in one of the early lists of links.

Other elements of the game that many players credited with being fairly successful were its use of real-time communication methods and a story that progressed in real-time, both attempts at trying to create an immediacy and level of believability to the in-game interactions. There was a certain amount of novelty and excitement the first time a character from the game instant messaged you or even called you on the phone, despite the fact that most of these communications were transparently artificial. Listening to pre-recorded calls or trying to converse naturally with chatbots quickly became tedious however, especially in comparison to the promotional claims for the game that promised the most interactive experience of your life. The technology was impressive, but the simulated human responses were ultimately lacking, as the chatbots were unable to respond to logical, well constructed, and relevant questions far too often. Instead of being interactive, the instant messaging conversations became the online equivalent of the pre-recorded phone calls, where all players could do was sit there and let the programmed character deliver its message, while trying really hard to pretend it was an actual person. Sadly, EA spent an incredible amount of money to have an automated chatbot system developed which ultimately failed and became one of the most unrealistic components of the game.

Reflecting back on the game and story theory covered in the first section of the book, it's clear that EA could have learned from the ongoing discussions about the conflict between interaction and story, and about the unavoidable shortcomings of using artificial intelligence to simulate human response. No matter how well the chatbot program was written, it was absolutely impossible to configure it for every possible question a player might ask in any given situation, so no matter how much money was spent on it, it was ultimately doomed to fail. One wonders if EA might have actually saved money by hiring real people to play these roles in instant messaging conversations instead of trying to use artificial intelligence programming that simply wasn't up to the task.

Another area where **Majestic** failed was in the conceit of a pay-per-play game that charged $10 per month for what amounted to fifteen minutes of game play each day. Unfortunately, it seems that this was pre-ordained from the start as part of Neil Young's stated desire to create something that didn't require you to devote hours to it every day in order to succeed. Many of Young's other comments in various places clearly reflect his desire to create something to compete with television, as reflected by his organizing the structure of the game into episodes and seasons. If you hold up the finished product, fifteen minutes of paid programming a day, it was an obvious bad bargain when compared to television. And the fifteen minutes of programming a day actually averaged out to be much less, as none of the **Majestic** episodes came anywhere close to lasting a full month. It seems like someone at EA didn't do the math before deciding to greenlight the game.

Perhaps the best thing about **Majestic** was its encouragement of the creation of fan sites and "mini-games," in something EA called the "BIOS Program." As mentioned before, many forms of entertainment spawn both fan admiration sites and fan fiction sites, and ARGs are no exception. The earliest examples were probably the fan sites created during **the Beast**, many of which were quite clever in their presentation of content that mirrored the themes and events of the game. **Majestic** fans were no different, and early in the game, actually while it was still in beta testing, the PM team noticed sites springing up that appeared to be very much in-game but weren't sites created by EA. Some of these sites were actually the first incarnation of one of my creations, the ChangeAgents, and marked the beginning of my first attempt at creating my own alternate reality game. This first game was merely an attempt to amuse myself and entertain my fellow **Majestic** beta testers, who were already complaining about the inordinate amount of down time in the game. It was so well received however, that when I admitted to the EA creative team that I was the person behind the ChangeAgents as part of the BIOS Program application process, they informed me that Neil and his team had spent a lot of time discussing and wondering exactly that.

The unusual thing about EA's approach to fan fiction and these fan sites was that they not only accepted it, they encouraged and embraced it, actually making several of the better BIOS stories featured side plots to the game itself. At its highpoint, the BIOS Program included thirty different websites, all built around peripheral characters in the **Majestic** world and each including either original stories based on these characters or self-contained small ARGs created by the players. My second ChangeAgents game, **Operation Mindset**, was created for the BIOS program and I created twelve original sites for the game. **Operation Mindset** was featured in the monthly newsletter and on the **Majestic** website for a month as the first player created "mini-game" done under the auspices of their BIOS program. It was this program that inspired me and others like to me to continue to create the independent alternate reality games that helped sustain the genre when company after company failed to find a sustainable business model for ARGs. In that, if nothing else, **Majestic** helped shape the future of alternate reality games for years to come.

Chapter 9: Lockjaw, Exocog, and ChangeAgents: Out of Control – Independents Come of Age

Spawn of the Beast

As mentioned in the previous chapter, alternate reality games have traditionally inspired their players to create fan websites or even miniature ARGs of their own. Such was the case with both **the Beast** and **Majestic**; as each has had former players go on to create their own games. Almost simultaneously, several different groups of former Cloudmakers had begun developing independent ARGs in the fall of 2001. The first of these games to launch was named **Ravenwatchers** but it ended prematurely, before it ever really even had a chance to develop. Right around the same time, on Sept. 19, 2001, an article appeared in the News section of http://www.wired.com detailing the efforts of another group of former Cloudmakers who were busy crafting their own follow-up to **the Beast**, a project code-named **Lockjaw**. The Wired article was just a sneak peek, announcing that the game wasn't due to launch until November of the same year. It did, however, include quite a few details about certain parts of the planned game itself, stating, "The game revolves around the secret activities of fictional company GanMed Biotechnical and its work toward developing a highly controversial genetic therapy to halt the aging process." The article went on to even name a few of the nascent Puppetmasters, quite a break from the traditional *TINAG* philosophy inherent in the top-secret development and launch of their model, **the Beast**. Nevertheless, the article did declare the intent of the PMs to launch **Lockjaw** stealthily, with the hope that "players will happen upon the biotech conspiracy-themed game on their own or through word-of-mouth, and that their first encounter with **Lockjaw** might leave it unclear whether or not they've stumbled onto something real or simulated." As it turned out, players had been alerted by the Wired article and commenced watching for the website they had discovered, http://www.ganmed.com, to go live, which it finally did in February of 2002. Almost immediately, a group of players calling itself the Jawbreakers set out to solve the mystery of GanMed Biotechnical.

Going Underground

As the GanMed Biotechnical site became active, the Jawbreakers quickly discovered a network of in-game sites and a story about a group of urban explorers called the DCMetroCrawlers, whose discovery of a hidden laboratory in the tunnels beneath Washington DC one night led to the death of one of their members and launched the investigation to discover what GanMed Biotechnical was really up to. The story cleverly included references back to **the Beast** and the

Cloudmakers, and eventually encompassed a dozen different websites plus a few additional sites created by players along the way. **Lockjaw** also included some wonderfully designed and executed puzzles, including an infamous puzzle that has come to be known as "where.gif" (after the image used in the puzzle). Where.gif is still brought up frequently in ARG disussions whenever puzzle design is the topic of conversation.

Undoubtedly, one of the strongest elements of the game was the incredible writing of the amateur PMs, as evidenced by the players' postings to the game forums throughout and after the game had concluded. The Puppetmasters were successful in creating both environments and characters that truly emotionally involved the players. Perhaps most impressive was that they accomplished this predominantly through static web content rather than real-time interaction. By static, I'm not implying that the in-game websites didn't change over the course of the game; they did, and the evolution of each site was part of the overall story of the game. And the game did feature real-time interaction - e-mail, live chat, and even online game playing with characters - but the fictional characters, companies, and towns of the game were primarily made believable through the written text of the game, the various parts of which came together masterfully to tell the stories of these people in a powerful way.

The game concluded in the middle of May 2002, at which time the six Puppetmasters - Andy Aiken, Bruce Cain, Clay Chiment, Derek

Jensen, Brooke Thompson and Krystyn Wells - revealed themselves. Overall, **Lockjaw** successfully recaptured many of the best elements of **the Beast,** with its intricate storyline and well written characters, its challenging and thematically diverse puzzles, and its development of an active and passionate community of players. The game also helped proved that a team of amateur ARG creators could independently produce a successful game, and that the genre of alternate reality games wasn't entirely going to be determined by the failure of EA's **Majestic.**

Back to the Future

While **Lockjaw** was running, yet another mysterious rabbit hole was discovered, this one apparently tied into the release of the upcoming movie **Minority Report.** In April of 2002 a post appeared in the Cloudmakers forum that included a link to a blog for a woman named Sarah. The initial entry was dated Wednesday, April 10, and the blog entries themselves were rather ordinary except for the use of the word "precog" several times. Most interesting though, was a link on the page that went to a company website, http://www.exocog.com. The entry page into this site looked authentic enough, unless you noticed the copyright line at the bottom that said, "© 2011 - 2013, Exocog, Incorporated. All rights reserved." Clicking through to any of the internal pages revealed the fact that the company was claiming to provide "precognitive services" with accuracy ranging from 89% to 97%. Needless to say, it didn't take the ARG crowd long to figure out there was a new game afoot.

Exocog was created as an experiment of sorts by Jim Miller and Miramontes Studios to learn firsthand how to conduct an immersive marketing campaign. In fact their website, http://www.miramontes.com, features a great post game analysis of both the development and results of the game. In it, Miller cites the two major inspirations for the game as **the Beast** and **the Blair Witch** online movie promotion. While not technically an ARG per se, Miller was impressed with **the Blair Witch** campaign's use of multimedia assets on a fictional yet realistically portrayed website to tell the back story of the upcoming movie. Additionally, the idea of using an immersive experience for a massive real time marketing campaign as **the Beast** had done intrigued Miller, but also raised some natural questions in his mind. In his analysis of the game he writes, "From a content perspective, what did these projects have to say about the relationships of games and stories? Further, these projects, especially the *AI* project, were real-time events. What is the nature of this real-time feedback from audience to creator, and how does a creator balance this feedback with the desire to maintain the original design of the project?"

Of course the last question involving the real-time feedback and balancing it with the creator's original vision is what I have termed "interactive authoring," and is precisely the means by which ARGs bridge the gap between stories and games.

The six member PM team for **Exocog** took a very novel approach in that they decided to make the game appear as if it were an

123

official promotion for the **Minority Report** movie, when, in fact, it was nothing more than a piece of fan fiction turned into a game and not sanctioned by the movie's creators in any way. The story was written so well and the sites executed so brilliantly though, that the players were still debating whether it was official or not right up through the end of the game. After drafting a story set in the pre-movie world of the **Minority Report,** the team laid out a general strategy on how to proceed. Again according to Miller's analysis, "Therefore, the next steps were to design Internet presences for each of the characters, build initial versions of them, and take them live on the Internet under real domain names. We would then announce the game in ways that would attract visitors, and evolve the content of the properties over the course of the game to tell the story. We needed a very clear – ultimately, day to day – plot outline describing what was happening to each of our characters throughout the five weeks of the game."

As mentioned, the game was planned to be relatively short compared to most ARGs, only five weeks, and it was all set inside of four websites. Costing only $150.00 total by Miller's own estimate, the game maximized the use of those resources to tell a compelling story. The **Exocog** team achieved this by effectively using carefully chosen storytelling techniques that Miller lists in his game analysis. One of the most interesting ones he calls "storytelling by out-of-game property manipulation." This is Miller's way of explaining the inclusion of real world items and assets into the fictional world of an ARG. An example from the **Exocog** game was the establishment of an Amazon.com account for one of the characters which, when accessed, revealed some important information.

Another extremely informative part of Miller's deconstruction of **Exocog** is where he details what the PM team learned from doing the game. One important lesson he cites was the importance of the player community that develops around alternate reality games. He writes, "We came to realize that what we were really doing, through our website and e-mail manipulations, was creating a social event. The people who came to the ARGN board may have gone there in search of information, but if they stayed, it was because they valued the sense of community that grew out of the players' shared interactions on the board."

Miller also tells future PMs "there's never enough content" and explains how they approached this problem. "We addressed this problem by taking some of the static parts of the game and making them interactive, with the new content coming from the *players*, not from us." Again, this is interactive authoring in action, and is one of the things that truly make ARGs different from any other form of entertainment medium.

Exocog can only be considered a success, both in terms of the marketing experiment the developers wanted it to be and as far as the free game that they provided the players. Combined with the success of **Lockjaw** which, coincidentally, wrapped up just about the same time,

Exocog gave further indication that the future of the ARG genre might just belong in the hands of the independent developer.

From the Ashes of **Majestic**

The Beast wasn't the only professionally produced alternate reality game that spawned successors, however, as Majestic's BIOS program had left a batch of amateur PMs with a taste for creating their own material too, including me. Disappointed with **Majestic**'s dramatic collapse, I actually stayed away from the ARG-related message boards and news sites for a while, and so missed the beginning of the **Lockjaw** game, much to my regret. Even without being actively involved in the genre for a couple of months though, I couldn't stop ideas for new games from percolating around inside my head. And so, when I casually returned to the ARG world and found a well-done independent ARG going on, it motivated me to get back in the game, so to speak.

Within a few days I had written the first draft of the third and ultimately final ChangeAgents adventure, something I christened **ChangeAgents: Out of Control (CAOOC)**. I realized that by using a property, the ChangeAgents, that everyone already knew, I was immediately losing most of the *TINAG* effect, since everyone would know it was a game right from the start. But my idea was to still try and create a sense of uncertainty and suspense by taking everything I had done in the previous two ChangeAgents' adventures and turning it upside down. Instead of heroes that were trying to free unsuspecting people from secret government mind control, I now wanted make players wonder if the ChangeAgents themselves were being controlled, and if everything they had learned in the two previous games was just another layer of deception.

I was also very aware as I started writing the story from the initial draft that I would need to go to special lengths to try and achieve any of the blurring of reality and fiction that characterized alternate reality games. Not only was the world of the ChangeAgents already established to be fictional, I was planning on incorporating a few other fringe concepts (as if mind control wasn't far enough out there on its own) and needed to find some way to put it all together in a believable package. The plan I came up with was to carefully insert as many real pieces of information, history, and background into the story as I could. Consequently, I devoted hours and hours to researching every element of my intended story, looking for any mention of similar themes or concepts I could find, and figuring out ways to insert these little slices of reality into my fictional world.

CAOOC was six weeks in development, much of that time spent in research on the Internet, both into the intended subject matter of the game and learning the skills necessary to do Flash, audio and video on the Internet, as well as some rudimentary server side programming for passwords and so on. I also came up with names and ideas for twenty in-game websites, and an outline for the intended three-month run of the game.

The game launched on June 1, 2002, when people who had played the former ChangeAgents' games received a cryptic e-mail:

Things are about to change . . .

We are sorry we have left your message unanswered for so long. Pressing matters and urgent preparations have kept us from responding to the many who have sought the truth. But time is running out and soon the choice will no longer be ours or yours.

Despite overwhelming odds and unimaginable dangers, our window of opportunity will soon be upon us. Are you ready?

Our need for secrecy is absolute. Can you be trusted?

the ChangeAgents

Hidden in the white spaces of the e-mail (one of **Majestic**'s favorite tricks) were three phrases - Iron Mountain, giants, and unseen war. Although they didn't lead anywhere concrete yet, the phrases did yield some interesting Google results having to do with top-secret government conspiracies. Two days later a follow-up message arrived:

Things are about to change . . .
the ChangeAgents

The events we have been fearing and preparing for are coming to a head. The forces arrayed against us have taken advantage of current affairs to escalate the struggle.
Very soon your direct help will be needed.
There is a path to education and earning trust.
In the next few days it will be fully open. Have you found it?

the ChangeAgents

Within days a hidden link was found on a page within the ChangeAgents' website that led eventually to the "path" the second e-mail had predicted and **CAOOC** really began. As I mentioned before, I had decided to make the ChangeAgents' motives and actions appear to be questionable, at least in the beginning of the game, and so I needed a new central character (or two) for the game to revolve around. Also, realizing I was fighting an uphill battle as far as believability of the game, I had also decided I needed to make this new character appear as human as possible as quickly as I could. I used two methods to accomplish this. First, I gave him a voice and found a way to let the players hear him speak. The voice was actually mine and I manipulated it with an audio program to sound higher and younger. Next I gave him a face, well, of sorts.

Since I was the only PM and my face was already known to way too many ARG fans, I couldn't use my own image for the role of Tommy, the lead character. But I also did not want to result to stock photos or even photos at all. I wanted Tommy to be a living, breathing person to the players, but didn't have the resources to use video and a live actor for everything I wanted Tommy to do and say. One of the things I do as a Puppetmaster is constantly search the Internet for new technologies that I can use somehow in my games to make them more realistic, entertaining, or interactive. As part of the research for

CAOOC I had found a website called FaceMail, which allowed you to create an animated face, record a message in your voice, and send it in the form of an e-mail. Even though the face was animated, it was very well done, and the fact that I could use Tommy's voice with the animated image made it acceptable. That FaceMail was a real service easily verified by the players made it believable and one of the slices of real life I had inserted into the game. So Tommy now had both a recognizable voice and face, even if it was animated. Many players later said that these two elements did exactly what I intended them to – made Tommy into a character they could believe in and care about.

Creating the various character voices was actually one of my biggest challenges for **CAOOC**. There are only so many modifications you can make to your own voice, even with the best audio software. I ended up using my voice for three different characters. For Tommy, I raised the pitch of my voice a few steps while leaving the tempo the same. For another character, I did the opposite and lowered my voice a step or two, also slowing it down slightly to give it a deeper and more menacing tone. And finally, for the third character, I used my voice pretty much as is, but added various delay and EQ effects to change it just slightly from normal. Unfortunately, that still left three or four other male speaking parts and a few female voices for characters I needed as well. To create these voices, I turned to a variety of different software applications. First, I had found a few websites that had online text-to-speech engines available on them, allowing visitors to type in a text passage, choose between different male and female voices, and then convert the text to speech. While some of the voices were too obviously artificial to use, by trying different settings on different sites, I was able to come up with enough acceptable ones for what I had in mind.

ChangeAgents: Out of Control ran until September of 2002 and was declared a success by the players and ARG community, many of whom were amazed that it was all done by only one person. In retrospect, there are many things I did wrong on **CAOOC** and I would do differently if I had the chance. Even though it was my third game, it was really my first truly independent one in the sense that it wasn't created for and aimed at the pre-existing **Majestic** audience (the first two took place while **Majestic** was still going). One definite mistake I made that I see other beginning ARG creators make all the time was to rush the launch of the game. When I returned from my short time away from the ARG world and found **Lockjaw** wrapping up an incredible run, I was so excited and motivated to make another game myself that I didn't take the time to prepare like I should have. I didn't even have a complete story written out; I did have an outline of the plot with a definite sequence of events and all the major events, but had only completed about two-thirds of the entire detailed story. I also only had a few weeks of assets and completed content ready to go when I launched the game. The end result was that I believe the game suffered in several ways because I anxiously and foolishly rushed the start.

One negative result was that it made running the game much more difficult for me than it had to be. Monitoring and managing an ongoing game is hard enough, especially with only one PM, but having to create content while you go just makes the whole thing insane. Also, it makes your work much more prone to errors, both from rushing to begin with and also from not having time to proofread anything properly. I made several stupid mistakes in puzzles and website content that should have been caught, in even a minimal proofing process, mistakes that affected both critical points of the game and caused me great embarrassment. It's not just errors in puzzles or on web pages though, hurrying the game like I did also caused the writing to suffer. In many cases, I was writing content and posting it without having the time to consider exactly how it fit in with what had come before, only to see a player's post shortly after they found it, explaining how it didn't make sense in some way. Quite often, this led to having to change things that were already done to try and cover for the mistake, something I could ill afford to do when I was struggling to create new content. I hardly had time to go back and change things already created, but was forced to nonetheless.

Don't get me wrong, I still consider **CAOOC** a success, and am very proud of what I accomplished. I don't think anyone else has or ever will again create a game of this magnitude by themselves. I obviously did many things right in making the game, as evidenced by the great player reaction and their sustained involvement throughout the game. I point out the mistakes I made only in hopes that future independent PMs can learn from them and not have to put themselves through what I did.

Chapter 10: Commercial Comeback?

Heartened by the success of several consecutive, well-made independent games, the ARG community had begun to rebound from the catastrophic failure of EA's **Majestic** and believe that there might be a future for the genre after all. When there were signs that several more professional ARG promotions were possibly starting up in the near future, things began to look even brighter.

Primetime **Push**

As the first wave of independent alternate reality games wrapped up in late summer 2002, a string of new ARG commercial ventures had already begun to be announced. Despite EA's embarrassing failure with **Majestic**, it seems there were still a few companies who believed ARGs could be part of either a viable business model or a major media production. Perhaps most exciting to ARG fans were the announced plans for a television show called Push, Nevada, that was being produced by Ben Affleck and promoted as including a online game or contest that sounded very much like an ARG. In fact, Affleck made reference to the genre of alternate reality games in several pre-show interviews, although many ARG old-timers were worried that he used the word "gimmick" when talking about the game that would eventually give away a $1,000,000 prize. Many others worried that having such a large prize involved would hurt the community of alternate reality game fans who had always worked together collectively to solve puzzles. It turned out that both concerns were justified.

The first episode of Push, Nevada aired on ABC on Sept. 17, 2002. The show was planned to last thirteen episodes and fans had been told in advance that each episode would contain one clue that would be critical to solving the final puzzle. Unfortunately, the show contained so many quirky plot elements and offbeat production techniques that it was hard to tell exactly what was a clue and what wasn't. The Internet content developed as the online component to the Push game was fairly well done initially, but ended up being underutilized and not really adding anything of substance to either the show or the solution of the final puzzle. In fact, one of the most talked about websites on the community forums was a fan site called http://www.speedhuntingclub.com, that I created just for fun, using an obscure business name mentioned in some of the early Push content. I originally just used the site to mysteriously hint at what I thought were key moments or themes in that week's episode, sometimes posting very brief video captures from the show moments after it was aired. Because I guessed right about a few things early on that I thought would become part of the Push story, the site gained an air of credibility it otherwise wouldn't have had. Eventually, I decided to use the site to promote my next game to the huge <u>Push, Nevada</u> audience, when it became clear that <u>Push</u> itself was doomed to end prematurely.

The <u>Push</u> storyline not only puzzled ARG fans but television critics alike. The large majority of the early reviews the show received were unabashedly negative, and the show began to lose advertisers a few weeks into its run, causing many people to question whether or not the show would justify the cost of making and promoting it as well as the $1,000,000 prize. Early into the second month of the show, ABC announced that the season had indeed been cut from thirteen episodes to seven, and that the final clue would be broadcast as part of a Monday Night Football telecast on Oct. 28, 2002. Fans of the show were almost universally disappointed with the final clue and the solution to the season-long puzzle, which had absolutely nothing to do with the <u>Push</u> plot at all. Despite the novel concept of marrying an alternate reality game to an ongoing television show, the ARG side of <u>Push</u> unfortunately never really developed and gave another black eye to the whole genre in the world of professional entertainment.

<u>Push</u> even generated its own fan-produced follow-up game, a project called **NoahBoddy**, which interestingly turned out to be just as disjointed and unsuccessful as <u>Push</u> was, ending in disaster after a less than stellar run.

<u>Nice Ride</u>

The one highpoint in this entire period of commercial experimentation with the ARG was a game produced for BMW nicknamed **:k:**. Launched in September 2002, the game integrated professionally produced short video clips featuring a BMW Z4, in an episodic action story that ended with a live event in Las Vegas, Nevada, on January 11, 2003. The highlight of the live event was one player winning a BMW Z4. The video clips were produced by Ridley and Tony Scott and directed by famous directors like John Woo, Joe Carnahan, and Tony Scott. While not strictly an ARG in my opinion, the online **:k:** game did incorporate many of the best elements of alternate reality gaming, and may have returned just a small portion of legitimacy to the entire concept as a marketing vehicle after a few highly public failures.

Searching for Success

In summer of 2002 another game that would eventually turn out to be an attempt at a pay-per-play model was just getting underway. Known by a few different names as it went through a rather rocky and confusing introduction, the game eventually came to be called **Search4E** and attempted to recruit players for a subscription program. **Search4E** started out for free, with no mention of any intent to charge for it in the future. After its somewhat shaky start, it showed some signs of great promise, as the early video assets and websites in the game were very well done. The game appeared ill-prepared for the initial success it had, however, as it soon lapsed into some periods of extended inactivity, periods that had players wondering at times if the game had ended unannounced. After one of those periods, the game came back to life by giving away some rare coins worth over $2000 to one player through an in-game online event. Shortly after that, the main website for the game announced plans for the game to begin charging on a monthly basis. The game developers had obviously learned nothing from the **Majestic** experience.

Even after **Search4E** began charging to play the game, it still suffered from inconsistency, in both scheduling and content quality, as some of the new material made absolutely no sense in context with earlier portions of the game. There were rumors on the ARG player forums that perhaps the entire game had either been sold to a new PM team, or had almost folded and had just a skeleton crew of people trying to keep it going. At one point, the PM team actually sent e-mails and posted messages begging for players to recruit others to play the game, and confirming that the number of paid subscriptions was way below what they needed to continue. It wasn't too long until all game activity stopped completely, although the game's meta sites are still up today, complete with Registration form and PayPal donation button, leaving many players wondering just what the hell happened, and if there would ever be a successful moneymaking ARG project.

TerraQuest

Yet another failed commercial venture from the same period was a game called **TerraQuest,** produced by MindQuest Entertainment. Like most commercial ARGs, the game threw the *TINAG* principle out the window and was announced via an article on CNET News.com on November 4, 2002. The article promised **TerraQuest** would unfold through six monthly installments, with each installment having a monthly challenge with a $25,000 prize. At the end of the six episodes there would be a grand prize starting at $250,000 and growing according to the number of players willing to pay the $25.00 monthly subscription fee. Apparently, MindQuest believed the monetary reward would be enough to overcome the problems that doomed **Majestic** to failure less than a year before.

On January 16, 2003 MindQuest announced it was canceling **TerraQuest** with the following statement:

To the Players of TerraQuest
We want to thank you for your enthusiasm in playing TerraQuest. While the comments from those of you who are players have been wonderful, there is simply not enough participation in the experience to keep this version of TerraQuest going. As a result, we will discontinue TerraQuest immediately.

This string of failures of high-visibility and, in some cases, heavily funded, ARG-related projects left many in the alternate reality gaming world wondering if there was any future left for the genre at all.

Chapter 11: Chasing The Wish

Even before I finished **ChangeAgents: Out of Control**, I was thinking about doing another game and I already had several specific goals in mind. I knew, first of all, that I needed to recruit help to create and run the game, especially since the game I wanted to make was much larger in scope than **CAOOC** had been. I also knew that I wanted to make real world items and interactions a vital part of the game, as I wanted this game to transcend the boundaries of the Internet more than any of my previous three games had done and, quite frankly, more than I had seen any other ARGs do. It seemed to me that real world interactions that were handled in an in-game way always became favorite parts of whatever game they were in. This was especially true when the players either found or received an actual item or artifact that had some *in-game* meaning or value. In **CAOOC**, I had distributed one small metallic disk that had a mysterious in-game symbol on it to several players and, for the most part, they couldn't stop talking about how cool it was. I wondered what a game might be like that incorporated dozens of such artifacts on a regular basis.

Another part of the "crossover" into the real world I had in mind was to try and produce what I felt a few previous games had promised and failed to deliver - a game that reached out and played with you. Imagine if a game really did send someone to knock on your door, or leave an item for you in a locker at your local mall. Or even if a real person called you and spoke to you, at length, as a character in the game in a realistic and believable way. How realistic an experience could a Puppetmaster make a game for the players?

My final goal in deciding to create another game was to write a cohesive and meaningful story, to do everything I could to create characters that had interesting and believable personalities, who acted and responded as if they really existed. I knew this wouldn't be easy, not only because it is a difficult thing for any writer to accomplish in the first place, especially in an experimental medium like alternate reality games, but also because of the *type* of story I wanted to write. I wanted to write a fable, a mythology of sorts, that portrayed the Internet as something akin to a new religion of the world, because of the time and attention man devotes to it. I realized that this type of story would make the fictional world I intended to create inherently less believable, making it even more important that the people in the world of the game appeared as real as possible.

The Wish Takes Shape

I spent six months writing and developing **Chasing The Wish** **(CTW)**, starting with approximately two months devoted entirely to working on the story. During a period of personal hardship in my life I had spent a great deal of time researching different ways in which people have traditionally tried to change their lives or even themselves through extraordinary or even supernatural means. As I researched this subject, I became increasingly intrigued with just how often historical individuals, who had achieved incredible things in their lives, credited something like a prayer or a wish as being somehow responsible. This line of thought led to a whimsical idea: what if there were a being, a person, who appeared to people in times of great need or historical importance and offered them one wish for whatever they wanted? What if this being appeared to all of us at one time or another, but we never remember because the being wipes the memory from our mind?

Out from behind the Curtain

One of my general rules for starting to plan an ARG that I commonly share with new Puppetmasters is to begin by writing down everything you'd like to do in a game, no matter how crazy sounding or potentially expensive it might initially appear. Don't limit yourself right from the start; instead, think big, and don't let the details of how you are going to do it affect your first drafts for the game. In the process of fleshing out the details of the story and the timeline of the game, you can then evaluate each idea and see if they really are possible.

143

One of the original logo designs for **Chasing The Wish**. Several different logos were used throughout the game but they all included the same key elements as this one – the reaching, outstretched arm, the six-fingered hand, a seven-pointed star, and the tag line "A place you cannot go, a secret you cannot know."

In many cases, it will quickly become apparent that some of your wilder ideas may be either too expensive or too difficult to accomplish for technical or logistical reasons. You'd be surprised, however, how many times this approach enables you to actually come up with a plan for achieving what might otherwise have originally appeared impossible.

The first several sets of **CTW** notes did exactly that, included anything and everything I thought would make an enjoyable, exciting, and incredibly immersive game for the players. The original story included things like burying items in people's backyards, having a character show up at players' homes, and distributing real handcrafted paintings, manuscript pages, and "magical" artifacts to players throughout the game. These elements were the first reason I decided I needed to have some form of registration for the game. For obvious legal reasons, I couldn't go as far into players' actual worlds as I intended to, without their permission. I didn't see anyway around this and didn't think players would mind, since they had been exposed to similar requests from the various commercial ARG games that had come before.

If it was a given that there needed to be a registration for the game, then it logically followed that the process of registration and therefore, the game itself, had to be both announced and actively promoted. You can't register players for something if they don't know it exists. Announcing the game in advance also had other advantages that were important to the planning of the execution of the game. If I wanted **Chasing The Wish** to interact with players as I've described, I had to know where they were located while I was still writing and planning the details of the game. The **CTW** game registration process allowed me build a player database with names, addresses, and phone numbers to use for any real world events or interaction I wanted to include. The registration also allowed players to select their own level of immersion or involvement with the game, an important consideration because some people just don't want to play a game that knocks on their door.

The final very important thing that announcing the game in advance did was allow me to recruit potential Puppetmasters to help create the game from the people who were registering. I decided early on that I was going to do something a little different as far as recruiting help for the game. I wanted to enlist two different levels of helpers. One level was people I called *artists*, who would create certain assets for the game, whether they were websites, images, programs, or actual real world items. This level eventually grew to include character actors too, helpers who played the role of the in-game personalities by answering e-mail, making phone calls, and so on. The other group I called *BTS* or *Behind The Scenes* helpers. These were the people who would help hide items around the country, help manage the player database, and perform other non-creative tasks like that. In the end, both groups came to be known collectively as *BTS* helpers, but there was clear distinction at least early on in my mind.

One final note about the BTS people – all along I intended on recruiting help to make the game, but I didn't plan on revealing to anyone more than their own little part in the game. This did two very significant things. The most important reason was it protected the secrecy of the story and the integrity of the later elements of the game. I wanted to minimize the danger of anyone deciding they didn't want to be involved any longer and ruining the game for others by prematurely revealing anything. Also, structuring the BTS team this way allowed the BTS helpers to still play **CTW**, even though they were remotely involved. They really didn't know anymore than the next player, except perhaps that they were the one who created the particular object players were trying to find at some point in the game. Even in cases where I had BTS helpers play out character roles, I gave them only the bare minimum of information and direction I thought was necessary, usually only a day or so in advance.

So, for what I believed were very good reasons, I pulled aside the PM curtain and created a meta, or out of game, site for **CTW**, giving details on how to register, when the game would start, how it would interact with players, and so on. There were even a few video trailers that contained vague but significant clues as to what the story would actually include. The site accomplished exactly what I wanted it to and the ARG world soon began talking excitedly about the upcoming game. Unfortunately, not all the excitement was positive.

Unintended Consequences

Like any online community, the social side of the ARG world tends at times to be filled with drama and separation, as cliques develop of players who are fans of certain games or not others, or even fans of certain game creators and not others. Luckily, the ARG community is actually much better in this respect than most other online communities I have been involved with, but we still have had our moments.

A few months before I even launched **CTW,** I was informed that several ARG "old-timers" (which usually means people who played **the Beast** and think no other game can ever live up to it) were extremely upset that I had revealed myself as the Puppetmaster for a game that hadn't even been launched yet, and that I was promoting **CTW** as a game. Some of them were even encouraging other ARG players to boycott the game in protest, in various chat channels and on their personal websites. Curiously, some of these people were former PMs themselves, who had been involved with other games like **Lockjaw.** If you'll remember, **Lockjaw** announced itself several months in advance through an article that even included the names of some of the PMs and entities from the game. In addition, some of these people were openly playing and discussing the commercial projects that were underway, all of which had either registration of some form or a meta site that announced the details of the game. Needless to say, I was surprised and confused by this reaction among a small segment of the ARG community, but was determined to not let it change what I intended to do. In retrospect, I think it had very little impact on the game anyway, and was more a matter of my feelings being hurt that people who I knew and respected and who were supposedly about nurturing this new *innovative* form of game, would work against someone else's efforts, based on their closed minds and fixed opinions.

The Fun Begins

For anyone who has never tried being a Puppetmaster before, it's hard to even describe to exactly how much fun it is to sit and watch the launch of a game you have created. ARG players get so excited when they solve or discover anything, and leading them down a trail that involves several puzzles and almost a dozen websites made for hours and hours of enjoyment on my part. It was thrilling to watch them in the chat room posting things like, "Look, I found another website! Is this part of the game? This is so cool!" And **CTW** truly did give them a lot of content to start the game. I deliberately wanted the players to feel almost overwhelmed with the amount of material they discovered that first night, as if they really had found a whole other world or, better yet, a part of this world they never knew existed.

Besides the amount of content, I also very carefully chose the setting of the game so as to take advantage of a pre-existing history and back-story. Remember the name Ong's Hat from the **Ong's Hat: Incunabula** project described earlier in this History section? Like I mentioned in that chapter, the mythos that developed around and from the Ong's Hat story has become one of the persistent legends of the Internet, and was already a blend of fact and fiction, making it the ideal starting point for a story intended to blur the line between the two even farther. Additionally, the Ong's Hat story had just the right blend of science and mysticism, something I was also hoping to achieve with **CTW**, having deliberately inserted mythological and fantasy elements in an otherwise modern story. I intended to present hard science and pure fantasy elements right next to each other, hopefully in a way that made the "science seem magical and the magic seem scientific," which by the way, is how one of the players described it, after the game was over. So, by placing my new fictional world in a location with a searchable and somewhat mysterious history, I gave the players a wealth of obviously related but out-of-game content to sort through at the beginning too. This created the illusion that the roots of the game stretched back way before even the early promotional announcements, and added a layer of believability to the launch.

I launched **Chasing The Wish** on February 27, 2003, one day ahead of the announced "latest start date" I had set for the game. I really wanted to start it a week or so earlier but had problems just getting all the last minute things done. I planned on the game lasting six months and had written a script that involved almost daily in-game interaction or events. I had also estimated a player base of around a few hundred people based on my previous games, but had over 1000 players registered a month before **CTW** even started. This made the launch itself a big deal, because the game began with e-mail from the main character, Dale Sprague, asking for help. I sent approximately 1200 e-mails that night to launch **CTW**, unaware that at least part of my hard work was in vain. As luck would have it, the mass-mailing program I was using malfunctioned and some of the registered players either didn't get the initial e-mail or received two copies. Not a very auspicious beginning to the game. Luckily, the players who did receive the e-mail were so primed to get started that, within minutes, the complete contents of the e-mail message were posted online and players were off and running, discovering the ten different websites prepared for the start of the game.

The opening e-mail:

Date: Fri, 28 Feb 2003
From: dale@synthasia.com
Subject: Please, please read this

Hi:
Please, even though you don't know me, I pray that you will take the time to read this message. I'm in trouble and have no one else to turn to.

A mutual friend suggested you as somehow who might be able and willing to help me, and said you were someone who was good at solving mysteries and researching things on the web. You see, my wife and daughter are dead and it's all my fault. No, not like you're probably thinking; I loved them and would never do anything to hurt them. But there's been a terrible accident. And now they're both gone. But you see, I know this sounds crazy, it wasn't supposed to happen this way. I was promised everything would be OK but it's all gone terribly, terribly wrong.

I can't explain here but if you are willing to try and help, I've hidden some informa-tion at my website, http://www.synthasia.com. I had to hide it because people are looking for any excuse and evidence they can find to prove me crazy.
In fact, that's why I'm sending you this now. I'm actually being committed to some kind of mental facility, tonight, against my will. The doctors have come a couple of times to the door and I've ignored them but I'm certain they will be back any minute, with the police probably to gain them access. They think I'm crazy because of what has happened and what I know. But I can't explain here; I'm not sure if the court orders they have allow them access to my e-mail or not.

Take a good look at my site; sometimes you can't see the forest for the trees. There's a journal of sorts there that I've hastily thrown together in the last few weeks, even before the accident. Things haven't been good for quite a while now.

If you decide to help, I may need someone to access my e-mails, as I may not be able to and I've tried to contact some people lately who may be able to help me besides you. I've set-up a form of access . . .

Damn, someone's at the door. I have to go. I must send as many e-mails as I can, quickly. Please help me. This isn't right. I promise, somehow I can explain it all to you but you must help me first.

Desperate,
Dale Sprague
dale@synthasia.com

The game included over two dozen sites during its six-month run and, at its peak, had over 2700 registered players. It cost me over $1000 personally to create and run the game, not to mention every spare moment of my life for over nine months. **CTW** received international press coverage, including articles in the New York Times, the BBC News, several major international newspapers and magazines, and many major online news and gaming websites. Some of the highlights of the game included:

- A live telephone press conference with several people portraying in-game characters, while interacting with over a dozen players at the same time;
- Over two dozen real world items created especially for the game, including original paintings, a puzzle disc, nine "magic" stones, and nine puzzle manuscript pages with beautiful calligraphy and illuminations. There were also rare and valuable antique books auctioned off as part of the game;
- Professionally produced video news segments reporting on key events in the game and featuring a fictional character from the game as the newscaster;
- Real world interactions in which three different items were handed over to players either face-to-face or hidden somewhere for players to find;

- A chatbot programmed especially for the game whose automated online responses were constantly monitored and interspersed with real time replies and later video animation to create the illusion of a sentient, self-educating, and constantly evolving cyber entity.

The game was not without its faults, as there were many times when I made mistakes in puzzles and content because I was either trying to do too much myself, or hurrying to create assets because I was running behind. One of my favorite mistakes happened when I was playing the parts of two different characters at the same time in an online chat, and I started off by typing a message that was obviously from one of the characters in the other character's instant messaging screen. It was immediately apparent to everyone in the room what had happened and caused me more than a few moments of panic and self-recrimination. Afterwards though, I couldn't help but laugh, because it was just so damn funny. Also, there were parts of the game where errors revealed puzzle solutions too early, spots where puzzles were too hard and entirely stumped the players, and sections that relied entirely too much on personal e-mail or individual instant messaging conversations to tell the story. Overall though, **Chasing The Wish** was incredibly successful, and was a wonderful learning experience for me in all aspects of creating and running a major league ARG.

Dave Szulborski

One of the hand-made illuminated manuscript pages created especially for **Chasing The Wish**. Six of these beautiful artifacts, each containing a secret puzzle, were distributed to the players throughout the course of the game.

One of several original paintings created especially for **Chasing The Wish**. The painting, entitled *The Tree of Life*, was auctioned off during the game and contained a clue in the form of mystic symbols painted onto the base of the tree. The symbols have been made white to make them visible in this image.

155

Chapter 12: MetaCortechs - ARGs Reloaded

In summer 2003, the online fan forums for the enormously popular **Matrix** movie franchise were already extremely active with discussions about the soon to be released third and final movie of the trilogy, when one **Matrix** fan posted about a curious website he had stumbled across, http://www.metacortechs.com. MetaCortex was the name of the company that the main character, Neo, worked for before being freed from the matrix in the first movie but, interestingly, it was spelled two different ways in the movie – MetaCortex and Meta-Cortechs. When the site was first discovered, it was nothing more than a Flash movie counting down to October 1st. Inside the Flash file, however, people quickly discovered six hidden links to websites, all involving the **Matrix**.

On Sept. 19th MetaCortex sent out a press release:

FOR IMMEDIATE RELEASE

Redland, WA - SEPTEMBER 19, 2003 - MetaCortex Corp. announced today the development of its new MetaVR entertainment system, for use in conjunction with its MetaGamex computer gaming console.

The MetaVR entertainment system is currently the most sophisticated Virtual Reality complex developed for the home entertainment market. Consisting of a set of MetaVR goggles, a stereo headset, infrared tactile sensor/emitters and an olfactory chest plate, the MetaVR system breaks new ground in providing absolutely immersive, lifelike, convincing gaming like nothing ever seen before.

Our new MetaVR system will take gaming a quantum leap beyond anything that our competitors have been able to create so far, stated Steven Walsh, CEO of MetaCortex. We're on the cutting edge of the gaming marketplace. We're very excited about the worldwide anticipation for this new system, and we've put a lot of effort into putting more of what players want into the MetaVR. Already, we are building substantial inventories in anticipation of consumer demand.

The MetaVR system uses new proprietary MetaCortex software to actually anticipate the players' moves, buffering what it thinks will happen in order to avoid any kind of perceptual lag on the player's behalf. This lag has been the primary limitation on the gaming community's willingness to wholly embrace true virtual reality systems in the past, since it has a tendency to make players nauseous, which clearly is not in our best interest as a developer, stated Walsh. However, all indications are that these anomalies have been completely eliminated from the core MetaVR operating system.

Providing sensory input to four of the five senses, the MetaVR system will let players see in stereo 3-D vision, hear in simulated surround stereo, feel objects when they're held or impact their bodies, sense temperature changes, and even smell their simulated surroundings. Players have yet to realize how important olfactory feedback is in the gaming world, because they take it for granted in the real world, Walsh continued. Imagine the adrenaline rush as, while you're exploring an alien world, you realize that you are smelling the sour musky odor of an invisible grungbeast. That smell could give you those precious extra seconds that may mean the difference between life and death, or at least having to start a level over.

MetaCortex has only recently made inroads into the gaming genre. Known for its expertise in developing business and information applications, the Company has made a huge impact worldwide, quickly becoming *the* force to be reckoned with in the computer industry.

For further information, contact:

MetaCortex
One MetaCortex Avenue
Redland, WA 98076
USA

It didn't take long for people to notice that neither the company itself, MetaCortex, nor the town where it claimed to be located, Redland, Washington, actually seemed to exist. They also found it curious that the press release imitated the **Matrix** movie by including both variations of the MetaCortex name. Finally, the product the press release was announcing, the MetaVR System, could easily be seen as an early version of technology related to the **Matrix** movies.

Now, more than ever, people were convinced that this was the beginning of a new alternate reality game, or at least a major online promotion for the upcoming **Matrix Revolutions** movie. Soon, the discussion found its way to the ARG fan forums, where the ARG community was just as fascinated with it as the **Matrix** fans were. Many ARG old-timers even anxiously posted that they thought this might, at long last, be the fabled sequel to **the Beast**, since that promotion also involved a major motion picture. As the countdown continued at the MetaCortechs site, both the ARG and **Matrix** communities waited anxiously to see what would happen.

The **Matrix** Revolution

A few days before the much-anticipated October 1ˢᵗ date, players tracked down the supposed web hosting service MetaCortechs was using, a company called Underscore Hosting. There were indications on this site that Underscore wasn't a real company, convincing people even more that this was an alternate reality game just waiting to launch.

When October 1ˢᵗ rolled around the website for MetaCortechs became active. The website appeared to be for a real company that billed itself as "the world's foremost software and information systems development company," whose products could be found on "over 80% of computer software worldwide." There was still nothing about the website to tie it directly into the **Matrix** films though, besides the name connection, except for two small additional clues. First, the site showed the company name as both MetaCortex and MetaCortechs in various places, a discrepancy that also appeared in the first **Matrix** film, as already mentioned. Additionally, there was a company directory on the site that responded to the name "Thomas Anderson" with the message:

Name: Anderson, Thomas

TRANSFERRED

No forwarding information available.

Thomas Anderson was the character Neo's real name in the film series.

The Truth Revealed

As the game began to unfold, one of the major lines of discussion and speculation had to do with who had created it and whether or not the game was an official promotion by Warner Brothers for the upcoming film. The material and websites that had been discovered so far were all so professionally done that many people were convinced that it was indeed the latest major studio ARG, if not the long awaited **Beast II**. Unfortunately, a breakdown in website security a few weeks into the game revealed a name that was traced back to a known independent Puppetmaster team, the same group that had previously done the game **Lockjaw**. While this information actually encouraged many of the long time ARG community members, because they knew it meant that the game would be very well done, many people from the **Matrix** community were disappointed and openly hostile at the news, feeling they had been deceived into providing personal information and participating in the game. Luckily, this controversy faded quickly, as the upset **Matrix** fans wandered away to continue waiting for **Matrix Revolutions** but leaving many fans of the film series who had become enamored of this new world called Alternate Reality Gaming behind to play the game.

The game itself included a great variety of multimedia assets and puzzles, including original songs and video clips, and also integrated real-time communications in the form of online chats and phone calls. **MetaCortechs** also incorporated some real world items in the form of CDs that were hidden in various cities across the country to be found by players. The game was created by a team of eight Puppetmasters and used sixteen different websites, lasting for eight weeks. Although not entirely an original idea (**Exocog** had done much the same thing before with the movie **Minority Report**) their decision to present the game as a possible official part of the **Matrix** franchise and time it to an upcoming movie release was brilliant, attracting a massive amount of potential new fans and players to their game and the ARG world. Because of the crossover into the **Matrix** universe, the game wasn't just played by the ARG community; there were large groups of **Matrix** fans around the world following along with the game on their own community forums and fan sites. The **Matrix** tie-in also generated a great deal of press coverage for the game. An article in the British newspaper The Guardian declared, "this was the most successful ARGs ever, with around 12,000 players and visits logged from 118 different countries." Of course, like any ARG, the game didn't sustain those numbers throughout the entire game, but still achieved an incredible level of success for an independent game.

For players who played the entire game, **MetaCortechs** created tremendous loyalty, as many players were inspired to create their own websites or artistic creations as tributes to the game and the PM team. A group of them even banded together after the game concluded to begin drafting an online book of the storyline, which has just recently been completed. In any case, the PMs of **MetaCortechs** provided two months of well-written and emotionally involving material for the players, and created a game that helped attract many new fans to the genre of Alternate Reality Gaming.

Chapter 13: Summer Heat - I Love Bees

The summer of 2004 was a time of waiting in the world of Alternate Reality Gaming; even though there weren't any major games currently under way, there were many signs of potential games right around the corner. A long running and sometimes trouble-beset independent game called **Acheron** had concluded in February, and in March there was an announcement of an upcoming game called **Project Syzygy**, which appeared to have some substantial financial backing, and claimed to be a "new type of immersive game, one that will change everything." Unfortunately, it wasn't scheduled to launch until early 2005. Spring also saw a few ARG-like promotions for upcoming major motion pictures, including **Eternal Sunshine of the Spotless Mind** and **Godsend**, but they failed to turn into full-fledged games. Another independent game called **AWARE** launched a *pre-game* in April, but was plagued with early problems and controversy in its initial months. And so, as the summer of 2004 dawned, many alternate reality game fans were sitting and waiting for the next big thing.

In early July, things appeared to be coming to life. A game named **El Centro**, which had been discovered a while ago and looked suspiciously ARG-ish, was showing signs of new activity. An auction found on E-bay for an asteroid (of all things) hinted at the impending start of another new independent game, called **Orbital Colony**. Coincidentally, on the same day the auction was discovered, July 16th, the webmasters of several prominent ARG-related sites received a strange package. The parcel claimed to be from a company called Margaret's Honey in San Francisco, California, and contained the traditional small bear-shaped plastic jar filled with honey. The little plastic bear held something else inside though too – a rabbit hole, in the form of nine cut-out letters that could be assembled to spell out "i-l-o-v-e-b-e-e-s" and several other possible phrases. Being the ARG fans they were, it didn't take long for the people who received the package to find the website http://www.ilovebees.com, which appeared to a website devoted to beekeeping created by someone named Margaret, appropriately enough. But there were weird things going on at the site, including an ominous pop-up message that appeared to be counting down to something that sounded menacing:

HALT - MODULE CORE HEMORRHAGE

Control has been yielded to the

SYSTEM PERIL DISTRIBUTED REFLEX.

This medium is classified, and has a

STRONG INTRUSIVE INCLINATION.

In 5 days, network throttling will erode.

In 19 days this medium will metastasize.
COUNTDOWN TO WIDE AWAKE AND PHYSICAL:

32:15:38:10:831

Make your decisions accordingly.

The site featured a link to a blog by someone named Dana, who turned out to be Margaret's niece and also the person who created and managed Margaret's website for her. In fact, the http://www.ilovebees.com site featured a plea for help from Dana, who couldn't seem to fix the mysterious and constantly increasing problems the site was having. One of these problems were images on the site that were corrupted due to text being hidden inside them. And so began the "next big thing" the ARG world had been waiting for.

Hold the Phone

Even when it became apparent that **I Love Bees (ILB)** was some form of alternate reality game, it still was a waiting game for a while, as the timer counted down to three different dates - Tuesday July 27th when "network throttling" was due to "erode", Tuesday August 10th when the "medium will metastasize", and Tuesday August 24 when something unnamed would be "wide awake and physical." Many long time ARG fans immediately latched onto the Tuesday dates as a hint that this might be the long-awaited sequel to **the Beast**, since that team of creators adhered religously to a schedule of updating every Tuesday, but others on the community forums urged them not to get their hopes up prematurely.

On Wednesday July 21st rumors began to circulate that the website address http://www.ilovebees.com appeared in the theatrical trailer for an upcoming video game release. The video game, **Halo 2**, was already one of the most anticipated releases of the year and was being developed by Bungie Studios for Microsoft, the creators of the original **Beast**. When the rumors were confirmed that the url did appear in the **Halo 2** trailer, many people took this as a sign that **I Love Bees** was indeed another ARG being done by Microsoft and, quite possibly, the same Puppetmasters who had created **the Beast**. Needless to say, scores of ARG old-timers, including some who hadn't been around at all since the days of the Cloudmakers, were beginning to become very excited, generating an increased level of activity in the ARG world. In addition, fans of the original **Halo** game had also caught on to this apparent promotion for the upcoming sequel and were joining the alternate reality game community forums by the hundreds. The game had yet to even really start and it was already creating more of a stir than anything else had in quite some time.

Tuesday July 27th turned out to be a disappointment for many of the players who were anxiously waiting for the game to kick into gear. While there was some new text on the **ILB** website, there wasn't the huge launch many expected, leading to new websites and the start of the real story. They resolved to wait out the next two weeks until the next countdown date, sustained by the e-mail messages they were receiving from Margaret's site and the occasional new entries to Dana's blog.

Two weeks later, on Tuesday August 10th, the second countdown phase ended and the "medium metastasized." Players soon uncovered many new examples of embedded text on the **ILB** site, as well as finding a bunch of numbers believed to be GPS coordinates, and wav files of a voice speaking. Another week later and the list of numbers had changed somewhat, with both deletions and new additions, as well as the inclusion of a specified time for each coordinate. After several more weeks of the coordinates being adjusted and endless speculation among the players as to what they might possibly mean, it was discovered that the numbers represented the locations of payphones across the continental US and that's when the fun really began.

For the next two months, the **ILB** players ventured forth to answer payphone calls from the game at hundreds of locations around the country. Their reward for answering the calls and giving the right information when asked was a series of audio files that cumulatively told a story. The payphone locations were called "axons" and the process of answering them making them "hot." The community teamwork and cooperation required to "enhottentate all the axons" was massive, but the huge player base of the game came together and succeeded each week in answering more and more calls, successfully working their way through the story. Amazingly, although the characters in the audio clips were presented in very brief segments and through their voices only, many of them became very real to the players, a tribute to the strength of the writing in the game.

During the three month run of **ILB**, many players were constantly waiting for the game to break out into other websites, as most other ARG games have used multiple websites to tell their story and create their fictional world. No one imagined that **ILB** could present a believeable and engaging world with only one main website, a blog, and hundreds of individual sound files, but the game not only succeeded in doing so, it became one of the most written about marketing promotions of the summer. There were a few minor bumps along the way, as some players were openly upset that the game didn't include many traditional ARG puzzles in the early stages, and others were frustrated when there were no calls to payphones anywhere near them. The Puppetmasters, in another clear example of the unique *interactive authoring* possibilities of alternate reality games, actually created a series of puzzles midway through **ILB,** in an effort to pacify this vocal minority within the ranks of the players.

The game ended with four real world "Training Events," in which a certain number of players were allowed to attend gatherings where they got to play **Halo 2** four days in advance of its release to the world. Although these events weren't conducted in an in-game manner, they still generated a massive amount of interest and excitement among the players. These events actually highlight a curious dichotomy that exists in many alternate reality games that are used for promotional purposes or tied into a known fictional universe. As soon as the **ILB** url was confirmed to be in the **Halo 2** trailer, it was obvious that the story just beginning to be told on the websites was fictional, theoretically destroying the immersive elements of the game. After that, there could not be any true *TINAG* feeling, as no one could believe what was happening in the game was actually real. Additionally, there were several segments of the game that also violated the principles of *TINAG*, including the endgame Training Events. Nevertheless, most of the players showed a great capacity for ignoring these non-immersive portions, and the fact that the events of the story were taking place in the universe of the **Halo** series video games. This obviously harkens back to the "dual consciousness" theory of Jay David Bolter and Richard Grusin discussed in the first section of this book. The strength of the game's writing was such that it was able to evoke a sensation of immersion in the players, despite their awareness of the fact that **ILB** was indeed just a game.

Son of the **Beast**

Once the game concluded the PM team was revealed to be the same team that had developed **the Beast** three years earlier, as many players had come to suspect along the way. The creative team of Sean

Stewart, Elan Lee, and Jordan Weisman, now operating as 4orty2wo Studios, had returned to produce a game that overshadowed even their earlier creation in terms of player numbers and international attention and press coverage. The team had a budget from Microsoft of $1,000,000 to produce **ILB,** but still went over it in creating the massive production. It's highly unlikely that **ILB** came anywhere near to generating enough actual sales of the **Halo 2** game to cover the investment it required, but there's no denying it created a small cultural phenomenon and launched both ARGs and the **Halo 2** game into the mainstream consciousness, at least for a brief while.

Chapter 14: David and Goliath - Urban Hunt

Fireworks weren't the only things exploding in early July 2004, as this summer would turn out to be the busiest time ever in the history of alternate reality games. As some people were anxiously watching movie trailers, looking for the latest signs of an alternate reality rabbit hole, others unexpectedly stumbled upon what appeared to be another ARG in yet another major entertainment medium – television.

While browsing through various online forums that regularly announce upcoming television reality shows, one of the former players of the **MetaCortechs** game found an entry that seemed interesting for a new show called **Urban Hunt**. The show involved a group of contestants traveling across the country on "missions" competing for a cash prize of $500,000. There was also a web-based component to the show, where people could apply to become "Online Advisors" to the contestants, which appealed to the ARG player, so she applied. In response she received the following autoresponse reply:

Urban Hunt!

Ready for an exciting adventure? Be alert at all times. A call could come at any moment. Never knowing when is part of the thrill of the hunt!

Making yourself known to us is just the first step. You now must wait for the call that can earn you fabulous prizes as you help, or foil, the missions of future contestants on our show. Their success, or failure, is in your hands. However, you must make the choices.

Online players are contestants' lifelines. Like it or not, our urban hunters know they must rely upon you to provide them with information. Only you can determine the direction of our contestants' future...and their future travels...so we wish you luck in your choices. Getting our contestants to believe in you is another matter entirely!

You are now registered for the online component of Urban Hunt. Net access is required. Email address on file must be current. Telephone numbers must also be up-to-date.

Good luck!

Everything seemed legitimate enough, until the person who applied noticed that there was a puzzle apparently hidden in the reply she received. By taking the first letter of every sentence, a website address was discovered – urbanmythology.net – and the stories on this urban legends website provided the first glimpse into the mystery that was to become **Urban Hunt**.

Urban Hunt

Urban Hunt was the latest game that I wrote and produced along with a team of five other fulltime Puppetmasters. We actually called the game **Dread House**, which was the name of the failed reality show that was at the center of the game's mystery, but the players named the game **Urban Hunt** since that was their entry point into the game. I spent several months after finishing **Chasing The Wish** contemplating if I even wanted to do another ARG and decided that, if I did, it would be to try and achieve the very specific goal of fully exploring the concept of *TINAG*, or *This Is Not A Game*. I wanted to create something that made people actually stop and question if what they were participating in was real or not.

Is it Real or is it . . . . ?

My initial goal when I first began thinking about an idea for a new game was to try and truly capture the *TINAG* feeling and have players wondering exactly what was real and what was not, and if they were even playing a game at all. Unfortunately, for many alternate reality games, the extent of *TINAG* is wondering if a possible rabbit hole that has been found is really a *game* or not. In too many cases, there never is a question of whether the events are *real* or not, because the game is set in a known fictional universe (**MetaCortechs** and **I Love Bees**, for example) or in the future (**the Beast**). Other games find other ways to make it apparent that they cannot be real, such as **CTW** announcing in advance that it was a game. All of these games, while incredibly enjoyable and well-made, fell short of the true potential of *TINAG* in my opinion, by never making the player question the reality of what he was experiencing. I wanted to try something that could finally bridge that divide and create a world that didn't require the players' willing suspension of disbelief. Instead, I wanted them to believe that everything that happened was part of their regular world.

Because I wanted this game to blur the lines between reality and the game to an extent that had never been done before, it made sense to build the story around subject matter that did that also. This wasn't too hard to do actually, as it seems our society is on a path to do just that – merge reality with fiction. Between reality shows that aren't real and urban legends that get accepted as real because they are repeated endlessly on the Internet, we have become a culture that doesn't know where its reality starts and ends. So those two areas where reality was already blurred, reality television and urban legends, became the basis for the game's story.

Building the Game

I chose six other Puppetmasters to help me create **Urban Hunt**, based either on the specific skills I already knew they had or just because I felt I could trust them. The goal we were trying to accomplish with **UH** made total secrecy essential during the development phase of the game. If people knew the game was coming, it would be much harder to convince them of the "reality" of any rabbit hole we would present. It was critical that everyone on the PM team keep absolutely silent about the game until it had concluded, which made trust an important consideration when choosing the team. Unfortunately, one of the people I chose as a Puppetmaster had to drop out shortly after we began working on the game, leaving us a core team of five other members and myself.

We started building **UH** in March, focusing on the seven websites that would be part of the launch, trying as hard as possible to make everything – the websites, the video clips, and the initial puzzles – as realistic as could be. That may sound funny at first, as the original material included a story about a haunted abandoned mental hospital, a machine that could read and visualize people's dreams, a crazy woman who communicated with the dead and wrote poetry based on their thoughts, and a television show that ended with the deaths of both the cast and crew but was never reported. Admittedly, these topics weren't necessarily the most believable of subject matter to begin with, but, by framing everything within the world of urban mythology, we anticipated the players' reaction and gave them an *in-game* means of accepting the content, while also establishing our central theme of blurring reality.

Although we were funding the game entirely ourselves and had little chance of recovering much of our personal investment, we deliberately decided to use some innovative but sometimes costly resources to enhance the illusion of the reality of the **UH** world. We knew we needed to make the initial websites appear unquestionably real and went to great lengths to try and accomplish this. We began by building a back-story trail on the Internet, months before the game was set to launch. Using the name of the character that supposedly created and ran the urban legends website in the game, we established accounts at several major legitimate urban legends websites and began making posts in whatever topics were currently being discussed, just to get the character's name on record long before the game began.

For the company that was supposed to be developing the **Urban Hunt** TV show and had also produced the earlier show that had ended in disaster, Tomorrow's Talk Studios, we used a domain name that had been registered three years earlier and had never been developed, to try and create the illusion that the company had existed for quite some time. We also went to the extraordinary lengths of hiring a virtual office service to act out the role of the real Tomorrow's Talk Studios when the game began. The virtual office added so many elements of believability to the fictional company that it was well worth the cost. It enabled us to send and receive packages and snail mail from a real address in New York City, an important consideration since we were asking people to send in audition tapes to apply to be on **Urban Hunt**. The virtual office gave us a verifiable address for our fictional company in an office building that housed some businesses in the same field, entertainment production, lending even more credibility to the company if anyone looked into it that deeply. Also, and perhaps most importantly, the virtual office provided live telephone answering services during business hours, in which they presented themselves as the actual Tomorrow's Talk offices. We provided the virtual office company with our fictional employees' names and company details, to present as seamless as possible illusion of a real company. And, with a few minor exceptions, it was incredibly successful.

To make the **Urban Hunt** TV show appear real, we drafted press releases for the upcoming show and sent them to actual websites that normally announce all the new reality TV shows for months to come. Without exception, they all believed the press release was legitimate and posted it on their sites. We also took advantage of the timing of a small reality TV gathering in Las Vegas planned for the same time as our launch, by printing up postcards that allegedly were recruiting contestants for the new show and distributing them at the reality TV event.

Finally, for the abandoned mental hospital we wanted to use in the game, I spent weeks researching real abandoned facilities until I found one that fit the profile and timeline needed for the game. Even after selecting the location, another PM spent hours and hours looking for any and all references to the hospital on the Internet, discovering some material that we incorporated into the storyline to add yet another layer of believability. I'm not suggesting PM teams plagiarize existing websites and that's not what we did. Instead, we found a site from a group of urban explorers who had actually been in the asylum we were using and wrote small elements of their descriptions into our characters and story events. For example, the urban explorers mentioned they found a room that had piles of torn up paper arranged in strange patterns, as well as many small sculptures and pictures of birds. We created a character that was a mentally imbalanced former caretaker at the hospital and described the "hidey holes" he created and lived in after the asylum shut down as being filled with torn up paper and bird imagery. So, the information on the urban explorers' website, which has been around for years and years, gave the players pause when they discovered it, and made them wonder just exactly what was real and what wasn't.

David and Goliath

We launched **Urban Hunt** in the middle of July of 2004, coincidentally just days after the **ILB** honey jars showed up, signaling the beginning of the massive **Halo 2** promotional effort. Of course, at the time we had no idea that those little jars meant that our independent game would be going head-to-head with what, for all intents and purposes, was **the Beast II**. Not that it would have mattered; with all the work and preparation we already put into **UH** and the schedule we had worked out, we weren't about to cancel or delay the game anyway. The stealth launch went well and even though many experienced ARG players suspected this was the start of a new game, the elements of realism we had built into the game gave rise to much discussion early on, questioning if this was even a game at all, exactly as we had hoped.

When it became clear that **ILB** was an alternate reality game promoting the release of **Halo 2**, the **UH** PM team predictably had more than a few discussions of how this would impact our game. We saw both positive and negative results of running concurrently to what was sure to be a massively funded and talked about professional effort. While there's no denying that the publicity and number of players that the ILB generated far overshadowed **Urban Hunt**, it also meant that thousands and thousands of new people were exposed to our game, as the legions of existing **Halo** fans rushed to join the ARG community. In fact, many players left **ILB** to join **UH** at various points; some openly posting that they felt **UH** had a much more immersive and engaging storyline and presentation. Some of them came just because of the puzzles which, early in the game, **ILB** was sadly lacking. The **ILB** Puppetmasters actually rewrote part of their game while it was in process to include a series of puzzles and try and appease players who were publicly complaining.

We also felt that **UH** offered a distinctly different and *truer* alternate reality game experience than did **ILB**. Promotional ARGs, by their very nature, are less immersive and inherently less believable than many independent games. This isn't a criticism, just an acknowledgement of the different styles and purposes of the two types of games. I don't think there was ever one moment during the **ILB** game where anyone thought they were actually answering a payphone call made by an artificial intelligence from the future. By contrast, there were many instances in **UH** where the players were seriously questioning if *in-game* content was real or not.

Endings

It's an interesting phenomenon in the world of alternate reality games that the endings of ARGs often disappoint some of the players and cause controversy on the player forums. The **MetaCortechs** game, for example, was incredibly well received and constantly praised by its players during its run, but nevertheless generated a rash of negative posts and comments when it ended. This certainly wasn't the first time this happened in an alternate reality game and quite often doesn't necessarily mean there was anything wrong with the writing. Some-times, it is just because certain players get so emotionally involved in a game that they don't want to see it end. In keeping with this great tradition, **UH** also caused some controversy when it ended, but for somewhat different reasons When I was first writing the **UH** story I really wanted to find some way to rekindle the *TINAG* feeling at the end of the game. Normally, as a game goes on, there is very little of this feeling left by the end, because all the players know undeniably it is a game, and that the characters and entities in it are fictional. I also thought it would be fun to copy the false endings you often see in horror films, where you think the movie has ended and the last survivor has escaped and then, suddenly, the killer resurfaces and extracts his revenge. We discussed the ending several times as a team and decided we wanted to do a finale that left players wondering if they perhaps had been deceived the entire time as to who were the good guys and bad guys, and even if the game had really ended at all. And so we decided to incorporate a false ending to the game with several plot twists along the way.

To do so, we staged what apparently was the ending, in which several main characters died and many questions were left unanswered. To make matters even more confusing and uncertain, the following day we posted a false set of credits for the game at the Tomorrow's Talk Studios website, claiming the entire production had been an alternate reality game promotion for their upcoming new show called **Dread House**. Many players were upset with the abruptness of the false ending and the issues it left unresolved and didn't hesitate to voice their opinions on the community forums, which we had anticipated might happen. Within another day or so, the main character who had apparently been killed during the false ending wrote to the players, letting them know he had survived and setting them up for the real ending. The real finale wrapped up most of the remaining unresolved issues and **Urban Hunt** concluded as originally planned on Halloween night, Oct. 31st, 2004.

Looking Back

In retrospect, **Urban Hunt** was both a successful and highly enjoyable experience for me and, hopefully, the rest of the PM team. I believe we accomplished the goals we set for the game and provided three months of solid, immersive entertainment for the players. The game did receive its share of press coverage including, like **CTW** before it, an article in the New York Times. Some of the highlights of the game included the level of reality blurring we were able to achieve, the interweaving of science and the supernatural in a mostly believable way, and the quality of the websites, puzzles, and assets we produced. **Urban Hunt** also included a novel first for the ARG world, an actual book that was published and sold as an *in-game* item. The book was a collection of poetry that had puzzles hidden in a great many of the poems. Unfortunately, this book was also the source of one of the most embarrassing moments of the game, as I inadvertently included a poem created by one of the other PMs that had the hidden message in it "insert puzzle here." She had created the framework for the puzzle, but I was supposed to add the actual hidden message and forgot to. Finding the "insert puzzle here" message caused some confusion among the players understandably and, after I stopped kicking myself about the stupidity of the mistake, kept me smiling through the end of the game because it was just so damn funny.

What I am most proud of about **Urban Hunt** is that we went head-to-head with a game produced by the team that had created **the Beast** and held our own. Besides the enormous budget **I Love Bees** had, it also had the advantage of being tied into one of the most popular video game franchises of all times and benefiting from the massive amounts of hype that went into promoting the release of **Halo 2**. Not too many independent games or development teams could have lasted against such overwhelming competition, and the fact that we not only did, but also were compared favorably to **ILB**, is an incredible accomplishment.

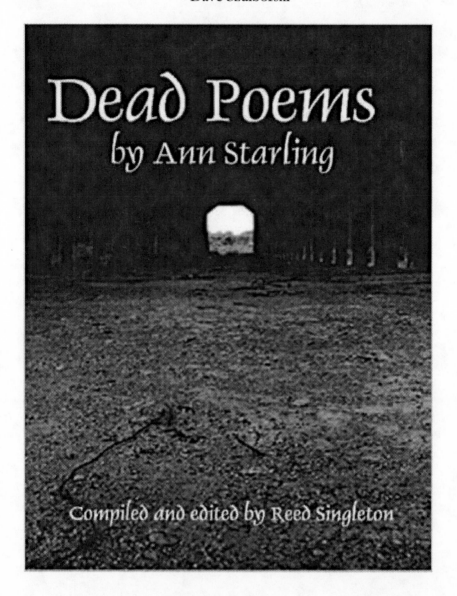

The cover of the book <u>Dead Poems</u>, written and published as an in-game item for **Urban Hunt**. Over one hundred pages long, most of the poems contained within had secret messages or puzzles encrypted into the text.

Chapter 15: The Current and Future State of Alternate Reality Games

Thanks to the overwhelming success of this summer's promotional alternate reality game **I Love Bees**, the genre of ARGs is more active now than it has ever been. By using an alternate reality game to help launch the hugely popular and long awaited video game **Halo 2**, the developers of **ILB** have helped thrust the genre into the mainstream consciousness in a way it hasn't been since the promotional game for the **A.I.** movie, **the Beast**. Unfortunately, the failure of **Majestic** right after **the Beast** dampened the enthusiasm for the genre at the time and certainly went a long way to discourage other professional companies from using ARGs as promotional or revenue-generating projects.

Today, however, not long after the **ILB** promotion has ended, the world of Alternate Reality Gaming seems poised to sustain the public interest and enthusiasm with several ongoing games and more scheduled for the near future. And it looks like the world of marketing may finally be catching on too, as there are more promotional campaigns going on now in the form of ARGs than ever before.

Dave Szulborski

Alternate Reality Games as Marketing

After years of disappointment and confusion in the field of online advertising, alternate reality games promise to bring new life and potential to Internet marketing. Compared to other forms of currently available web-based advertising, nothing has the power to create and sustain consumer interest in a product like ARGs. The **Halo 2** promotion **I Love Bees** is a great example, as the campaign successfully created and maintained a highly active and motivated online community for over three months, leading up the release of the video game. Not only that, the promotion actually motivated people to take action, by getting them to leave the medium carrying the message (in this case, the Internet) and go out in the world and accomplish something. All in all, the results of **ILB** were quite remarkable for any advertising campaign, let alone an online promotion. Additionally, by using a new and innovative marketing technique, at least to most people, the alternate reality game also generated a massive amount of free publicity over and above what Microsoft had already budgeted to market the **Halo 2** game.

Other companies have apparently noticed the success of **ILB** too, as there are more and more ARG-like promotional campaigns surfacing all the time. Currently, there are major marketing efforts being conducted by Nintendo, Sharp Televisions, and Stella Artois, and many websites for major motion pictures and television shows that use elements of ARGs in their design. The shows <u>Alias</u>, <u>24</u>, and <u>Smallville</u> have all incorporated online content into their shows in various ways, with hints that more extensive projects may follow. And finally, there are several companies looking to produce alternate reality games as commercial products in the near future, and probably many more nobody even knows about yet. Besides movies and television shows, ARGs would be ideally suited for promoting novels, music CDs, live shows, and many other products and services that have yet to be explored. Another highly visible success like **I Love Bees** is probably all that it would take to have even dozens and dozens of additional companies jumping on the bandwagon.

The Demand for Better Online Content

"I think that the world of interactive online entertainment is going to mature over the next five years pretty dramatically. We'll look back and say that the things we imagined as interactive entertainment -- games, predominantly -- are a relatively small segment of the online entertainment pie. **Majestic** is interesting because it bridges the gap between storytelling and game play, and does it on top of the platform that is the Internet. And it brings together, for my generation, the three things we have connected with over the last 30 years: stories, whether movies or television; gaming, interactivity and computing; and communications. It synthesizes those three things and creates a compelling platform upon which you can tell multiple stories." **Majestic's** Neil Young from an interview published on Salon.com

Despite being wrong about **Majestic** being the vehicle to cause it, I do believe Neil Young was right when he said that interactive online entertainment is in the process of maturing. As the technological capabilities of the Internet continue to advance and high-speed access continues to become more pervasive around the world, consumers of online entertainment are constantly going to demand more complex and better quality gaming experiences. Digital gaming itself is rapidly expanding, as reflected by figures that show that the video game industry now generates more revenue than either television or movies. As it becomes possible to deliver truly immersive and engaging entertainment on the Internet, more and more consumers will turn to the web as their primary source for entertainment. Alternate reality games are capable of delivering those experiences now, and are not dependent on advances in graphical display, artificial intelligence programming, or connection speeds. More than any other genre of digital online gaming, alternate reality games seem capable of delivering the experience consumers want now and into the future.

Another insight into the future of alternate reality games comes from Steve Peters, the creator and Webmaster for the website http://www.argn.com, which serves as one of the central news sources for the world of Alternate Reality Gaming. Steve has appeared on television, radio, and innumerable online locations speaking about ARGs and about specific promotions such as the recent **I Love Bees** game.

"My interest in what's become known as Alternate Reality Gaming began when I saw a piece on CNET's television show about a strange promotional web-mystery revolving around the film **AI: Artificial Intelligence**. It seems that there had been some strange clues embedded in the film's trailer, which led to a phone number and a website. The show pointed me to Cloudmakers.org, and after spending an evening exploring the websites, sending emails, calling phone numbers and basically getting caught up with everything, my curiosity piqued. A few days later, when I was called on my cell phone by a character from the game, I was hooked. I found myself totally caught up in solving the mystery of who killed Evan Chan, and the online universe spanning multiple websites, challenging puzzles, compelling story, and best of all, a cool community of people from all over the globe, puzzling, dissecting, speculating, solving and progressing the story. The game lasted most of the summer and when it was over, I knew I'd been part of something totally new and unique, a new form of entertainment and storytelling, and I loved it.

Upon reflection, I realized that community is key when it comes to alternate reality games. The synergy that occurs when a group of people accomplishes something that they could never have done individually is an amazing thing to see. Without a community, the player base of a game can never achieve critical mass, so one of the challenges for these games is the need to depend on the players to be resourceful enough to set up their own space in which to work and coordinate efforts. During **the Beast**, the Cloudmakers used Yahoo Groups as their meeting place, which was adequate at the time, but with the later addition of banner ads it became pretty cumbersome. During **Lockjaw**, which was a second ARG developed by some Cloudmakers in the months after **the Beast**, Yahoo Groups kept going down and was getting really laggy. As a result, we set up a forum on my company website using a popular open source forum application to use as a backup when Yahoo Groups went down. It turns out that this board became the impetus for the Alternate Reality Gaming Network. I wanted to set the forum up somewhere other than my business site, so I registered argn.com and put things there. Little did I know that argn.com would spawn an entire community based around Alternate Reality Gaming. Since then, argn.com has amazingly become the nexus of ARG, functioning as a portal to point players to the various games, sites and communities that are currently online.

Since then, we've seen dozens of alternate reality games come and go. Some were successful, but many have imploded before they've been able to complete their run, leaving players dazed and disappointed to say the least. I'd say the two main challenges facing new Puppetmasters are: a) underestimating the amazing amount of work and 12/7 dedication needed to successfully pull a game off; and b) being unable to build a substantial enough player base to support the game and gain critical mass, which is especially important in the case of pay-to-play models. Every instance of pay-to-play games I've witnessed so far have been cancelled midway through, due to the number of players falling far short of the projected need to sustain the game. I'm not saying this isn't a workable revenue model yet, I just think these games have been a little ahead of their time. I look at games like **Majestic, Search4e** and **TerraQuest** as being very innovative, but unfortunately they couldn't attract and sustain the numbers they needed to survive.

Currently, this whole genre is really still in its infancy. I liken where things are now with television in the early 1950's. Television was a new medium, and producers played around and tried innovative new techniques to tell their stories. Some caught on, some didn't. Some worked great, some were dismal failures. Look at how Desi Arnaz revolutionized everything by developing the 3-camera shooting style that has become standard to this day. Everyone thought he was crazy, but he was able to look ahead and find ways to utilize the medium to a fuller extent than anybody else. This is still happening with alternate reality games. The authors are still trying out unproven techniques, finding out where the boundaries are, what works and what doesn't, and hopefully why. The successful games of the future will not only build off of successful and proven techniques, but also learn from previous misfires. The ultimate goal will continue to be, first and foremost, good storytelling. After all, this is the basis for what draws us. We learn to truly care about the characters whose lives we're following. The puzzles and interaction are like special effects in films, in that they're most effective when they're there to support the story, making logical sense, as opposed to being just dropped in for their own sake.

The future holds quite a bit of promise, with more and more aspects of society becoming truly networked together. Who knows? Maybe a game could reach out and have your refrigerator make you a drink, or get a pizza delivered to your door (now there's an idea!). I anticipate seeing ARGs used more and more as effective promotional tools for films/television/novels, etc. and becoming a more mainstream vehicle very soon. In addition, I hope to see the non-promotional games become a popular and accepted form of entertainment in their own right."

Steve touches on several key points in his look forward, including the idea that, for alternate reality games to truly be successful in the future, someone still needs to develop a workable business model for ARGs as a commercial entertainment genre. The novelty of using ARGs for marketing promotions is sure to either wear off eventually or become diluted through the overuse success is sure to bring, and so, without a viable method or platform for producing alternate reality games that can at least cover their expenses, the genre will ultimately return to a small niche community in the world of online gaming.

One of the main obstacles so far to accomplishing this has been the public's ignorance of or misconceptions about what alternate reality games actually are. I remember when **Majestic** was first announced and being advertised in advance of its launch, I read several different quotes that all included something like, "Who would want to pay for a game that intrudes into your life and calls you in the middle of the night?"

Obviously that one line is all they could recall from the **Majestic** ads and formed the basis of their misconception about the whole genre. Even to this day you can find old reviews and online analyses of **Majestic** that blame this aspect of the game entirely for its failure. These people, in their ignorance, are mistaking a player's voluntary immersion into the world of an alternate reality game with the involuntary intrusion of a phone call in the middle of the night. They are two entirely different things.

The other problem with attracting new people to the genre, especially in terms of a pay-per-play scenario, is the inherent complexity of the form of alternate reality games. I don't mean the games or storylines are necessarily complex but I am instead referring to the very concept of the ARG itself. It's extremely difficult for the average person who hasn't experienced an ARG to comprehend what it will be like. They can quickly become overwhelmed and disinterested when someone starts trying to explain by saying things like, "Well, it uses e-mails, telephone calls, and instant messaging to talk to you, it can have dozens of websites you have to check for updates all the time, and there are really hard puzzles that it takes whole communities to solve." While all those things may be in some sense true, it doesn't make ARGs sound very accessible or enjoyable. And, if people don't know or understand what they are getting in advance, they aren't going to buy it. That's why ARGs are an extremely tough sell to anyone who doesn't truly know what they are.

That's the purpose of this book – to try and give the average person who has never even heard of alternate reality games an easy and painless way to learn about them. Many people are too intimidated to join an online community as a newcomer and start asking questions to try and educate themselves, and this method is almost impossible for something as complex as ARGs anyway. So, hopefully, this book will give the non-ARG fan a starting point and a path to follow towards getting involved in the world of Alternate Reality Gaming.

Part Three:

Alternate Reality Games

in Practice

Dave Szulborski

Chapter 16: Puppetmastering - Picking Up the Strings

Having detailed why I am qualified to do so, I am going to break the sacred Puppetmaster Code of Silence and reveal to you the secrets of making an alternate reality game in this section of the book. While I had my tongue firmly implanted in my cheek while I typed the line above, it really is not too much of an exaggeration, as Puppetmasters, the people who create alternate reality games, have come to be looked upon almost like magicians or celebrities in the ARG community. And yet, what they do and how they create the games they make is still pretty much a mystery to the average ARG fan. Some ARG community websites do have sections with short "Puppetmaster Guides," including rudimentary information on some things necessary to create an alternate reality game, but most of them are limited and out of date. For the most part, the details of what really goes into making an ARG, how you go about doing it, and what Puppetmasters go through in the creation process, have never really been divulged in a public forum.

I don't mean to imply that Puppetmasters really do possess and jealously protect some secret knowledge or anything; it's really more of a case of there just being so many things to do and so many details to consider, that no one has ever sat down and tried to put them all into even a list, let alone a coherent How-to-Guide. So that's exactly what this section of <u>This Is Not A Game</u> is intended to do – provide both a basic summary of how to get started trying to make your own game if you are so inclined, and give a brief behind the scenes look at what it's like to be a Puppetmaster. The fact that amateur game developers can and regularly do create their own games truly is one of the most unique and wonderful things about the whole genre of alternate reality gaming. Even more remarkable is that many of these independent games have been on par with the professional efforts done by major companies. I don't know any other art or entertainment form where non-professionals can and do produce pieces rivaling the work being done by the "experts" in the field.

First though, let me give you a brief summary of my experience with alternate reality games and why I am qualified to even attempt the difficult task of writing an ARG How-to-Guide.

<u>Becoming a Puppetmaster</u>

My first real exposure to alternate reality games was the Electronic Arts' experiment **Majestic**, in late spring or early summer of 2001. I had heard about **the Beast** through various Internet sources shortly before first discovering **Majestic**, but never bothered to look into it, something that I still regret to this day. By the time I realized how unique and exciting the whole **Beast** concept was, the game was virtually over, and the massive number of posts about the game made it an almost impossible task to try and catch up at that point. I do remember skimming through many of the posted messages, however, as well as skipping through the various guides and articles that had been written about the game, and having the feeling, just from that brief exposure, that I had missed something truly incredible.

I don't recall exactly how I first found **Majestic** but I believe it was while doing some Internet research on conspiracy theories, a subject that has fascinated me ever since I first read the Illuminatus! trilogy by Robert Shea and Robert Anton Wilson in high school. In any case, I soon applied and was accepted as a beta tester for the game, and was therefore allowed to play **Majestic** for free, before it was released to the general public. Undeniably, **Majestic** was a flawed game, as was explained in the ARG History section of this book, but it still was groundbreaking in many ways, not the least of which was opening my eyes (and many others', it seems) to the possibilities of using the Internet to tell stories in a manner I never before dreamed possible. Despite the long hours of waiting between periods of activity in the game, I was absolutely captivated and engaged when the **Majestic** utility would come to life everyday and I'd get my chance to see some new story content. It might have been an e-mail message or perhaps a phone call from a character in the game; it didn't matter, it was thrilling in any case to have elements of the game reaching out and interacting with me.

I also quickly became enamored of the online community that developed around the game, as the beta testers came together on the discussion boards provided by EA to solve puzzles and discuss the events of the day. Such Internet communities had obviously existed for quite some time for just about any interest you could think of, but the **Majestic** community was my first real exposure to them. Needless to say, I was hooked, as evidenced by my continuing involvement in this just developing genre of games ever since.

Even before **Majestic** came to an end, I began my career as an amateur ARG creator. As coincidence would have it, I had just begun to teach myself web programming, which in those days consisted of little more than basic html, with a little Macromedia Flash thrown in. I had also just begun to record my own original music on my home computer. Right around the time the beta testers were just concluding Episode One of **Majestic**, I had what I thought was a rather clever idea. It seemed a shame to have this captive audience of **Majestic** players who, for the most part, were incredibly excited about the game, sitting around every day for twenty-three hours or so with nothing really to do. And so I took it upon myself to try and entertain both them and myself for a while.

I came up with the idea of recording a few songs under the alias of a fictional band name, since the new technology I was learning at home allowed me to multitrack the various parts of a song myself and make it sound like an entire group. I named this group **the ChangeAgents**, and made up a storyline that had these musicians using their music to fight against secret government mind control programs, which, of course, was a central theme of **Majestic**. Although I didn't use any of the main content – names, characters, etc. – from the actual **Majestic** game, I admittedly did everything else I could think of to make people believe that the ChangeAgents were somehow related to the game. I even chose the name "ChangeAgents" and wrote it the way I did so that it included "eA" in the middle of it, a not so subtle hint at the Electronic Arts' name. Next, I made one of the songs I created sound like it had been recorded live, and placed the name of a certain country club that had been mentioned in a throw-away manner during the beginning of **Majestic**, in the credits of the song. Within a few weeks, I had all the pieces in place – three songs posted on a now defunct amateur music site called http://www.mp3.com, and six websites I had created for the game. I launched my first alternate reality game by using AIM conversations with other beta testers to say, "Hey, check out this website someone told me about. Do you think it might be part of **Majestic**?" Again, not too subtle but effective, and my career as a Puppetmaster was off and running.

Games I've Created

Beginning with the very first ChangeAgents adventure during **Majestic**, I have created and successfully run five alternate reality games, three of them by myself and two of them with team members or some other form of behind the scenes help. I honestly don't think anyone else in the world comes close to that in terms of experience in ARGs, professional or amateur. My list of games begins with three ChangeAgents stories, including the one I've already mentioned, which somehow never did receive an official name. The second ChangeAgents game, **Operation Mindset**, was created in August of 2001 as an official part of what Electronic Arts called the "BIOS Program" for **Majestic**, which encouraged fans and players of the game to create their own fictional content centered around one of the peripheral characters in the game. The entire program was carefully monitored by the actual creators of **Majestic**, and they even singled out certain fan creations by promoting them in both the EA newsletter and on the official **Majestic** website. Some **Majestic** players wrote short stories about the characters they choose, others, like myself, created original mini-games that took these minor characters and the overall themes of the game in entirely new directions. My game consisted of twelve websites and an intricate storyline, with personalized e-mail, instant messaging, and telephone interaction, and was featured as the headline story in the EA newsletter and on the **Majestic** website, where it was highly praised by both the developers and players of the real game.

I conceived and began developing the third ChangeAgents game, **ChangeAgents: Out of Control** (hereafter abbreviated as

202

CAOOC), in May of 2002, inspired in part by the successful conclusion of another independent game called **Lockjaw,** which I stumbled upon near the end of its three to four month run. I had wandered away from the ARG community for a short while after the second ChangeAgents adventure wrapped up and **Majestic** ended prematurely. I hadn't really even considered making another game, believing EA's failure in the genre to be the death knell for the entire sub-section of gaming. When I discovered **Lockjaw** I realized two things: there were others out there who loved playing (and making) these games as much I did, and that amateur games like **Lockjaw** could be just, well, damn good. Don't misunderstand me, I was and still am immensely proud of the first two ChangeAgents games, but I never realized that amateur games could stand on their own, without a major professional effort like **the Beast** or **Majestic** running simultaneously, until I saw the success **Lockjaw** had. And so **CAOOC** was born.

I worked on **CAOOC** for approximately six weeks, learning the new technologies I needed to be able to create the story I had in mind, and developing the twenty web sites that made up the world of the game. The game launched in June of 2002 and lasted for almost four months, wrapping up in September. Obviously my most ambitious game yet, **CAOOC** was well-received by the ARG community and, after I revealed I had been the solo Puppetmaster of the game, many people found it hard to believe it was all created by one person.

Besides teaching me that an independently produced and funded ARG could be successful at levels I hadn't imagined previously, **CAOOC** also taught me that trying to do something of that scope alone is an almost suicidal undertaking, and I swore never to do it again. So when I began to imagine an even more involved and ambitious game, I knew I needed to recruit some help.

In February 2003 I launched **Chasing The Wish (CTW)**, a game I spent months planning and developing. Little did I know at the time the phenomenon **CTW** would turn out to be. As explained in the ARG History section, **CTW** broke new ground in the amount and methods of real world interaction incorporated in an alternate realty game, and garnered international media attention and acclaim, including articles in the New York Times and the BBC News. Although I still did almost all of the two dozen in-game websites myself, for the first time I also employed behind the scenes (BTS) helpers, people who fulfilled various roles and tasks throughout the game. Some people played character roles for me, assuming the responsibility for personally answering e-mail, engaging in AIM conversations, and even acting as characters in telephone conversations or conference calls. Other BTS assistants created the real world items which were integrated into the game, which ended up being close to three dozen unique and hand-made items I had various artisans craft just for **CTW**. Many of the hundreds and hundreds of players who wrote me to thank me for the game after it concluded claimed it was a life changing experience for them, and something they will treasure for the rest of their lives.

My most recent game was **Urban Hunt (UH)**, which began in July of 2004 and concluded on Oct. 31st, 2004. One of the great joys for me in working as a PM over the last few years has been the opportunity to recruit new people into the small but ever-growing ranks of game creators. Some of them get overwhelmed by the whole experience and the amount of work and dedication involved, but many find the same thrill and creative satisfaction that I do in creating ARGs. After writing the original script for **Urban Hunt** I recruited a team of fellow Puppetmasters to help me create the game. With a core group of six Puppetmasters, we worked as a team on the game for five months before beginning its planned three-month run. The game, like **CTW** before it, received international media attention, including another mention in the New York Times. Perhaps **Urban Hunt's** greatest achievement, however, is that it ran simultaneously as the enormously hyped and extravagantly funded **Halo 2** promotion, **I Love Bees**. With but a miniscule fraction of the **ILB** $1 million budget and development staff, **UH** not only managed to take players away from **ILB** (albeit admittedly in small numbers compared to the massive player base of **ILB**), but also caused the **ILB** creators to change their game, when players began comparing the clever and well-crafted puzzles in **UH** to the apparent lack of them in **ILB**. Not too bad for a team of amateur game makers who created and funded the game entirely on their own, while working other full-time jobs and with no hope of ever receiving any compensation for creating the game.

Chapter 17: Puppetmastering - Creating a Game

One of the most frequent questions I am asked by ARG fans who want to make a game of their own is where the ideas for the games themselves come from. In other words, how do you set about coming up with a story idea for an alternate reality game? Much like trying to explain what an ARG is, this certainly isn't an easy question to answer. For me, story ideas come from everywhere, and I am almost overwhelmed with the number of ideas I have for stories that I think would make engaging ARGs. Perhaps it is because I have immersed myself (sorry, couldn't resist) in the world of alternate reality games that I literally see no end to the possibilities for good story ideas in the daily events that go on around me. Most of these ideas, if I actually took the time to sit down and try and work them out, would probably prove unfeasible to create, but the point is that you can find inspiration just about anywhere. I realize that just saying that isn't too much concrete help at this point, so I'll also suggest a few places where the aspiring game maker might turn for potential story ideas.

Starting Points for Story Ideas

The first place I would recommend any aspiring ARG creator to look when starting out to write a game is past ARGs. Although the genre is still relatively young, there have been dozens of games concluded, successfully or otherwise, with a wide variety of subject matter and styles between them. Researching past games not only lets you know what has been done before, but also what kinds of stories or styles have worked best. A large portion of the early work on an ARG involves research, and this is no exception. Read everything you can find about completed major alternate reality games, starting with the forum posts about the games on the major ARG community sites. Almost all significant alternate reality games have a player-produced guide or Wiki that normally contains both a chronological listing of events and a compiled storyline. Pay extra attention to any parts of the games that were particularly well received or praised by the players, and try to figure out what about those parts made them so successful.

I'm not suggesting you sit down to write a story set in the future just because **the Beast** and **I Love Bees**, two undeniable ARG successes, were, only that gaining an understanding of what methods have worked in the past to deliver certain types of content can give you a great head start when thinking about your own story.

Because alternate reality games are so intricately related to written stories and the narrative tradition, another great place to begin searching for story ideas is in the wealth of different narrative forms that have developed throughout history, including such things mythology, folklore, literature, film, and even history itself. Most of my games have involved characters and story elements taken from and inspired by all these different forms of narratives. For example, when I first began writing **Chasing The Wish** and conceived of the idea of a somewhat mythical figure named "The Wish" who appeared to people in times of need, I spent weeks researching every possible connection between wishes and mythology, fairy tales, and children's books I could think of. But I didn't stop there. I looked for any references to wishes in serious historical texts, religious, and mystical books, and even television shows and films. That research generated a great deal of the content that eventually turned into parts of the actual storyline for **CTW**.

One specific example was the name and very idea for the main antagonist in the game, the Sons of Don. In the game, they became the sons of Don Marzano, a wealthy construction magnate who had ties to organized crime, but they were actually named after the "sons of Don," who fought at the mythical battle of Caer Nefenhir in Celtic mythology. And the name Marzano was chosen both for its mythological connotations (Mars being the god of war) and because of an interesting history associated with the real family name, discovered while doing genealogical research.

So, just beginning with the seed of an idea and following it up with research can spawn a wealth of plot and even character ideas for your game. If you are having trouble coming up with even a beginning idea, you can always start by modeling your world or story after a piece of fiction that you are particularly fond of. Some of the most successful ARGs ever produced, both independent and professional, have been set in or tied into existing fictional worlds. I'm not suggesting you try and adapt or recreate your favorite novel or film as an alternate reality game, but there could be a particular character or plot point that you feel deserves a separate story line of their own. Use that as your starting point. The two most successful marketing based ARGs – **the Beast** and **I Love Bees** – were both original stories that took place in and were derived from an existing piece of work, the movie **Artificial Intelligence: A.I.** and the video game series **Halo**, respectively. Placing an ARG in a pre-defined world like this has enormous advantages, especially to the novice game designer, because so much of the background and setting has already been created for you, in terms of the actual game world in which your story will occur. You don't have to try and explain the history and overall conditions of the world in an in-game way when potential players of your game are either already familiar with it from the previous fictional works, or can easily learn more about it with a little research on the Internet.

The fact that these existing works probably already have substantial fan bases can be a huge asset for a game as well, one which several independently produced games have used to great advantage. The creators of the **MetaCortechs** game brought thousands of new players to the world of ARGs by setting their original story in the world of the popular **Matrix** films. Likewise, an earlier amateur game, **Exo-**

cog, gained early attention and attracted players by cleverly integrating its plot into the world of just debuting film, **Minority Report**.

Of course, there are always concerns about using elements of anyone else's copyrighted intellectual property, but so far, most games that have tried this approach have been considered "fan fiction" by the copyright holders, and, in some cases, even encouraged by the creators of the original material. While using other people's creations as a basis for your game can be a way to jump-start your creative process and the development and player base of your game, a developer needs to be extremely careful how he presents the game and addresses the material. Be sure not to imply in any way that the game is an official part of the existing work, or that the work's creators have had anything to do with the creation of the game. Also, any use of copyrighted images or company and character names taken directly from the book or film should be avoided, except in the most peripheral of ways. For example, in the **MetaCortechs** game, the name Thomas Andersen, which was the character Neo's real name in the film series, was only used as a name for an employee who no longer worked for the company in-volved in the game. The creators used the name to help tie their story into the world of the **Matrix**, but didn't make the character from the films an actual character in their game.

There are a few other sources you can consider when trying to come up with a storyline for your game. One possibility is the field children's books; in many ways, Lewis Carroll's <u>Alice in Wonderland</u>

can be considered a precursor to the whole genre of Alternate Reality Gaming. And I personally know many people longing to play a Dr. Seuss ARG. Another possible source is history, as there are many historical incidents already culturally linked to various conspiracy theories that are prime material for making into a game. The key, at least from my personal experience, is to come up with an initial idea, or better yet, several possible ideas, and then start doing research. Take notes and take your time; don't expect a fully developed, wonderfully original story to just pop into your mind. It takes work and perseverance, and the openness to try and discard multiple ideas along the way.

Considerations When Developing the Story

It is essential to keep the very unique elements and features of alternate reality games in mind when developing the story from your original idea. Writing an ARG is not like writing a book, despite the fact that the experience of playing a game is sometimes compared to "playing" an interactive novel. The most obvious difference is the fact that a traditional book uses only one medium, one method of communication, the printed word, whereas alternate reality games use multiple media to tell their story. It's essential that a writer consider the medium (or media) being used to deliver his story while he is writing it, as a screenwriter of a film and a novelist can and, in fact, must approach the same scene in a story from two entirely different points of view. A movie maker has so many more options than a novelist – visuals, spoken dialogue, special video and audio effects, emotionally charged music, and so on – that the entire approach to writing has to be different. The choices an alternate reality game creator faces make a screenwriter's job look easy, as he has to juggle not only the same kind of video and audio assets as a movie maker, but also written pieces in the forms of websites, web blogs, and e-mail, as well as all the other multimedia capabilities made possible by the Internet. Additionally, almost all alternate reality games find it either desirable or necessary to include puzzles, in one form or another. And that's not even considering the added dimension of real-time interactivity possible in an ARG. All of these added possibilities need to be considered when the ARG story is being written, and it makes the process of writing an ARG a totally unique and challenging experience.

So how do you factor all of this into the writing and development process? I am admittedly biased, due to my experience as a solo creator of ARGs, but I firmly believe that, for a game to achieve the potential inherent in the genre and become the true story-game hybrid discussed in the Theory section of this book, the story must be crafted in a fashion different from all other forms of writing, even from other forms of video games. The ARG creator must not only draft the story, but also begin creating the mechanisms of delivery simultaneously. Again, referring back to our game and narrative theory concepts, this means the ARG writer, to some extent, creates the story and the discourse at the same time, as two separate and distinct items.

In traditional narrative written forms this is done automatically, as the writer creates only one piece, the story, and employs literary techniques to achieve the discourse level of the narrative. In other words, by choosing first person, past tense, etc., the author determines how the reader experiences the discourse. In film, the discourse is the end result of the collaboration between what the screenwriter wrote and how the director approaches and frames the individual scenes and shots. In both of these examples, the creator is working in only one medium, so the decision of how to deliver the content is not part of the creative process, except on the level of *techniques* within the medium; e.g., should it be a long shot or a close-up?

In ARGs, the discourse needs to be an entirely separate consideration for the writer while he is constructing the story. The ARG creator must consider not only what he wants to say, but also which media at his disposal is the best way to say it. Would this be a good spot to include a video clip? Is there some way I can naturally integrate a puzzle into this part of the story? These are the things I think about *while* I write the story itself. Quite often, I find that the process of writing the story actually suggests to me such things as what domain names I might possibly want to use for the game (more on domain names shortly). It is, of course, possible to write an entire plot and then try and add the various elements of an ARG later, and I often do that to flesh out or expand certain parts of the game, or to incorporate the ideas and work of fellow Puppetmasters in team situations. I recommend as strongly as possible, however, that you try to do this during the writing process. It just seems to make the game and technical elements fit into the natural flow of the story much better when the game is written that way in advance.

Characters in Alternate Reality Games

Developing an easy-to-follow method for creating believable and engaging fictional characters is way beyond the scope of this book. There are tons of resources available covering that subject, although the debate still continues as to just what does make a character realistic. So my focus, for the most part, instead of being on character *creation*, will be on character *presentation* in alternate reality games. I will touch on a few properties I believe are essential for realistic fictional characters, but only in terms of how those traits can be expressed through one of the digital media commonly used in ARGs. What kinds of things can you do to make the hopefully believable character you've created and written into the story appear that way in the game?

Let me start with one general suggestion, based on my experience from creating five games. Keep the number of *main* characters in your game as small as possible. There are several reasons for this, not the least of which being, it's hard enough to create one believable character, let alone three. Secondly, it's much more difficult for players to keep track of characters and what they do and say in an ARG, than it is in a book or even a film, but for different reasons. I've read books that featured large casts of characters, all approximately afforded the same amount of character development and writing time. In many cases, I find myself frequently flipping to the back, hoping there's a glossary or an index of some type there, a scorecard to help me keep the names and relationships straight. If the book doesn't have one, I often flip back through parts of the story I've already read, looking to find where the character was mentioned previously and try and remember how he fits in. A lot of times in ARGs you don't have that luxury. While some of the content appears on websites and appears unchanged for the course of the game, much of it is ephemeral and either disappears or is changed in short periods of time. While ARG community sites and fans often construct guides to the games which sometimes include information like this, it certainly destroys the in-game illusion of reality if the player has to constantly refer to out of game sites to keep the story and characters straight. It is the online equivalent of flipping to the glossary or index, which always destroys the flow of a novel for me.

One final reason for keeping the number of characters low is interaction. If you create believable characters in your game, players will want to interact with them. If your player base is in the hundreds or even thousands and you are trying to achieve the impression of realistic and personalized interaction from a multitude of characters, you are setting yourself up for a nightmare in terms of logistics. Just to give you an idea, in past games where I had a character who was regularly interacting with about 200 people via e-mail, it would take me at least five or six hours to send out minimally personalized e-mail messages to all those players. You can, of course, choose to use automated methods of doing this, by using either an autoresponder that sends the same reply to everyone or programming scripts that can insert certain words, such as names or the subject line from the player's e-mail, into the reply to try and make them appear as if a person sent them. Most ARG players won't be fooled, however, and you risk damaging the illusion of reality you've worked hard to create.

Characters can be portrayed in a great number of various ways in ARGs, meaning you can use any and all of the various media available on the Internet to help create your characters for the players. For players to truly respond and relate to a character, they have to believe the character is real, which implies the players have some conception of who the character is and, more importantly, why he does the things he does. There has to be enough information for players to at least think they understand the character and how he fits into the events of the game. This generally requires establishing a history or back story for the character, which can sometimes be delivered by the character himself, either through a web page with an "About Me" section, a web blog that the character uses as a diary, or even through correspondence (e-mail and instant messaging for example) with the players. Alternately, the same information could be delivered by another character in the game. Another method is to spend time before the game even launches leaving a "trail" around the web, evidence of the character's prior existence. For example, for the **Urban Hunt** game, one of the main characters was the webmaster for an urban legends website, so we had registered the character by various identifiable nicknames at a bunch of legitimate urban myth web forums and made a trail of posts, all dated before the launch of the game. In any case, it is important to make the players believe that the character existed and was actually doing things before they started interacting with him.

Another great benefit to using a blog or another simulated diary of some sort for a character, is that it reveals to the player the inner thoughts and dialogue of the character, a critical part of establishing a realistic and believable fictional person. According to Andrew Glassner in Interactive Storytelling: Techniques for 21st Century Fiction, "Great characters lead two fascinating lives at the same time. The *outer life* is their presence in the world and is described by what they do and say . . . . A character's *inner life* is his self-awareness, composed of feelings, beliefs, self-image, self-doubts, hunches, intuitions, and the millions of other mysterious and often ill-defined and contradictory forces that work within him." It is this deeper layer of character, his *inner life* as defined through his self-awareness and sense of agency within the game, that goes a long way in making the character real for the players.

I have one final suggestion about how characters are introduced and presented in the game. It's immensely helpful to provide a picture of the character as early as possible. Players cannot relate to, and consequently care about, someone unless they have a mental image of that person. But just using a picture you found of a good-looking guy somewhere on the Internet and placing your character's name underneath it probably isn't the best idea, either.

Many ARG players are compulsive researchers and won't rest until they find the source of every image, sound, and Flash file used in a game, especially if they realize somehow that it is an independently produced and funded game. Finding a picture of the same person who you "grabbed" to play your character on another website can be an illusion-destroying moment for everyone involved. One classic example of this happened during the **MetaCortechs** game, when a picture of the girl who was supposed to be the central character in the game showed up in a spam e-mail advertisement in players' mail boxes not too long into the game. The game creators had found the girl's image on a royalty-free image website, and apparently, so had the mortgage company who was sending out the ads. The lesson to be learned is that, even though they are necessary, you need to be very careful which images you choose to represent your main characters. If possible, use pictures you know can't be found online, like relatives or friends, but be sure to ask their permission first.

Anticipating Interaction Points

One of the main goals of alternate reality games is to engage the player in the events and with the characters of the fictional game world, motivating them to want to participate to the fullest in exploring and interacting with your creation. A predictable yet often overlooked corollary to this is that, if you are successful in achieving this level of player involvement, there will be definite times where the players want to and expect to be able to intercede and direct the action in the game. If they know that the character John Doe is going to be killed if he goes to Chicago this weekend, and they have come to care about John or just believe that he is important to the game, they will try and stop him from going. And don't underestimate what lengths they will go to, either. In the example I gave above, if the players had previously discovered a graphic showing John Doe's plane ticket to Chicago, complete with the ticket number and the airline name and phone number, I guarantee you many of them would try calling the number to cancel his reservation before he could leave. Or, perhaps try sending him an e-mail, saying something stupid like they had personally planted a bomb on that flight, in hopes of discouraging him from going. Unfortunately, within a day, that e-mail would be posted somewhere on a community forum site and anyone who saw it and didn't realize it was part of a game would understandably be concerned and try to take action. Always remember, ARG games can and do sometimes have real world effects and consequences, because of the unique position they take of trying to pass themselves off as real.

This doesn't mean that the players desire to influence a game is bad, quite the contrary. That's exactly what an ARG creator wants, but, like everything else about creating a game, the possibilities just need to very carefully considered and planned for. In fact, giving the players' the feeling that they have changed the game in some significant way, even if it is just another illusion, can be both a powerful motivating and rewarding factor for the players. It is the theory of immersion and agency in action and is one of the common factors in many successful games. One of the most talked about and fondly remembered parts of **the Beast** was when players discovered a phone number they could call and talk to a live actor to try and persuade him to help save a character's life. Although it is almost certain the character was destined to be spared according to the script anyway, players felt as if their interaction and participation had saved him, and it became a defining moment of the game for many of them.

While you write your story, look for opportunities to motivate the players by providing them parts where they believe they can and do affect what happens in the game. If you are particularly ambitious, these points can be written in as actual branching points in the game's story, where an entirely different set of events follow because of the players' choices. Be warned though, this is far from an easy thing to do. It's a somewhat dangerous path to try also, especially if you have content from both alternate paths created and posted online in preparation for the interaction point. There's always the chance that players could somehow discover the content prematurely or even simultaneously, which would be embarrassing not to mention extremely harmful to the illusion of reality. The few times I have tried to do this I have experienced mixed results and choose now to restrict this technique to very short and limited spots. I hate creating material that never gets seen anyway, and if you make a couple of long branching alternate story lines, you almost guarantee that will happen. There are other, safer ways of creating the same effect, without taking the risks associated with branching storylines, and without wasting precious development time.

Write Out Everything in Advance

The final point I'd like to raise about writing a story for an alternate reality game is to make certain you write out the entire story, from start to finish, in advance, before you start even developing any other assets, and definitely before you launch the game. Not that you don't start thinking about the other assets while writing, I'm talking about actually creating them. Get a notebook (I normally end up with a half dozen or more through the course of an average development cycle) and write down everything in as organized a manner as possible. Take it from personal experience, having a great idea for a game and writing only a couple days' worth of material before launching it is not a blueprint for success. It can be done, but the question I would ask is, "Why?" In the long run, you are just making things extremely difficult if not near impossible for yourself.

Take your time and do it right. No one is waiting to play your game anyway, no matter how great or groundbreaking you think it is. If you are doing right, they don't even know about it yet. Write it out. Read it. Take notes. Rewrite it. Show it to other people, friends who don't know anything about ARGs. Proofread it. Have others proofread it. Play test it. And when that's done, repeat the above process. Believe me, one careless mistake on a puzzle or critical in-game communication can do more damage to both the players' enjoyment and your ego as a game creator than three weeks of success can do to build them up.

Organizing a Team of Puppetmasters

Almost all ARG games today are made by a team of creators or Puppetmasters. Although I've created three games entirely by myself, I probably will never do it again for several reasons. The primary reason is that the potential audience for a game has grown so large that one person alone cannot create enough content and manage enough interactions to make a successful game, without damn near killing himself. Additionally, most games require such a diverse range of skills to create them, that one person normally just doesn't have enough of them to do everything himself. So recruiting and organizing a team of Puppetmasters is obviously the best way to go.

It's really not too difficult most times to find enthusiastic and moderately skilled volunteers. Players who experience a well-done game frequently become avid and passionate ARG fans and have a strong desire to peek behind the curtain, trying their hand at helping to create a game. Unfortunately, not many people can afford to devote the time required to be a PM on a complicated and lengthy game, so sometimes it is a matter of finding a core team of PMs and supplementing them with additional behind the scenes helpers, people who play limited roles or fulfill specific functions or tasks. Many of the ARG fan sites have areas where people who want to get involved as Puppetmasters can post their interests, skills, and availability, so that is a good place to start looking for potential teammates.

There is no ideal size for a Puppetmaster team. It really depends on the details of the game you intend to create, in terms of both length and scope, and the skills needed to make the content you want to include. If you plan on making a relatively short game and stick to fairly simple web pages and limited interaction, you can probably get away with a team of just a few people with moderate web making, graphic design, and programming skills. I'm writing this, of course, from the perspective of a writer, so if you are a graphic designer with no writing skills you would include recruiting a writer in the process, too.

To make a larger and more involved game, you'll definitely want to recruit at least a half dozen or more team members and make sure they have abilities that complement each other well. If you want to include video and audio assets in your game, be certain to find someone who has both the equipment and skills required to produce those pieces. Also, a team will need at least one person who has good graphic design skills and programs, such as Adobe Photoshop or Macromedia Fireworks, to create the images needed for the game. Basic web design skills (html, cgi, php) are a must for a few members of the team, as most games encompass a multitude of sites and should use a variety of styles and web technologies. More than likely, you'll need someone who knows Macromedia Flash fairly well, or a similar program, especially if you intend to create any realistic looking flashy or hi-tech websites.

Your game may require a variety of performance related skills, such as voiceovers or even full fledged acting of roles. It may be appropriate in some cases to include music in some of your websites or in-game events, so a person able to create or at least edit music files is a valuable asset to the team. You can also include people who have very few computer or Internet skills on the team, since there are an innumerable amount of organizational and operational details to be taken care of. There are domain names to be registered, hosting accounts set-up, screen names registered for various instant messaging programs for all the main characters in the game, phone numbers for the fictional companies you may be using, and on and on. There is more than enough work to go around for anyone who has the motivation and energy, regardless of their experience or skills.

To give you a real life example, my game **Urban Hunt** was created by a core team of six "fulltime" Puppetmasters, with a couple miscellaneous people helping out in minor roles along the way. The game was five months in development, not counting the months I spent conceiving, researching, and drafting the story even before recruiting the team. The game included eighteen websites in a three month run. The PM team included people with specific skills in video creation, graphic and website design, puzzle creation, technical writing, and even proofreading. And even with all of the time we put into preparation and all of our cumulative skills, there were still times during the run of the game when we were dangerously close to falling too far behind.

PM Team Logistics

Here are a few basics you need to consider as far as how the team might function. First, out of necessity, I would absolutely recommend that every member of a PM team agree to and sign a Non-Disclosure Agreement (NDA). This is a contract between the team members not to disclose anything about the game or its contents until the entire project is over. The intent is to protect the intellectual property that the team members are creating, and also to preserve the secrecy of the development process so critical to the *TINAG* effect. NDAs don't have to be overly complicated or lengthy and you can actually find samples from which to start creating one by searching the Internet. An amateur team does not have to pay a lawyer to create an NDA, although they might want to consider it, if they are planning on investing a good deal of personal funds into the project. If desired, the NDA can also spell out who owns the intellectual property of the game once it is finished, how any funds generated by the game will be accounted for and distributed, and any other business matters the team feels are necessary.

It's always worked best for me to establish a regular team meeting schedule, the frequency of which is, of course, dependent on the availability of the team members and the amount of work you are trying to get done in a certain period of time. Even though such meetings sometimes seem to be repetitive and time consuming, the communication and feeling of being a team that they generate are well worth the effort. If you happen to be the team leader, make sure you solicit input from all the members of the team as much as possible. If you are a team member, be certain to voice your opinion whenever you feel strongly about something, and try and listen to other member's opinions with an open mind. Most team meetings will probably take the form of an online chat, so setting up a secure team channel on IRC or an equivalent may be necessary. Additionally, a secure online forum where the team can posts ideas, progress reports, To Do lists, etc., can also be a tremendous resource for the team. In both of these cases, the key word is secure; the last thing you want is to spends months developing a game, creating a complete record of it on a team forum, only to have all of it discovered by someone shortly after the game launches.

Funding an Independent Game

It is theoretically possible to create an alternate reality game without spending any money, as there are more than enough free resources on the Internet to create a basic ARG game. Unfortunately, using many of those free resources would be an immediate give-away as to the fictional nature of the game, especially in the areas of domain names and website hosting. You could use any one of innumerable free web hosting sites available, but almost all of them force you to accept either pop-up or banner advertising as part of your site. While there are obviously certain types of websites that could appear real on those free hosting servers, if you are creating what is supposed to be a top secret government agency web site, I'm not going to believe it's real if it has pop-up ads. So, unless you are willing to settle for a fairly limited and sometimes unrealistic game, you need to be ready to invest at least a little bit of money to fund it.

The list of expenses you'll incur while creating a game begins with registering domain names. Domain names are the names of the websites you intend to use within the game. Sites like http://www.godaddy.com offer domain name registration for about $9 per name, but other sites charge up to $20 for the same service, so be sure to look for the best buy you can find. You may also want to consider using a site that offers private name registration, otherwise the contact information required to register a domain name can be a dead giveaway as to who is behind the game. You are required to submit authentic name and address information when you register a name for a website, so the private services allow you to hide your real information in the website records. Private registration will add approximately $9 to each domain name registration, so expect to pay a minimum of $18 to register each domain name required for the game, if you choose the privacy option.

You'll also need a hosting service for each website you plan on including in the game. There are literally thousands to choose from; just search for them online and you'll see what I mean. Like I mentioned previously, some of them do offer free website hosting, but they have the drawbacks mentioned plus they may be extremely limited in both storage size (how much space you have to store your files), and web traffic permitted (also called bandwidth). I am not going to try and recommend any specific website hosts, although I have experience with more than I care to admit. Just do some research and check out thoroughly any hosting services you are considering using. There are way too many disreputable hosting companies out there not to take the time to check into any you may be thinking about. I would recommend that any service you select have a working telephone number on their site for customer service, and should offer twenty-four hour, seven day a week support. Many hosting companies list only an e-mail address or an online, ticket-based support system, both of which always leave you wondering just when and if someone will get back to you. There are many critical points in most ARGs where you cannot afford to have a website go down for no apparent reason, without any way of contacting the hosting company in real time. So choose one with a published telephone number and call it before you sign up for their service, just to make sure it works and is answered as advertised.

The cost of hosting a site with a reputable company is dependent on exactly the requirements of the site you intend to develop. By looking around, you should be able to find a decent hosting company who will host a small basic web site for no more than $5 to $10 per month, a medium sized site with more advanced functionality for $10 to $15 per month, and a large, fully loaded site for no more than $20 per month. Many hosting services offer discounts for multiple month or even yearly contracts, so that may be a way to reduce your hosting costs. Some hosting companies also offer multiple domain hosting plans, meaning you can host more than one site on their servers as part of one account. Be careful though, as many of these plans place all of your web sites on the same physical server with a non-dedicated IP address. Without going into an overly technical explanation, that means players could discover any sites you have on the server prematurely, by using various tools and techniques freely available on the Internet. If you can afford it and have the time for the extra research and set up work, placing each of your websites on separate servers with different companies may be the best option.

Those are probably the only two expenses that are absolutely essential and unavoidable, although there are many other things you can spend money on if you want to create a more professional-looking and enjoyable game for the players. You may want to establish working phone numbers for a few entities within the game, and you can find national services online that offer a phone number with voice mail system for $10 to $15 per month. There are many online sources where you can buy pre-made website templates from extremely basic and affordable to incredibly flashy and expensive. Again, it really all depends on the story you are trying to create. Pre-made web templates are a great way to give variety and a professional look to your sites, as well as having the extra benefit of cutting the development time needed for the game. You can also purchase other assets for the game online; things like royalty free video clips, images, and original music and sound effects. There are also sites that offer database and newsletter management services which can make the Puppetmaster's job much easier in the long run. Finally, you may also want to consider buying professionally made programs and scripts for certain applications within your game. If there are any specific skills your PM team is missing, there is a good chance you can find what you need on the web, for a price.

Depending on how ambitious your game is, you might also plan on paying to have a few unique real world items created for the game. I did this for **Chasing The Wish**, and the amount and quality of real world items players got to receive, find, or buy, really distinguished the game from previous and subsequent efforts. The amount of money I spent to have a few original paintings, artificial stones, manuscript pages, and other items created for the game turned out to be an excellent investment.

Sources for Revenue Within the Game

The sad but true fact is that there has yet to be a successful revenue generating business model for alternate reality games. The few that have tried any form of pay-per-play method have all ended in failure, including Electronic Art's **Majestic**, which had the weight and resources of a major league game company behind it. All of the successful games, including those done by major corporations for promotional purposes, have been games players could play for free. It's actually rather difficult to imagine a scenario anyway that would allow you to charge for a game in advance or on a subscription basis and still maintain the complete illusion of reality and the *TINAG* effect. If players don't know it's a game, the developers behind it, how long it will last, or other critical elements of the project, would they even be willing to pay anything to play it anyway? This doesn't mean there aren't opportunities for independent game creators to try and raise revenue from the game in an attempt to recoup their investment, just that PM teams need to be creative in finding ways to do it in a believable in-game manner.

2Perhaps the easiest and most time-tested method so far in ARGs has been the practice of selling merchandise, or *swag*, for differ-ent websites within the game. Many companies do this in real life on their websites anyway, so, if done properly, it seems a perfectly natural thing for an in-game website to do also. There are a few different services that make this extremely easy for the PM team, the most popular being http://www.cafepress.com, although they do take a significant amount of the selling price of the merchandise to cover their costs. This means you have to sell one Hell of a lot of tee shirts to come anywhere near covering the costs of an average, fairly lengthy, and moderately complex alternate reality game. But every little bit helps, and if you can manage to integrate a few merchandise shops believably into the storyline along the way, you should be able to generate at least a small revenue stream.

Another method of producing revenue in an in-game manner is to hold online auctions on websites such as E-Bay for real items that are somehow tied into the storyline. This has been done in quite a few different games and is generally well received by the players, who are excited about being able to get their hands on real world items, despite the sometimes rather transparent attempt to raise money by the developers of the game. One of the keys is to make the items you are selling either very unique and interesting, or critical pieces to solving something and progressing within the game. Auctioning something like a mouse pad that the players can already buy on a merchandise site within the game is probably not going to work very well. However, an original painting that was supposedly done by one of the characters in the game and that may also hold important hidden clues will probably be a very popular item. I used this method with excellent results in **Chasing The Wish** and raised a modest amount of money by selling several paintings made especially for the game, as well as antique books and other items carefully integrated into the story. Of course, doing this does raise some questions and possible difficulties about how you go about sending items in an acceptable in-game way. After all, if the character selling the item supposedly lives in New York and you, the Puppetmaster, live in Texas, you may have to find an accomplice or a service to handle the shipping for you, or accept the fact that players will shortly be posting about and discussing the discrepancy between the postmark and the in-game reality. I address this in a little more detail in the next chapter where I go over how to run a game.

233

Dave Szulborski

A few more possible avenues of revenue generation that haven't really been explored in the ARG genre yet are product placement within games, advertisements on fictional in-game sites from legitimate real world companies, and corporate (or private) sponsorship of a game. Product placement, inserting an image of a product or showing someone using the product within the reality of the fictional presentation, is being used more and more all the time in feature films, and could conceivably be done in alternate reality games effectively as well. If you think about it, that's actually what both **the Beast** and **I Love Bees** were, very complicated and lengthy stories with discreet product placements for the movies **AI** and the video game **Halo 2** throughout. In these cases, the product placements were the subtle references to the movie or game worlds, designed to make people want to go see **AI** or buy **Halo 2**. Even with an independent alternate reality game, however, there's no reason to believe a few carefully inserted product placements couldn't generate some revenue without affecting the illusion of reality at all. In fact, they might actually enhance the overall *TINAG* effect, since similar product placements have become such an integral part of our everyday lives.

A similar approach would be to place a few real ads of some sort on select in-game sites. There are many different possible types of ads that could be used – pop-up ads, banner ads, and even ads from services such as Google - which can be placed in a frame on the side of a website and generate revenue whenever anyone clicks through. Obviously, ads like this would not be believable on certain kinds of in-game websites, so PMs need to think carefully about where they might fit. Most real world companies don't put ads from other companies and / or products on their sites, so you probably don't want to have a fictional company in your game do it either. If one of the in-game sites is an online magazine, gaming forum, or news site however, it may be perfectly realistic for there to be ads appearing on their site. This method is not something I would recommend overdoing within a game, but it is a potential source for adding another revenue stream to your ARG.

The final option I'd like to suggest is securing a financial sponsor for the game, a company or person who is willing to help finance the game, usually in exchange for some type of recognition once it has completed. I'm not talking about situations where a major company like Microsoft contracts a professional development to create a game, but instead, the possibility of a small independent but highly creative and ambitious team of PMs going out and actively seeking sponsorship from companies you think might be interested, for whatever reason. It doesn't have to be a single sponsor, and it doesn't have to be large amounts of money, either. In many cases, the PM team can secure services for free from various businesses in exchange for giving or sending traffic their way during the game, by mentioning their website in an in-game manner, or by giving them a credit at the end of the game. The **Urban Hunt** team did this with great effect with http://www.lastwishes.com, a legitimate online service that offers automated and pre-arranged death announcements for anyone wishing to notify distant friends and relatives of their passing. One of the **UH** characters arranged for a Last Wishes announcement to be sent to the players upon his apparent death, leading them to some new information, and eventually helping them to discover he wasn't really dead after all. The Last Wishes website agreed to provide the service completely free of charge and took care of many of the details for us in exchange for being listed in the credits of the game and the exposure they received for their service by participating in the game.

As you can see, although no one has yet come up with a profitable business model for alternate reality games, there are potential sources of revenue that can be used in realistic, non-disruptive ways. It actually becomes part of the writing process of the game and adds just another element an ARG writer needs to consider while crafting his game. I highly recommend that you create and stick to a budget for the game. As a team, you need to decide in advance how much money you are willing to spend to create the game and exactly where it is coming from. Any changes to the budget once it has been agreed upon should be discussed and re-approved by the entire team of Puppetmasters. For all intents and purposes, you need to treat the financial end of the game as a business, even if it is just an amateur production.

<u>Domain Names – The *Non*-Human Characters in Your Game</u>

I touched briefly on domain names as far as their cost earlier, but there are other important considerations when choosing and registering domain names as well. First are the names themselves. Good domain names are sometimes hard to find, as many people have spent the last few years speculating on domain names, by buying up every possible useful combination and logical name they could think of. Many times as you write your story and create names for the fictional characters and companies you wish to include, you'll discover that the names you want have already been reserved by other people, especially in the "big three" category of .com, .net, and .org names. I've often had to go back and modify or change completely a name I had written into an early draft, because I couldn't find and register anything like it for a domain name. But there's no denying that the names you choose and use in your game can have a great impact on the overall player experience, so an ARG creator can't just settle for any available names he can find.

In a very real way, your in-game websites and, by implication their names, become almost like supporting characters in the story. It's quite interesting and informative that for many past games, the players you talk to remember the website names more frequently and with less prompting than they often do the names of the characters from the ARG. For this to happen though, the names, like everything else in an alternate reality game, have to be logical and believable. This is one of the strongest arguments for not settling for free hosting services, because they don't allow you to use dedicated domain names likehttp://www.mysite.com, but instead force you to accept a name formatted at the end of their main site name, like http://www.hostingcompany.com/mysite. The presence of the hosting company's name in your website address totally destroys the intended illusion of reality if the site is supposed to be a legitimate and functional business.

Even if you do register your own names however, they still need to be consistent with the image you are trying to portray for the site. Most companies and businesses try and name their companies in a way that expresses something about what they do in the name itself, so if you are trying to pass off one of your sites as just a straightforward, normal operating business, calling it something like http://www.mysterioussecretcompany.com isn't going to work. In a similar way, the names you use need to convey a sense of what the websites are about and express the personality of the company or character they are for. It's a delicate balance though, because you don't want the website name to expose too much about that company that you intended to reveal later in the game.

Once you find the names you want and confirm they are available by checking on a domain registration website, you can start the registration process. You may want to think about the timing of the registrations however, as the dates the names were first created and registered will be visible to the players if they check the official "WhoIs" information for the website. "WhoIs" is an Internet service through which anyone can check and see who owns a particular website name and when it was created. If your game uses twelve different websites and the players discover they were all registered on the same day, it's an easy deduction for them to realize they are all in-game. As an ARG creator, I like to take the opportunity presented by the introduction of every new element to the game, such as a newly discovered website, to reintroduce the *TINAG* factor to some extent. In other words, every time the players find a new website, I want them to wonder if it is real or not, if it is part of the game or not, and just exactly what they are supposed to do with what's there. If they can easily go and check the creation date and see it matches every other site in the game, any work you've done on trying to create the *TINAG* feeling is wasted. So even if you have decided on all your website names when you begin registering them, make a schedule for doing so and spread them out. Chances are, if the domain name hasn't been taken by the time you thought of it, it will still be around a week or two from the time you register the first batch. You can get away with registering a few names at a time if you make sure they are spread out *time-wise* throughout the game. In other words, in the first batch register one name from the beginning of the game, one name that will be found towards the middle, and one domain name from near the end of the game's run. That way, the common date of registration is a lot less noticeable and damaging to your overall efforts.

Website Hosting

Again, even though website hosts were discussed briefly earlier, there are some important things to keep in mind when choosing them that aren't necessarily directly related to cost. One very important consideration is the decision you'll need to make as to where the sites can be hosted, in terms of believability and continuity within the plot. Does it really make sense that the hero's website and the villain's website are hosted on the same server? Perhaps, but you'd better make a case for it before the players discover it (and they will), or they won't believe it. Also, if an in-game website is supposed to be for an ancient secret mystical brotherhood with extraordinary powers and resources at their command, would they host their site on http://www.thecheapestserver.com? These are all things to bear in mind when making the decision of benefit versus cost, and if you can really afford to use the cheaper service just to save $2 or so per month.

Another key element is website security, and this actually has a few different facets to it. The first is the possibility of premature discovery of your websites. In most games, the websites are revealed gradually, they are part of the overall mystery of the story, and are often used as rewards to players for solving a particular puzzle or tricky part of the ARG. It's absolutely critical therefore that the players not be able to find these sites before the creators intend them to, and this can happen in a variety of ways. As has been previously mentioned, if all your websites are on a multidomain hosting service that uses non-dedicated IP addresses for all your sites, players can potentially find sites before you want them to by using techniques such as reverse domain look-ups and other readily available applications on the Internet. If you still decide to employ a multidomain host because of the other benefits it offers, then you'll probably not want to post any material from the sites that haven't been revealed yet, until you are ready for the sites to be found. If necessary, you can upload the pages somewhere else, to a temporary server location for proofreading and play testing by your fellow PMs.

Hosting them on the same server isn't the only way sites are found early, unfortunately. There are a few other errors you can make that allow the too clever ARG players to find material before its time. One thing I've been known to a do a few times that causes this is the way I label images, web pages, and even directories sometimes, on my websites. When you are developing a game, you are normally juggling so many different assets and components that you forced to try and use some logical scheme for naming the pieces you are working with. Sometimes, because you are fully aware of how the plot plays out, you unconsciously choose names that inadvertently give away parts of the later story. For example, in an early ChangeAgents game, I used a mysterious symbol throughout the game that was supposed to be a marking used by a top-secret organization. Unfortunately, when I created the image in the first place, I named it after the organization itself, right in the name of the file. It made sense to me at the time, but I forgot to change the name of the image when I first used it on a web page in the game. Within a few minutes of posting the graphic, the players had found the website for the top-secret group, a site I hadn't intended to reveal until the final weeks of the game. Needless to say, after calling myself every name I could think of for about a half an hour, I had to sit down and rewrite a great deal of what was supposed to follow. Strangely enough, for some reason though, I took the time to go back and change the file name and re-post it, like I thought the players might just forget what they had seen and the site the had found or something. Ah, the innocence of a naïve rookie game maker.

Speaking of image and file names, another aspect of website security is the ability to protect your site, in part or in full, with some sort of password protection. This is another way of avoiding premature detection of specific sites; make the entire contents of the site password protected and thereby inaccessible. Most good web hosting companies provide you with an online control panel for your website, which makes it very easy to use their built-in password protection for parts or your entire site. Unfortunately, this can sometimes be an unintended tip-off as to the site being part of the game but just not ready yet, so it's another judgment call the PM team needs to make.

I do highly recommend that you at least protect the various directories of your websites. Simply put, web servers store your website files in directories, just like your home computer does. While the exact structure of the directories changes from server to server and is dependent upon the operating platforms they are using, normally your web pages will be stored in what is called the root or top-level directory for your site. In addition, the various other elements you upload to make up your site generally are stored in separate directories depending on what they are. For example, pictures normally get saved in an

"Images" or "Graphics" directory, cgi and php scripts in a separate directory, and so on. On many web hosting company servers these directories are unprotected, or visible, to anyone who knows how to look at them, unless you deliberately go in and change the settings for the directories. In some cases, your website control panel will have an automated feature to do this for you; you simply have to choose "Protect Directories". In other cases, you may be required to create a blank index page for each directory you want to protect or hide, which will prevent inquisitive players from being able to view the list of the files in the directory that happens when a directory doesn't have an index page.

The Role of Puzzles

A strange dichotomy has formed around the use of puzzles in alternate reality games. While there is no denying that every ARG that has been produced has included them in one form or another, statistically, a large percentage of the players in each game can't and don't even try to solve the more difficult puzzles in a game. On this basis, puzzles could be considered a necessary evil, except for the fact that some players consider puzzles the best part of an ARG and others, even though they don't personally try and solve the in-game puzzles, seem to enjoy watching the other players solve a well-made and well-integrated puzzle. And that is really the key to how the puzzles in a game are received by the player base. If puzzles or puzzle-like activities are carefully made, incorporated in the game in a meaningful and logical way, and rewarding to the players in proportion to the effort required to solve them, they become enjoyable experiences and can become highlights of the game. This happens far too infrequently however, as both parts of the two-step process are extremely difficult – creating a good puzzle and integrating it into the game in a believable way. So what makes for a good puzzle in an ARG? To answer that, we need to first look at what purposes a puzzle serves in a game and some examples of how puzzles have been used in past games.

Perhaps the most obvious reason for using a puzzle in an ARG is because it is expected. This seems like a contradiction to all the times I've mentioned that the goal of an ARG is making the player believe the game is real. If they don't know they are playing a game, why would they expect to encounter a puzzle somewhere on a "normal" website? The unavoidable truth is that, even in the most carefully planned and run game, at some point, players will understand they are playing a game. That doesn't mean, however, that you can't achieve the level of believability and immersion I have been claiming ARGs need to strive for all the time. The "dual consciousness" explained in the game and psychological theories earlier in the book make it possible for immersion and awareness of the game to occur simultaneously. Who among us hasn't shifted forward or to the side in their chair, as they tried to dodge something with a character in a video game on their computer screen? We know we are involved in a game but our body still responds in an immersive manner, reflecting the depth of our engagement in the game. So, despite some level of immersion and involvement with the fictional world of the game, the ARG player will know he is playing an ARG and expect it to include elements he has experienced in similar games.

A recent experience that strongly illustrates this "expectation factor" happened in the **Halo 2** promotional game, **I Love Bees**. According to their post-game interviews and chats, the creators of the game didn't intend to include any overt puzzles in the game, over and above the few things they did to make it appear as if an external AI had somehow been trapped inside someone's personal website and was trying to communicate with the outside world. The inclusion of hidden text within image files on the website could certainly be considered puzzles, as could the very manner in which the story was slowly and gradually revealed through short audio clips, but the primary content of the story had no other puzzles in it. It wasn't until the PMs noticed that players were bemoaning the lack of puzzles and actually leaving **ILB** to play other games, that they quickly decided to rewrite parts of the game to include puzzles for the players to solve. So, in a very powerful and significant way, the players' expectations changed the course of the game.

There's another very good reason puzzles are found in ARGs. They serve to help regulate the progress of players throughout the game. ARGs are fundamentally different from most of the other types of games or narrative forms we've compared them to in this book in that they are intended to last for specific lengths of time, normally at least a month or two. None of the other entertainment or storytelling forms mentioned share this feature. It's true that it can take a reader a month or more to finish a book, or for a player to finish a regular video game, but it's not something the creators of the game schedule and try to manage in the same way. In both of these examples, the actual time it takes for the player or reader to finish the work cannot be accurately predicted or managed by the creators.

Yes, authors can make their book a certain length and writers of certain forms of narrative pieces are often given specific word counts for their assignments, but those are measures of content, not completion time. Likewise, video games are often promoted by their amount of content with phrases like "ten hours of game play" in their advertising. While that sounds like an estimate of how long it will take a player to complete the game, there is really no way for the creators to know how long it will take anyone to actually finish the game, since there are so many possible mitigating circumstances. In the case of both the book and the video game, the participant receives all the content in one package and the time it takes him to work through it is out of the developers' hands.

Alternate reality games function differently, as the creators develop content that they intentionally plan to deliver to the audience over an extended period of time. In some ways, this could be compared to dramas that are presented in a serial format, television soap operas for example, but they are still substantially different because television shows have the artificially imposed but strictly regulated restraints of time slots. The fact that the shows are created in deliberate half hour or one hour episodes regulates the delivery of the content to the viewers, but in a way that is obviously unnatural and unreal. Life doesn't usually happen in nice neat time segments like that. So a fictional work that is attempting to mimic life as closely as possible needs a different method of regulating the flow of content to its audience. Puzzles can serve that function quite well.

Actually, some alternate reality games have attempted to use a more episodic format for delivering their content but, in most cases, this predictable and artificial scheduling has been one of the least immersive and most artificial portions of the games. For example, both the **Beast** and **I Love Bees** adopted a regular schedule for content updates that players came to know and respond to almost instinctively. Every Tuesday (and Fridays too, for **ILB**) there would be a great flurry of activity at the fan forums as players posted the new content that they knew would be coming, and had been waiting for since the previous regular update. **Majestic** also employed a little more flexible but still fairly predictable schedule, as the players knew that, once a day, normally within a known range of hours, the game would come to life and deliver its small dose of content for the day. To make it even worse though, the game also labeled and delivered the content as "episodes," complete with silent periods between episodes that could last days or even weeks. While some players appear to like the concept of predictable and timed updates because it allows them to time their participation in the game to fit into their busy schedules, the idea obviously completely destroys the illusion of reality for the game, at least from that perspective.

Puzzles, if handled properly, are a way for Puppetmasters to pace the players' progress through the game. They are the "cliff hanger" endings of episodic dramas, keeping players involved with the game as they wait for the next batch of content to be discovered or delivered to them. They can also simultaneously serve a dramatic purpose by giving the players a real feeling of involvement with and agency in the game. If the puzzle is presented as something critical to the progress of the game and, in particular, a character the players have come to identify with, giving the players an opportunity to directly impact the story and help that character can be a powerful tool for creating immersion within the game. This aspect of puzzles is also reinforced by the fact that puzzles normally include a reward of sorts at the end, either new content for the game, or the resolving of a dramatic conflict within the plot. These rewards are motivating factors for the players to keep going on in the game, and provide great incentive for them to try and solve the mysteries hidden within. Puzzles are often the reflection of those mysteries, the symbolic representation of the secrets that players hope to learn at the end of the game.

A pretty clear example of how ARG writers include puzzles to help regulate the flow of the game can be found in the post game interviews the main writer of **the Beast**, Sean Stewart, did about his

248

experience in creating the game. He has said that they created and categorized the puzzles according to the length of time they thought it would take players to solve them, specifically so they could place them accordingly and help control the pace of the game. Unfortunately, for even the most experienced puzzle creator, estimating how long it can take a player or a community of players to solve a specific puzzle is almost harder than making the puzzle itself. I am always amazed when the players solve a puzzle in an hour or so that I thought would take at least a few days, or when they struggle for a week or longer with something I thought was embarrassingly easy (embarrassing from a creators' standpoint, not as a reflection on the players).

Even though it's far from scientific or accurate, I still think of puzzles in terms of how long they will last for the players when I am figuring out where they fit into the timeline of the game. Sometimes, if I know there won't be any other new content in the form of website updates, e-mail correspondences, etc., I will place a puzzle in the story to give the players something to do in the meantime. As always though, the critical thing to making puzzles work, whatever you've intended them for, is to make sure the puzzles are well made and naturally integrated into the story.

<u>What Makes a Puzzle Fit?</u>

There are so many variables that go into the highly subjective judgment of whether a puzzle will be considered successful or not that

I am not even going to attempt to define what makes a good puzzle, or try to explain how to go about creating one. I have included a piece entitled "Anatomy of a Puzzle" in the Appendix, which walks you through the creation of a puzzle and what the creator was thinking about when it was made and solved. If you are interested in learning more about the creation process of a puzzle, please read that essay. As with many of the other aspects of ARGs already discussed, I'm going to limit the discussion here to what makes a good puzzle in terms of how it fits in with the story line of the game.

A well-disguised puzzle called "The Twisted Path," created by Dave Szulborski for **Urban Hunt**. The key to solving the puzzle lies in turning the sequence of left and right turns into a binary pattern of 1's and 0's.

Puzzles must fit naturally into the game; otherwise they become disruptions to the façade of reality and transparent attempts by the game creators to manipulate some aspect of the players' experience. Integrating puzzles naturally involves two things: making sure the content and logic of the puzzle is compatible with the material and themes of the game, and also making sure the puzzles are presented in ways that are believable in terms of both the reason for being there and the timing of their appearance.

By content compatibility, I mean that a puzzle should reflect and build upon themes, ideas, and content already presented in the game. For example, there was a semi-ARGish game produced and sold commercially a short while ago called **In Memoriam**. For parts of the game, it mimicked an ARG by using websites, e-mail, video clips, and other Internet based assets to tell the story of a missing journalist in a fairly interactive and entertaining way. Unfortunately, interspersed throughout these well-done segments were the game's versions of puzzles, which often took the form of fairly one-dimensional arcade type mini-games. These games had little or nothing to do with the rest of the content, and totally destroyed the positive effect the rest of the game's content was creating. These puzzles, which did not fit into the theme and presentation of the rest of the game, made the overall experience a negative one, especially for players who had come to the product expecting an alternate reality game.

The logic of the puzzle, meaning the manner in which the creators intended it to be solved, must also fit into everything else that has happened or will happen in the game. If all the puzzles in game have been solvable from content included somewhere in the game or at least somewhere on the Internet, it's unreasonable to suddenly throw in a puzzle that requires the players to track down and physically locate a rare book that only exists in three libraries across the country. The players are not going to realize that is what expected of them and know how to proceed. When the solution is revealed, they are almost certain to be both displeased and openly critical of the puzzle.

The timing and manner of presentation of puzzles are also vitally important to making them believable and logical parts of a game. Like any other component of a carefully planned and constructed narrative piece, timing of puzzle placement can either significantly enhance or damage the dramatic effect of a scene. If your teams' great writing and months of planning have succeeded in creating a level of immersion or sense of flow in the players as they are working their way through a good deal of content, the very last thing you want to throw at them is a puzzle that may totally stump them for days. Not only will it disrupt the progress they are making, it will also discourage them from investing themselves too heavily in a game in terms of time, effort, and emotion, especially if it prevents them from finding or doing anything else until they solve it. Such a scenario is also completely unrealistic; rarely in real life does one obstacle (in this case, a puzzle) completely halt all other aspects of your world. Even if you can't figure out exactly how you are going to pay that big bill due next week, there are still many other things going on in real life that require and fight for your attention. To have everything in an ARG come to a complete stop while players work on particularly difficult puzzle reminds everyone that this is indeed just a game.

Finally, the way a puzzle is integrated into the story is perhaps the most important element of making it believable and enjoyable for the players. There has to be a logical reason for a puzzle to be included, which isn't necessarily an easy task. After all, you don't often stumble across things that are true puzzles in your everyday life. You can spend hours and hours creating the world's most creative and clever puzzle, but it is absolutely wasted if it shows up on a web page where it makes no sense for it to be. A puzzle needs to make sense in the context of the game in terms of content, timing, and placement. There has to be a reason that the twelve year old boy in your story has a puzzle leading to classified government secrets on his website.

For example, in the very first game I created, the earliest ChangeAgents story, the finale of the game consisted of a simulated interface in which the players had to insert pass codes and pieces of data in a specific sequence, to prevent the bad guys from winning and achieving their goals. It basically was just a multi-step puzzle that players had to use prior discoveries and clues to solve. The interface was supposed to appear as a software application of sorts, housed on the villains' computer network, and I invested a great deal of time

253

making a Flash-based interface that queried scripts and data on the web server as the player progressed through the puzzle. As a novice web designer and Flash programmer, it really was an impressive accomplishment, and I was very proud of it. Unfortunately, due to my ignorance of the details of web hosting at the time, only one of the sites I had set up for the game would actually allow me to use the server side assets I wanted to use, and it was the ChangeAgents' site, the heroes' site, not the villains'. Not realizing it would be big deal, I went ahead and put an entry page of sorts for the interface / puzzle on the villains' site, and then forwarded the players automatically to the main Flash movie, which was hosted by necessity on the ChangeAgents' site. Consequently, after the players had solved the puzzle I had spent hours and hours preparing and was so very proud of, all most of them could talk about was how unrealistic it was that most of the puzzle material was hosted on the ChangeAgents' website. Not one of them mentioned that they thought it was a good puzzle.

Mechanics of the Game

One of the most powerful features of the Internet is its ability to use so many different forms of technology and media to present content. Web-based content can be truly multimedia and integrate written text, static images, moving images (either animation or video), audio, computer-generated simulations, and various methods of real-time communication, such as e-mail and instant messaging. Additionally, there are so many different programming options available to the web designer, from simple html and its derivatives like xhtml, dhtml, xml, and more every day it seems, to more complex server-side programming like cgi, php, perl, and visual basic for example, that ARG creators have an amazing amount of tools and techniques to choose from. These tools and various forms of media and programming are what I am calling the "mechanics" of an alternate reality game.

It is way beyond the scope of this book and this ARG "How to Guide" section to try and explain the differences between all the various methods and languages you can use to create a website. There are thousands of printed books and online resources available that can help you get started in learning html and the various software programs you can choose from – Microsoft FrontPage, Macromedia Dreamweaver, and many other commercial and shareware programs. Instead, I will concentrate on how an ARG creator decides what programs and methods are right for the various components of his game, and the things he needs to consider in making those decisions.

Form Matching Function

There is one basic principle extremely useful in deciding whether a site needs to be simple html or Flash, whether a content update works best as a video clip or e-mail. It's something I call "form matching function." What it means is that the first consideration in designing any game asset, whether it is a web page or an interactive software interface for use in the game, is to think about what purpose it serves, what it is supposed to represent or convey in terms of the story of the game, and how real world websites or Internet applications accomplish the same function. If a website is supposed to create the illusion of a real functioning business, the site should have everything a site for a real business would have. The best way to know what that might be is to search the web and find companies that are engaged in the actual business your functional company is supposed to be in. See what their sites look like, what features they offer, how complex they are in terms of html versus Flash, and so on. These real sites will be the models for your fictional websites.

Some of the common elements this might include are things like personnel names for important positions within the company, a background (history) and vision statement for the company, and functional contact information, including at least one e-mail address that you, the PM team, intend to respond to. Actually, most companies, unless they are very small, will have more than one e-mail address on their site, so again, you'll need to make a deliberate decision between balancing the amount of realism you want and the amount of time you think you can afford to put into in-game interactivity and responses. Depending on the type of business, you may want to include a street or mailing address for the company. Many service-oriented companies that do their business primarily through the Internet don't include a specific street address so, if it is not necessary, avoid it, as it can raise some complications and possible difficulties. For one thing, no matter where you locate your fictional firm, you can count on at least one player being within driving distance and actually going there to see what is really at that address.

If you decide to use an address as part of your company's contact information, one approach you can use is to make it entirely fictitious, meaning the street name or even the town itself should be made up for the game. Unfortunately, this can be an easy confirmation for the players that the company is fictional and a reminder that they are only playing a game. I tried a slightly modified version of this technique for **Chasing The Wish**, in hopes my fictional town might appear a little more realistic and survive at least the first few rounds of Internet research by the players. I started by finding a town whose existence was somewhat in question even in real life, as it appears on some maps and in some versions of history but not others. Believe it or not, there are many more places like this around the United States than you can imagine. Just Google "forgotten towns new jersey" (or any other state for that matter) and see how many hits you come up with. I chose one such "forgotten" town in New Jersey, Ong's Hat, which conveniently already had a rich history of mystery and weirdness about it, and created a fictional community, located in the old Ong's Hat location. In my story, the town had just changed its name to Aglaura, in an effort to get a "fresh start." Because of the recent name change, which was explained right from the start of the game in the History section of the town's website, players accepted the fact that they couldn't find any record of the new name on the web. The real name of Ong's Hat, however, provided a wealth of pre-made back-story and local history for me to incorporate into **CTW** and build upon. This method actually proved so successful that midway through the game, I began receiving e-mail messages to the Aglaura site from New Jersey state officials, asking me exactly where the town was located because they hadn't been able to find it for their tax and governmental records.

Another method I commonly employ for creating moderately believable fictional addresses is to research the real location I want to set the fictional company or character in, right down to neighborhoods and streets that might be appropriate. If I want to place a fictional high-end nightclub in Newark, New Jersey, I'll start by searching for similar real businesses in Newark and trying to see if there are any real patterns to where they might be located. Even if there aren't, this process will at least start yielding potential street names to work with. Once I decide which street name I want to use, I'll research addresses on that street, looking for opportunities to place my fictional business. If my company is a small business, I may look for industrial centers or office buildings along the street, check out suite numbers within those facilities, and then create a realistic looking suite number for my fictional firm that doesn't have real business located there. Other opportunities could be things like breaks in sequential addresses along the street; you may notice that you can find businesses for the 7200, 7300, and 7500 blocks, but nothing in the 7400 block. That could indicate something like an empty lot or park or other undeveloped property, and might be a good spot to place your company. The final step in selecting or creating any address is to search for it on the Internet, to make sure there isn't a real company at the exact address you choose.

Real companies commonly have working phone numbers too. Traditionally, many ARGs have tried to simulate this by using phone numbers set up with an answering machine or voice mail box to collect player messages, and at least give the appearance someone may actually hear them. There are many national services you can find online that will give you a functional phone number, in many cases in the city of your choice, so it can even be made to match your fictional location. These phone numbers generally come complete with voice mail services for around $10 to $15 per month. Unfortunately, not too many real businesses have phones they don't answer, at least during standard business hours, so this alternative, although the one most PMs have opted for, isn't necessarily the most realistic option.

For my latest game, **Urban Hunt**, we decided to try a more expensive but vastly more realistic approach. For the main company in the game, a fictional television production firm called Tomorrow's Talk Studios, we contracted what's called a *virtual office* for a few months. A virtual office is a service that provides live telephone answering services that pass themselves off as an actual office, not an answering service. Additionally, they can also provide mail receiving and forwarding services, so that our fictional company could receive audition tapes for their upcoming reality show that was part of **UH's** plot. Companies that provide virtual office services are not as easy to find as businesses that just provide you a phone number and a voice mail system, and are quite a bit more expensive, ranging in price from $125 per month up to $500 per month. You also need to be careful in choosing one, as some of the companies offering this service are little more than glorified answering services and don't offer a realistic front for your business. For **Urban Hunt,** we felt that the expense was well justified, as the fact that players could call a phone number and speak to a live person who at least tried to give the impression they were an employee of our fictional company really heightened the *TINAG* effect at the beginning of the game and provided countless hours of discussion in player chat rooms and forums. Many times players raised the possibility of whether or not the company might actually exist, a rare event for an ARG.

The point of making the contact information included on the site as believable as possible is the "form matching function" principle; you plan and construct the website to match the function it is supposed to fulfill if it were real. This is a fairly simple rule to follow when creating the websites for the game, but there are other areas where "form matching function" applies as well, although not in such a clear manner. One area is how the players interact with the characters and the world of the game. The methods used to communicate between the ARG world and the players should be carefully selected to fit in with the story continuity and, as much as possible, reflect the *reality* of the game world. Here's a hypothetical situation to illustrate this point. Imagine your main character in the game is on the run, pursued by enemies, carrying nothing but the clothes on his back. Every few days, however, the players get e-mail from him that includes pictures or perhaps even short movie clips of things he has seen. The players are almost certain to question several elements of this scenario, such as how the character is getting online and sending e-mail every couple of days, how he is taking or getting the pictures and movies he is sending, and so on. While it's entirely possible that the player is stopping at Internet cafes or wireless hot spots along the way, and has purchased a digital camera that allows him to take both movies and pictures, unless this has been established in the context of the game his communications will seem immediately unbelievable. It would be better to have him send perhaps one e-mail during that same time, with a short and simple text message saying something like, "I will be out of touch for a while. I'll get in contact again when I can."

Another example of the "form matching function" principle could be the manner in which a main character responds to the players' e-mail. If you are depicting the character as someone who has reached out for help in some manner, it would be a good idea to take the time to personalize all of the character's responses, instead of using a pre-written autoresponder or a "cut and paste" message to everyone. A person seeking help would more than likely be thrilled to receive e-mail in reply to their request, and would sit down and read and reply to each one individually. A PM thinking only in terms of what information the character's reply needs to contain may mistakenly decide to just cut and paste a paragraph and mass mail it to everyone. The individual player may be excited when they first receive the message, but when they see that everyone else received the exact same reply, the character becomes a little less believable and a little less worth caring about. There are times when autoresponders and identical messages to all the players can be used effectively, but this isn't one of them. Luckily, although it is undeniably time consuming, it isn't too difficult to compose one initial message, as a template of sorts, and then insert small bits of personalization in each e-mail before sending it. This can be as simple as mentioning the player's name or referring to something specific that they mentioned in their original message.

One last important note about the mechanics of an alternate reality game has to do with making sure the assets you create for the game are compatible with both the Internet browsers the players may be using and the computer systems they are likely to have. Different web browsers have different capabilities, as do different computer operating platforms, so an ARG creator needs to familiarize himself with the various possibilities and their limitations. Obviously, the only way to be certain that the content you created works and will be presented as you envisioned it is to try it in different web browsers and on different types of computers, but there are also some basic rules you can discover and learn with just a minimal amount of research. Some web browsers can't display certain image formats, others don't allow dynamic frames and layers found in dhtml. That's just a small sample of the basics you can learn and apply even before you start proofreading and testing your creations. It's infinitely better to know the limitations you are working with and accommodate them in the design phase, then to catch them during testing and have to re-create significant portions of your work.

Also, some of the newer Internet technologies and media available to the ARG creator may not function in older browsers or, more importantly, on the older computers some players are likely to have. Another part of this same issue are the different Internet connection methods and speeds that various players will have, which will limit the size and types of the files that will work on their systems in a reasonable amount of time. It's very easy when creating interactive and animated Flash websites or simulated interfaces to end up with a finished file that is much too large for players still using dial-up Internet connections. It can be the best website anyone has ever created, but if it takes more than a minute or two to download, a large portion of your player base may never see it.

So, like many other aspects of alternate reality gaming, planning and creating the game mechanics for an ARG is a juggling act, an attempt to balance the desire for ultimate believability and player immersion with the limitations of the technologies and methods available for presenting the content. The ultimate goal is the illusion of reality, and ARGs are truly a unique opportunity to create an immersive experience exactly because the mechanics used in the game aren't artificial but instead, the same means by which the players interact with their everyday world.

Dave Szulborski

Planning Interaction

I've addressed several times already different ways in which the players traditionally interact with the characters and world of an alternate reality game. I believe it is critical that the PM team decide, as soon as possible in the development process, the boundaries of the interaction they are going to employ in the game. Some PM teams seem to make a conscious decision to minimize forms of real-time contact, such as phone calls and instant messaging, and instead, rely on website updates and e-mail as the basis for the players' interaction with the fictional world. This has many advantages, not the least of which being that the game becomes less ephemeral, and sometimes easier for the masses of players to follow. If a critical piece of information is given out via a real-time method, there is no visible record of it, unless the player who receives it posts about it on a community forum. Even then, if other players don't see the post shortly after it is made, it can easily get buried under the volumes of posts that can occur on a daily basis for a popular game. Posting the same information as a website update or distributing it through a minimally personalized mass e-mail insures as much as possible that everyone gets to see it first hand, without relying on the post of a fellow player.

As with anything though, there are also negatives to limiting interaction in this way, as many players seem to enjoy and prefer when a game interacts with them through real-time methods. There's absolutely no way of getting around the fact that including real-time communica-

264

tions at times in the game almost always makes for a more realistic ARG experience, since our real lives more closely resemble the real-time communications model. Some of the best moments of the game for many **Majestic** players were the phone calls they received during it, even though they were all pre-recorded and non-interactive. Players also tend to get excited about being contacted by a character through instant messaging, and planned group chats with in-game personalities always attract large numbers of enthusiastic players.

For many ARG players, instant messaging has become a way of life, a standard part of their daily routine and, in many cases, their primary means of communication with many people who are important parts of their lives. Consequently, instant messaging is a very believable method for an ARG character to use to talk to the players, but only if the PM team treats the instant messaging conversations as what they truly are – dialogue. Far too often, the in-game instant messaging interactions are poorly handled, reflecting the approach that they haven't been really treated like dialogue and carefully written. Instead, there seems to be the attitude that, since it is supposed to appear to be a character just talking, not reading from a script, it's acceptable to just improvise the conversation as it happens. PMs need to remember that every appearance by an in-game character and every word he says (or types) becomes part of the cumulative image the players have of the character. The words the character uses and the message he is trying to convey in an instant messaging conversation are no less important than the website content or fictional blog you spent weeks writing, editing, and proofreading. Instant messaging conversations need to be written out as dialogue, at least as a framework for the actor portraying the character to follow.

But there's a level of interaction capable of making the ARG even more believable and engaging, and that is real world interaction. Yes, the methods already classified as real-time, e-mail and phone calls, are also communication forms used in the players' everyday lives, and therefore can also be considered "real world" interactions, but for our purposes here I am referring to interactions that enable the game to go beyond the boundaries of electronic communication and therefore *feel* more real to the player. This would include such things as face to face personal or group meetings with actors portraying characters from the game, or real world items that players either receive or have to seek out and find. Interactive experiences such as these are powerful tools for creating unparalleled levels of belief and immersion in the fictional reality of the game. Interestingly, the real world interactions don't even necessarily have to be done within the confines of the *TINAG* principle, as evidenced by the events held as part of both **the Beast** and **I Love Bees**, two hugely successful and popular ARGs. In both of these games, the players were alerted in an in-game way to real world events being staged for the games, but the actual events themselves were not conducted in an entirely in-game manner. Nevertheless, these events were hugely popular with the players who attended. These players apparently had no problem in justifying the contradictory in-game and out-of-game aspects of the interaction.

266

In **Chasing The Wish** I tried to use a few real world encounters in addition to the large number of real world items incorporated into the game as previously described. One of these was a treasure hunt of sorts, in which players had to deduce the real world location of a hidden item from a character's travel journal, and then go out and retrieve the item. Even though there was no face-to-face interaction, the episode still helped create the illusion that the **CTW** world existed outside of the digital illusion created through the Internet content. Another previously mentioned independent game, **MetaCortechs**, also used this technique by hiding CD-ROMs around the country for players to search out and find.

I also included a few face-to-face encounters in **CTW** though, where players had to meet with people portraying characters in the game to receive physical items that had played important roles in the story. In each case, the actual person to person interaction was kept brief, just long enough to hand over the important in-game artifacts, but the encounters and the items the players received were universally cited as being elements of the game that helped make it more real for the players. Planning and actually carrying out real world events like this isn't easy, but by including a few well-planned real world interactions in your game, you can definitely make it more realistic and immersive for the players.

Additional Resources

A lot of different resources available to help Puppetmasters create their games have been mentioned in terms of cost and how they help to achieve certain desired effects, but I feel it is important to summarize and reiterate once more that a novice ARG creator really does have a tremendous amount of resources at his disposal, many of them free and available online, to use in helping create his game. The diversity and availability of websites, tutorials, and downloadable shareware programs is such that the lack of skills or software should not be an obstacle for anyone looking to make a game of their own. There is a list of some of the better resources you can access on the Internet in the Appendices of this book, covering everything from simple web design and programming, through encryption and decryption tools and resources. But don't limit yourself to what's been included in this book, as there are always new and exciting developments going on in all of these fields constantly. So use the search services on the Internet to stay up-to-date on the programs and assets available freely that you can use to craft your game.

There are resources beyond the Internet to consider as well, such as the telephone answering and virtual office services mentioned earlier. Other things not brought up before include things like post office boxes that allow your characters to receive snail mail and packages from the players and also act as a front for mailing things out. I've toyed with the idea several times of placing small classified ads in real newspapers across the country that would serve as part of a rabbit hole into a game but have yet to attempt it. It wouldn't be too difficult to accomplish however, as there are services available to help you do that as well. My point is that Puppetmasters should think big when planning and drafting their games. Don't be afraid to dream about including elements that will allow your creation to truly stand out from other games that restrict themselves to what's been done before. If you have an idea that transcends the limitations of the Internet and helps immerse your fictional world into the lives of the players, put it into the script and then go ahead and think about how you can possibly pull it off. If you automatically eliminate any real world interactions or items from your game just because you think they might be too hard to do, you've chosen right from the start to make your game less believable than it could possibly be.

Chapter 18: Puppetmastering - Running a Game

Even if you take your time and get everything you think you need ready before launching your game, there are still a whole host of new responsibilities and things to do once the game begins and continues through its run. Some of these things we have touched upon peripherally while discussing how to plan and create an ARG, but others are unique to managing a game once it is live. This section will address various aspects of managing, monitoring, and modifying an ARG in process, and discuss the unique aspects that set ARGs apart from any other form of narrative or gaming experience.

<u>Operating as a Team</u>

It is essential that the PM group function as a team while a game is in progress. There are so many different tasks to do even after the content has been completed, that organization and delegation of duties among the PMs are critical to the successful ARG project. Teamwork and organization require communication, which is why I have suggested that the PM team hold regular weekly or bi-weekly meetings once the game is in progress. Getting together and discussing

how the game is going, what the players are saying, and who is responsible for what in the immediate future, will guarantee that all the PMs
are all on the same page, and that they all understand what they personally are responsible for. Having a synopsis of the game's story and
timeline posted at the secure team forum can be a great help to the
team in figuring out where they are and how they are doing. It's virtually impossible to make a hard and fast schedule completely in advance
for a multi-month game that depends so heavily on what the players do
along the way, but an approximate timeline can certainly be made as a
guide for the PMs to follow as the game unfolds.

It also makes sense to utilize the team forum for keeping track
of the other tasks that need to be done and assets that need to be
created, by having "To Do" lists or something similar on the site. This
is also a good place for Puppetmasters who may be temporarily out of
tasks to post that they are available to help anyone else who might need
it. Separate sections of the forum can also be dedicated to the password
and log-in information for all the game's websites, e-mail and ftp
accounts, and anything else that requires secure access. There may be
times when the PM normally responsible for maintaining and modifying a certain website won't be available as players discover some critical
mistake or overlooked piece of unintended information. You won't
want to wait for that particular PM to become available again and
instead, will need to have the necessary information available to other
members of the team to fill in as necessary.

This Is Not A Game

The development phase of an ARG is filled primarily with creative acts for the PM team, but once a game launches the focus instead turns to more mechanical and sometimes terribly repetitive tasks and duties. There may very well still be development and asset creation going on too, but there is a whole new list of things the team needs to be aware of and taking care of on a daily basis. To start with, there are all the aspects of monitoring the game and player progress through it. This includes reading everything posted about the game at the various ARG community forums at the minimum of a daily basis. You'll probably want to do it much more frequently than that, however.

Additionally, the team will almost certainly want to have someone, a team member or just a discrete behind the scenes helper, sitting in and logging the IRC chat channel that the fans traditionally create and spend a great deal of time in for alternate reality games. If the PMs have done a good job in remaining anonymous up to this point, then any one of them can probably serve this purpose and you may want to establish a schedule for who will be in the player chat room when.

Alternately, you can have one PM remain in the chatroom all the time, automatically logging everything that is said, without having to actually sit in front of his computer the entire time. Any Puppetmasters who are in the player chats should avoid making any comments that could be construed as guiding the players or promoting the game. At some point, the players will know the identities of the PMs and won't appreciate the PMs doing things like that in retrospect.

Protecting Puppetmaster Anonymity

If the identity of the PM team is known or suspected during the game, the team will have to take additional precautions when participating in various forms of online interaction, or risk exposing or confirming their involvement. This applies to IRC chats where the connection and location information displayed by the IRC utility can quickly identify a known Puppetmaster to experienced ARG players. It can also apply to e-mail however, as many e-mail applications automatically include identifying information in what's called the header of the e-mail message. Luckily, there are a few different ways of getting around these potential breaches of security and hopefully obscuring the PMs' identities until the game concludes.

The first line of defense, at least for the e-mail problem, is to find and use hosting services that provide webmail interfaces for the e-mail accounts associated with your website. Many webmail interfaces automatically obscure the header information that reveals where the e-mail originated, so PMs are safe to log-in to the webmail interface and read and respond to players' messages. Not all webmail interfaces do this, however, so it may be something you want to specifically ask the hosting service before you sign on with them. Also, be sure to check that it actually works, by sending test e-mail messages to the other PMs before sending anything out to the players. You may want to consider turning off the images or the html altogether when receiving e-mail, through the "Options" or "Preferences" tabs on the webmail interface, because a clever player can use images, even tiny ones, in his e-mail message to identify the IP address of the computer that opens the e-mail and views the image.

Unfortunately, there are no settings in the IRC chat interface that allow you to do anything similar and eliminate the exposure problem inherent in Internet chatting. The AOL instant messaging (AIM) software does allow you to effectively obscure your identity and location, which is why that is all many PMs use for the real time instant messaging communication within their games. AIM makes it very easy to establish multiple screen names and portray an in-game character in instant messaging conversations. Actually, it is so easy to do that I would recommend, as part of the development process, that someone on the PM team take the responsibility of writing out all the character names and possible AIM screen names that could be used for them, and going through the process of registering them, even if there are no definite plans to use them at that point. It's not unheard of for overly enthusiastic or simply malicious players to make up screen names or even e-mail accounts and try to pass themselves off as characters from the game. It's critical that the PM team try and anticipate the opportunities for this to happen and take any steps they can to prevent it from occurring. At the very least, if all the names the team has registered are posted on the team's forum, there will be a way to immediately identify and confirm any imposters participating in the game.

Protecting the PM's identity while chatting on IRC can most easily be accomplished through an *anonymizer*, which is either an online service provided through a website or a downloadable software program. You can find examples of some anonymizers to try out in the resource list in the Appendix of this book. Most of them function in very similar ways, using proxy servers to hide your actual Internet connection from fellow IRC chatters. Some of them are effective for eliminating the e-mail header problem as well, but not all will, as many online anonymizer services disable the Java and JavaScript that certain webmail interfaces rely on.

One last concern about PM anonymity involves any phone calls the team may be intending to make. CallerID machines and services are so commonplace now that most players will be able to see the number of the phone the PM is using to make a call. Once again, thankfully, there are a few ways around this. The first method is to simply dial "*67" before dialing the phone number you want to call. In most cases this will effectively block the CallerID service the receiver might have. Many of the Internet-based voice mail services have features that allow you to use the numbers you have gotten from them for receiving calls to make outgoing calls too. This can be particularly effective because the call appears to be coming from a phone number the players recognize from the game and associate with the character or company calling. Finally, there are websites that provide CallerID "spoofing" services, which means that, by using them, you can make the call appear to come from any number you desire. This is even more flexible than the outgoing call features normally found with the voice mail services and offers the potential to do things like hide puzzles or clues in the spoofed number.

<u>Monitoring the Game</u>

Many of the regular and sometimes tedious tasks associated with running an ARG fall under the heading of monitoring the game. Besides the aforementioned regular reading of player posts and logging of the game's chat channels, this entails all the things normally required to run and maintain a website. PMs need to check the e-mail accounts for the websites every day, or as often as possible, and respond to them according to their content and the pre-written script for the game. It can get tedious to reply to seemingly meaningless e-mail messages from players sometimes, but if they are writing to a website that you want to appear to be a legitimate business, you may have to respond to a great many of them just to maintain the illusion of reality. Sometimes, there will be extended periods written into the story in which a certain character is not supposed to respond to players' messages until something else happens first, but besides that, it is important to maintain some sense of regular communication between the characters and the entities in the game.

Puppetmasters should also frequently monitor the usage statistics for their websites, as these numbers can provide valuable insight into the way players are viewing and interacting with your content. All good web hosting companies provide a built in statistics feature that allows the website owner to see how people have visited their website, what browsers they were using, the IP addresses of the visitors, and the geographic location of those IP addresses. Many control panels that come with your hosting service will have a more advanced statistics programs giving you an even more detailed look of who has been to your site and what they did while they were there. Besides built-in web statistic programs there are also a multitude of other companies offering packages to do the same thing for your websites, either through online consoles or software applications downloadable to your computer. These packages offer an amazing array of features and can track a visitor's path from page to page of your site, show you how long they spent on each page, and in some cases, if they interacted with any elements on the page. Monitoring website statistics also helps the team avoid additional charges that can occur if a site exceeds its contracted usage terms.

Of course, besides monitoring e-mail and web site usage, PMs also need to regularly check the voice mailboxes for any phone numbers they have set up for the game. Even if you don't intend to respond to any phone calls until a certain prescribed time in the story, it's important in many voice mail systems that you regularly listen to and clean out the incoming messages, otherwise the mail box may become overfull and not accept any more messages. Not only is this not realistic, but it also alerts players to the fact that no one is listening to their messages and, by implication, that maybe it isn't worth the players' time to actually do things like call the numbers in the game. PMs need to avoid, at all costs, anything that discourages players from exploring all the built-in interaction of their story and fictional world, or anything that shatters the illusion of reality, so regular maintenance of voice mailboxes needs to be a priority.

There are, of course, special situations that occur in a game that may require some additional temporary forms of monitoring, or at least an increased effort in using the regular monitoring sources. For example, real world events and item distribution require such careful planning and implementation that PMs may want to devote extra time and energy to monitoring the players by any means they can during those periods. One of the real world encounters in **Chasing The Wish** involved me driving approximately eighty miles from my home to hand over a special artifact from the game to a few players. Even though I thought I had planned everything out thoroughly and considered every possibility for what could go wrong, I still decided to have one of my behind the scenes helpers stay logged into the community forums and chat rooms, so I could call her at a moment's notice, and see what was being said in either of those places. That forethought ended up saving the whole situation, as I got a frantic call from my helper when I was about halfway there, telling me that the players were already in the general vicinity of where we were supposed to rendezvous and they couldn't find the specific location. The players had set up the same sort of communication system I had and were calling in updates to people sitting at home posting on the boards and hanging out in chat. As it turns out, the location I had chosen and even researched on the Internet was an old antique shop that had just been demolished a week or so before. Luckily, with the help of my behind the scenes assistant, we were able to locate an alternate location in a short period of time and she called the players I was supposed to meet, pretending to be a character from the game and telling them of the change in plans. Without the special arrangements I had made, the whole real world event would have been disastrous.

<u>Regulating Flow</u>

Another special form of monitoring involves watching the players' attempts to solve puzzles during the course of the game. Because they are often used to regulate the flow of an ARG, puzzles are normally worth a little extra attention in terms of monitoring. The first very obvious reason to monitor the community reaction when they encounter a puzzle is to catch any errors you may have made. Everything should have been proofread or play tested two or three times by this point, but that's still not an absolute guarantee that all the mistakes have been found and corrected. Because of the inherently deceptive nature of puzzles, it is extremely easy to make a mistake encoding or encrypting a message that you can't see in the finished result. Sometimes, either due to miscommunication or poor proofreading, encryption errors don't get caught, leading to a terrible puzzle experience for both player and Puppetmaster alike. This is another example of the player subconsciously being told that his time and effort in playing the game are not worthwhile.

Constant monitoring of the players' work to solve a puzzle can often alert you to any previously overlooked mistakes, before they become apparent to the player, who is still part way through the decoding process. A creative PM team may be able to salvage the puzzle if the error is noticed early enough, by rewriting the payoff or final solution of the puzzle.

Puzzles also need to be watched closely as far as the time they take for the players to complete them. This is especially critical when the puzzle is being used by the PMs in attempt to regulate the players' progress through the game. If a puzzle was intended to take the players several days and they complete it in a few hours, the PMs may need to be prepared with some filler material to hold them over in the mean-time. Conversely, if a puzzle contains a key piece of information that the PMs wanted the players to find in twenty four hours and it's now going on three days, the Puppetmasters may be forced to give the players a hint, hopefully in an in-game way. Hints are always an awk-ward situation, as they can easily turn into a reminder of the artificiality of the entire puzzle process, and highlight the fact that they are just tools of the ARG creators. That's why I suggest having a few hints prepared in advance for key puzzles, especially ones that are time dependent in some way. They need to be as planned and carefully scripted as the puzzles themselves, in order to appear natural and believable in the context of the story.

Monitoring Expenses

PM teams also need to monitor their expenses. I've already described how too much website traffic can lead to unforeseen expenses but the same thing can happen with the voice mail system and virtual office services, as well. Most of them come in packages with pre-set limits, so it is important to keep an eye on how they are being used and, if necessary, make some kind of in-game adjustment to try and prevent unbudgeted expenses. Finally, PMs need to constantly evaluate how the length of the game affects their expenses and budgeting. If you've planned on three months worth of monthly bills for website hosting, phone services, and so on, and the game stretches into a fourth month, you've already exceeded your budget by one third. For anything that is a regular monthly expense, such as website hosting or voice mail services, going beyond the intended duration of the game can be costly indeed. If the added length of the game cannot be avoided, the PMs may have to consider turning off some of the services that are no longer critical to the plot of the game.

As mentioned earlier though, the key to being financially responsible in running an alternate reality game is to create and stick to a budget. The PM should know what it costs to run the game for a month and consequently what the results of extending the end of the game would be.

Chapter 19: This Is Not A Game

This is not a game. After a long and unavoidably complex exploration of the world of alternate reality games, we find ourselves back to the underlying principle of the genre and the title of this book – This Is Not A Game. But now, perhaps, we have a new understanding and appreciation of exactly what the phrase means in relation to ARGs, in a few different ways. What began as a simple catch phrase for the idea that an alternate reality game should never admit it is a game, has come to encompass and convey a myriad of truths about ARGs on multiple levels. On each level, "this is not a game" accurately captures both the scope and potential of alternate reality games, in a way that seems almost eerily prescient, considering the rather straight forward origin of the phrase over three years ago.

By Definition, This Is Not A Game

We began by looking at established academic definitions for both games and stories and discovered that ARGs didn't fit comfortably or completely in either class. On first glance, it didn't appear that alternate reality games were truly games or stories, although they obviously incorporated many key elements from both forms of entertainment. Interestingly though, by breaking down the mechanics and techniques of ARGs, it became apparent that they did indeed include all of the things necessary to be defined as a game, but they integrated those elements in new and powerful ways. So, instead of using "this is not a game" as a means of disqualifying alternate reality games as games because they *lack* certain key components, it is perhaps more realistic to use the phrase to mean that, even though they are games, the word "game" doesn't really apply because it cannot capture the full potential inherent in ARGs.

In a similar way, the academic definitions we used for narratives or stories also now seem limiting when applied to alternate reality games. Originally, the inclusion of interactive sections in ARGs seemed to preclude them from being considered a form of true narrative expression, at least by those definitions. The unique feature in alternate reality games of *interactive authoring,* however, enables the ARG creator to script and manage the interactive sections in an entirely realistic and believable manner. Additionally, interactive authoring also potentially overcomes the problem of creating believable, interactive characters in a game or interactive fiction environment, something previously thought impossible by most theorists. In a very real way, alternate reality games very much appear to be an entertainment form that combines the best and most powerful aspects of both games and stories, but even that fails to capture their true potential.

This Is Not A Game, It's Big Business

In another sense, "this is not a game" describes the vast, but as of yet, largely unrealized potential of ARGs as part of a successful business plan. Although there has yet to be a successful revenue-generating game, the bare fact that Microsoft has spent over $1,000,000 a piece to produce two separate alternate reality games in the space of the last three years almost automatically elevates ARGs to the level of "big business." Not to mention the many other major corporate promotions going on right now modeled after ARGs or incorporating ARG-ish elements. These promotions are not nearly as extensive or expensive as something like **I Love Bees** or **the Beast**, making them affordable parts of the multi-million dollar ad budgets associated with most major product or motion picture launches, especially considering the potential benefits. Even if you use the money spent on **ILB** as the example, what other form of marketing can actually create an active online community of thousands if not hundreds of thousands of potential customers, and sustain that interest for months at a time for a single $1,000,000 investment? Not only did **ILB** accomplish that, it also motivated thousands of these same people to leave their homes and drive, sometimes for hundreds of miles, in the hopes that a payphone somewhere might ring and allow them to hear a minute or so of a recorded message. Could there be a more powerful illustration of the potential of ARGs as marketing tools?

In addition to the possible marketing application of ARGs, I believe it is only a matter of time until a company develops a business model that allows them to present alternate reality games as a successful pay-per-play venture. There are several critical factors, some of which have already happened, that may allow future commercial ARG projects to succeed where others have failed. For one thing, the Internet as a whole has become much more of a "pay as you go" entertainment venue. Internet users are more accustomed to and accepting of the idea of paying for quality entertainment content on the web. Unfortunately, there are very few forms of Internet-based entertainment that come anywhere close to delivering a similar immersive experience that a movie or even a book is capable of. Alternate reality games can provide exactly that experience and, arguably, on an even more realistic and meaningful level. The delivery costs of producing a major alternate reality game project have probably actually decreased over time, as the ubiquitous computer technologies of high speed Internet access and incredibly powerful home computers have made it easier to deliver content in a multitude of forms and media to the player. A well planned and budgeted ARG that utilizes some of the revenue stream suggestions in Chapter 17 of this book should, theoretically, be able to be successful with only a modest monthly or per game subscription fee.

The Game of Social Engineering

There's another aspect to alternate reality games that we've barely touched on in this book but to which the phrase "this is not a game" also has relevance, the idea that the collective efforts of an ARG community could be used to solve societal problems or bring about social change. Beginning with Jane McGonigal's seminal piece in this area, "This Is Not a Game: Immersive Aesthetics and Collective Play," looking at ARGs "as a potential tool for harnessing collective action" has grown to become an increasingly interesting and active discussion among scholars and social theorists alike. Many people are now starting to see the network of interconnected human minds via the Internet as some kind of potential "collective super consciousness," comparing it to the massive computing power provided by the interconnecting of thousands of home computers through the SETI project.

As cited in McGonigal's piece, this "collective" aspect of an ARG community is actually very similar to what French philosopher and social theorist Pierre Levy calls *collective intelligence*, in his 1997 book Collective Intelligence: Mankind's Emerging World in Cyberspace. Levy defines collective intelligence as "a form of universally distributed intelligence, constantly enhanced, coordinated in real time, and resulting in the effective mobilization of skills." In describing how such a collective intelligence might function in a self-organized group, Levy writes, "the members of a thinking community search, inscribe, connect, consult, explore......Not only does the cosmopedia make available to the collective intellect all of the pertinent knowledge available to it at a given moment, but it also serves as a site of collective discussion, negotiation, and development." By *cosmopedia*, Levy is referring to what he also calls "the Knowledge Space," which for our practical purposes

289

is the Internet, the means by which the ARG community comes together and interacts to solve elements within a game. Levy's description quoted above, even though it is presented only as a theoretical possibility in his book, is an almost perfect description of how the player base of an alternate reality game actually functions. Interestingly, although Levy admits that the framework necessary for a true collective intelligence to develop doesn't exist yet, one of the areas he points to with the potential to make it happens is "digital interactive media" or, more specifically, hypertext and interactive fiction.

One very real manifestation of the principle of "harnessing collective action" can be found in the phenomenon called "Smart Mobs," as explained by Howard Rheingold in his groundbreaking book Smart Mobs: The Next Social Revolution. The official website for the book, http://www.smartmobs.com, summarizes the concept by saying, "Smart mobs emerge when communication and computing technologies amplify human talents for cooperation. The impacts of smart mob technology already appear to be both beneficial and destructive, used by some of its earliest adopters to support democracy and by others to coordinate terrorist attacks." By Rheingold's definition, the community of players of any ARG could indeed be called a "smart mob," as one of the central goals of a well-designed alternate reality game is to bring about, if not in fact require, cooperation between the multitude of players. Some ARG puzzles are specifically constructed as to be unsolvable without the community's cooperative efforts.

Besides being just a philosophical concept, however, smart mobs have taken on actual physical manifestations as well, in events where large groups of people show up unexpectedly at public places and conduct some strange exercise or performance of sorts. These events are entirely organized and publicized by the smart mob communities on the Internet and, for the most part, their purpose remains a mystery to the uninformed public who witness the performances. Certain events in the world of Alternate Reality Gaming can also be seen as physical manifestations of the smart mob principle, most recently the large groups of **I Love Bees** players that gathered around payphones throughout the country waiting to answer an in-game phone call. While both the actual smart mob and related ARG real-world events that have taken place so far have all been entirely harmless, there is no denying the possibility that such events could be used for negative purposes, making it critical that ARG Puppetmasters consider very carefully any real world implications of the events in their games.

So "this is not a game" may apply to alternate reality games on yet another level, in a way that may have profound and lasting societal implications. Although still relatively unexplored, this aspect of alternate reality games is sure to bring continued discussion and deeper exploration in the future.

Hyperstition

Another nascent philosophical concept with possible relevance to alternate reality games is *hyperstition*. A hyperstition can be loosely defined as a fictional work or belief system that somehow gradually takes on the appearance of reality. Obviously based on the concept of superstition, hyperstition is distinguished by being predominantly digitally spawned and proliferated. A perfect example is the already mentioned pre-release marketing effort for the movie the Blair Witch Project. The clever and carefully crafted campaign succeeded in creating the perception that the fictional back story for the movie told on the Internet was real, before most people became aware it was all a promotional effort.

One of the primary proponents of the new idea of hyperstition, http://www.cold-me.net, claims that "the practice of *hyperstition* necessarily involves three irreducible ingredients, interlocked in a productive circuit of simultaneous, mutually stimulating tasks," going on to define these three ingredients as "numogram, mythos, and unbelief." Interestingly, all three of these ingredients can also be found in ARGs, in one form or another.

"Numogram" can be summarized as the gradual revelation of a belief system or secret knowledge through a numerical and / or symbolic system. In other words, the hidden knowledge is contained in a puzzle of sorts, which requires the active effort of the student (or in the case of the ARG, the player) to uncover and understand. "Mythos" is explained as the cumulative knowledge or narrative that is gathered from multiple sources that "produces a coherent but inherently disintegrated hyperstitional mythos while effecting a positive destruction of identity, authority and credibility." And finally, "unbelief" in terms of hyperstition is defined as "pragmatic skepticism or constructive escape from integrated thinking and all its forms of imposed unity," resulting in the "attainment of positive unbelief." In hyperstition then, "unbelief" becomes the philosophical equivalent of Coleridge's willing suspension of disbelief, as the audience puts aside the knowledge of the fictional basis of the material in order to further their enjoyment by choosing to believe it is real, at least for a short period of time.

Though couched in somewhat esoteric terms these three concepts and the overlying principle of hyperstition almost perfectly describe both the intent and methodology of most alternate reality games. On one level, the three ingredients necessary to produce hyperstition can easily be compared to the techniques used by Puppetmasters in creating ARGs. The idea of numograms, of course, reflects the way in which ARGs incorporate puzzles and use them to reveal critical pieces of information and points within the plot, while the concept of "mythos" perfectly describes the method in which the content of an alternate reality game is delivered via a multitude of vehicles – websites, e-mail messages, online chats, and so on. Together, the cumulative story told by these different assets within an ARG tells the narrative and forms the "mythos" of the game. The second part of the "mythos" concept – "effecting a positive destruction of identity, authority and credibility" – would make a perfect creed for an ARG Puppetmaster team, as that is exactly what they strive to do in creating and running a game.

"Unbelief" finds it's equivalence in the underlying ARG principle of *TINAG*, or *This Is Not A Game*. "Unbelief" in an alternate reality game is created through its immersive qualities, as the depth of the world created and the believability of the characters within the game encourage players to "escape from integrated thinking" which would remind them that they are only playing a game and achieve that state of "positive unbelief." By combining all the different methods used to try and create the illusion of reality for their fictional worlds, the Puppetmasters are actually attempting to have their games become just that – hyperstitions – in a very real way.

So again, the phrase "this is not a game" takes on new meaning, as the ARG creators of today may be writing the superstitions and mythologies of tomorrow. The powerfully pervasive nature of ARGs keep their players involved with them for years, as evidenced by the still active and loyal community for **the Beast** years after the game itself has concluded. If hyperstition continues to grow and be accepted as valid philosophy of the new digital media, alternate reality games are almost certain to be looked on as embodiments and validation of the entire concept.

A Game and So Much More

Finally, the catch phrase "this is not a game" also has deep personal meaning to many fans of the alternate reality game genre. At least a few ARGs have engendered such a powerful and emotional response from their players that the popular concept of "playing a game" doesn't even come close to describing the experience. Witness the legions of fans from the original **Beast** that still gather online to discuss various aspects of the game and reflect on how the experience has yet to be equaled, or the dozens of players of **Chasing The Wish** who wrote to me afterwards and claimed that the game literally changed their lives. For these players, the months they spent exploring and interacting with the alternate realities created by these works became something much more than just a game or an interactive story they participated in.

In a very real way, these players remember the time they've spent interacting with ARGs as a valued part of their lives, like the treasured memories of a particularly enjoyable vacation or an emotionally significant period in their past. So when they say, "this is not a game," they are not being delusional or trying to fool themselves or others into thinking that what the events and characters of an ARG are ultimately real. Instead, they are expressing the deep significance an alternate reality game can have for them on many levels. ARGs can become a source of personal revelation and transformation, while simultaneously enabling their participants to forge strong and lasting social connections with an active, self-motivated online community.

295

It's this potential that has made Alternate Reality Gaming one of the most exciting and rapidly expanding genres on online entertainment in recent years. With potential to affect real change in the fields of marketing, online gaming and entertainment, and even social consciousness, alternate reality games stand on the brink of indeed becoming something much more than just games.

Appenidx A: Bibliography

Part One: Alternate Reality Games in Theory

Chapter 1: Game or Not a Game?

Definitions of a Game

Huizinga, Johan (1955). *Homo Ludens: A Study of the Play Element in Culture*. Boston: Beacon Press.

Caillois, Roger (1961). *Man, Play, and Games*. New York: Free Press.

Suits, Bernard (1967). *What Is a Game?* Philosophy of Science, Vol. 34, pg 148.

Avedon, Elliot and Sutton-Smith, Brian (1981). *The Study of Games*. New York: John Wiley & Sons.

Crawford, Chris (1982). *The Art of Computer Game Design*. Washington State University Vancouver.
[http://www.vancouver.wsu.edu/fac/peabody/gamebook/Coverpage.html]

Juul, Jesper (1993). *The Game, the Player, the World: Looking for a Heart of Gameness*. Presented at the Level Up conference in Utrecht, November 4th- 6th, 2003. [http://www.jesperjuul.dk/text/gameplayerworld/]

Salen, Katie and Zimmerman, Eric (2003). *Rules of Play*. Cambridge, MA: MIT Press.

Steurer, Jonathan (1992). *Defining Virtual Reality: Dimensions Determining Telepresence*. Journal of Communication, 42(4), 73-93.

Rules and Winning Conditions

Thomas, David (2004). *I Love Bees, or do I?*. From http://www.buzzcut.com, July 29, 2004.
[http://www.buzzcut.com/article.php?story=20040729200330772]

Brown, Cody (2004). *Admiring the Bees*. From http://www.avantgaming.com, August 20, 2004.
http://avantgaming.com/archives/2004_08.html]

Game Mechanics and Components

Bateson, Gregory (1979). *Mind and Nature: A Necessary Unity*. New York: Dutton.

Bolter, Jay David and Grusin, Richard (1999). *Remediation: Understanding New Media*. Cambridge, MA: MIT Press.

·McGonigal, Jane (2003). *This Is Not a Game: Immersive Aesthetics and Collective Play*. Presented at the Digital Arts & Culture 2003 Conference Proceedings. Melbourne, May 2003.

Kittler, Friedrich (1995). *There is No Software*. From http://www.ctheory.net, Oct. 18, 1995.
[http://www.ctheory.net/text_file.asp?pick=74]

Chapter 2: Immersion in an Alternate Reality

Definitions of Immersion

Wagner, Richard (1849). *The Art-work of the Future*. The Wagner Library.

Coomans, M.K.D. and H.J.P. Timmermanns (1997). *Towards a Taxonomy of Virtual Reality User Interfaces*. Presented at International Conference on Information Visualisation (IV97). London.

Murray, Janet (1998). *Hamlet on the Holodeck*. Cambridge, MA: MIT Press.

Ryan, Marie-Laure (2001). *Narrative as Virtual Reality. Immersion and Interactivity in Literature and Electronic Media*. Baltimore, MD: Johns Hopkins University Press.

Poynter, Steve (2002). *Immersed in the News*. From http://www.poynter.org, June 6, 2002. [http://legacy.poynter.org/centerpiece/immerse/immersive.htm]

Salen, Katie and Zimmerman, Eric (2003). *Rules of Play*. Cambridge, MA: MIT Press.

The History of Immersion

Campbell, Joseph (1988). *The Inner Reaches of Outer Space: Metaphor as Myth and as Religion*. New York: Harper Collins.

Grau, Oliver (2003). *Virtual Art: From Illusion to Immersion*. Cambridge, MA: MIT Press.

The Power of Immersion

Nell, Victor (1988). *Lost in a Book: The Psychology of Reading for Pleasure*. New Haven, CT: Yale University Press.

Techniques of Immersion

·Mateas, Michael (2003). *Interaction and Agency.* From grand-textauto.gatech.edu, Aug. 6, 2003.
[http://grandtextauto.gatech.edu/2003/08/06/interaction-and-agency/]

The Illusion of Immersion

·Bolter, Jay David and Grusin, Richard (1999). *Remediation: Understanding New Media.* Cambridge, MA: MIT Press.

Immersion in Alternate Reality Gaming

McGonigal, Jane (2003). *This Is Not a Game: Immersive Aesthetics and Collective Play.* Presented at the Digital Arts & Culture 2003 Conference Proceedings. Melbourne, May 2003.

Chapter 3: Game or Interactive Story?

Defining a Story

Kim, John (2004). *Immersive Story: A View of Role-played Drama.* From http://www.darkshire.net.
[http://www.darkshire.net/~jhkim/rpg/theory/narrative/immersivestory.html]

A Ludologist's Point of View

Eskelinen, Markku (2004). *Towards Computer Game Studies.* Published in *First Person: New Media as Story, Performance, and Game.* Cambridge, MA: MIT Press.

Cameron, Andy (1995). *D I S S I M U L A T I O N S: illusions of interactivity.* Millennium Film Journal, No. 28.
[http://mfjonline.org/journalPages/MFJ28/ACINTRO.HTML]

The Narratologist's Story

Murray, Janet (2004). *From Game-Story to Cyberdrama.* Published in *First Person: New Media as Story, Performance, and Game.* Cambridge, MA: MIT Press.

White, Hayden (1961). *Critical Responses: The Narrativization of Real Events. Critical Inquiry* Vol. 7, No. 4.
[http://www.uchicago.edu/research/jnl-crit-inq/issues/v7/v7n4.html]

Mateas, Michael (2004). *A Preliminary Poetics for Interactive Drama and Games.* Published in *First Person: New Media as Story, Performance, and Game.* Cambridge, MA: MIT Press.

Perlin, Ken (2004). *Can There Be a Form between a Game and a Story?* Published in *First Person: New Media as Story, Performance, and Game.* Cambridge, MA: MIT Press.

Chapter 5: Interactive Authoring

The Power of Interactive Authoring

·Meadows, Mark Stephen (2002). *Pause & Effect: The Art of Interactive Narrative.* Indianapolis, IN: New Riders.

Part Two: Alternate Reality Games in History

Chapter 6: Alternate Reality Game Pre-History

Immersion in Literature

Aarseth, Espen J. (1997). *Cybertext: Perspectives on Ergodic Literature.* Baltimore, MD: Johns Hopkins University Press.

Norwich, John (1990). *Oxford Illustrated Encyclopedia of the Arts.* New York: Oxford University Press.

Ong's Hat: Incunabula

Unger, Denny (2001). From http://www.darkplanetonline.com, Aug. 14, 2001.
[http://www.darkplanetonline.com/whatreally.html]

Incunabula.org [http://www.incunabula.org]

Chapter 7: A Vision of the Future – **the Beast**

Birthing the Beast

Stewart, Sean (2001). *Introduction to the A.I. Web Game.* From http://www.seanstewart.org.
[http://www.seanstewart.org/beast/intro/]

The Interactive Trail

The Beast Puppetmaster team (2001). From http://www.cloudmakers.org.
[http://jeaninesalla.cloudmakers.org/credits/note/note.html]

The Legacy of **the Beast**

McGonigal, Jane (2003). *This Is Not a Game: Immersive Aesthetics and Collective Play.* Presented at the Digital Arts & Culture 2003 Conference Proceedings. Melbourne, May 2003.

Chapter 8: A **Majestic** Failure

Brown, Janelle (2001). *Paranoia for Fun and Profit.* From http://www.salon.com, Aug.10, 2001.
[http://archive.salon.com/tech/feature/2001/08/10/majestic/index.html?x]

Pre-game Hype

Majestic (2001). Designed and produced by Electronic Arts, produced for the Internet and for the PC.

First Signs of Problems

Morris, Chris (2001). *Innovation at risk?* From http://www.cnn.com, Dec. 19, 2001.
[http://money.cnn.com/2001/12/19/technology/column_gaming/]

Chapter 9: Independents Come of Age

Spawn of the Beast

Rojas, Peter (2001). *A Conspiracy of Conspiracy Gamers.* From

http://www.wired.com, Sept. 19, 2001.
[http://www.wired.com/news/games/0,2101,46672,00.html]

Back to the Future ·

Miller, Jim (2002). Exocog: a case study of a new genre of storytelling. From www.miramontes.com.
[http://www.miramontes.com/studios/exocog/index.html]

From the Ashes of **Majestic**

ChangeAgents: Out of Control (2002). Designed and produced by Dave Szulborski, produced for the Internet.

Chapter 10: Commercial Comeback

TerraQuest

TerraQuest (2003). Designed and produced by MindQuest Entertainment, produced for the Internet.

Chapter 11: **Chasing The Wish**

The Fun Begins

Chasing The Wish (2003). Designed and produced by Dave Szulborski, produced for the Internet.

Weathers, Gray (2003). *The Title Game.* From http://www.chasingthewish.net. [http://www.chasingthewish.net/j3f12p19e1i2a11h2c22k8n15m7.html]

Chapter 12: ARGs Reloaded

MetaCortechs (2003). Designed and produced by Project MU, produced for the Internet.

The Truth Revealed ·

Losowsky, Andrew (2003). *Puppet masters.* From Guardian Online, Dec. 11, 2003. [http://www.guardian.co.uk/online/story/0,3605,1103884,00.html]

Chapter 13: The Bees of Summer

I Love Bees (2004). Designed and produced by 4orty2wo Entertainment for Microsoft, produced for the Internet.

Chapter 14: David and Goliath

Urban Hunt (2004). Designed and produced by Team Dread House, produced for the Internet.

Chapter 15: The Current and Future State of Alternate Reality Gaming

The Need for Better Online Content

Brown, Janelle (2001). *Paranoia for Fun and Profit.* From www.salon.com, Aug.10, 2001. [http://archive.salon.com/tech/feature/2001/08/10/majestic/index.html?x]

Part Three: Alternate Reality Games in Practice

Chapter 17: Puppetmastering – Creating a Game

Characters in Alternate Reality Games

Glassner, Andrew (2004). *Interactive Storytelling: Techniques for 21st Century-Fiction*. Natick, MA: A.K. Peters. Chapter 19: This is Not a Game

The Game of Social Engineering

McGonigal, Jane (2003). *This Is Not a Game: Immersive Aesthetics and Collective Play*. Presented at the Digital Arts & Culture 2003 Conference Proceedings. Melbourne, May 2003.

Levy, Pierre (1997). *Collective Intelligence: Mankind's Emerging World in Cyberspace*. New York, NY: Perseus Books.

Rheingold, Howard (2002). *Smart Mobs: The Next Social Revolution*. New York, NY: Perseus Books. [http://www.smartmobs.com/book/book_summ.html]

Negarestani, R. (2004). *Polytics*. From http://www.cold-me.net. [http://www.cold-me.net/polytics/]

Appendix B: Alternate Reality Game Resources

Alternate Reality Gaming Community Forum and News Websites

http://www.argn.com

http://www.unfiction.com

http://www.argtalk.com

http://www.deaddrop.us

http://www.arginsider.com

http://www.cloudmakers.org

http://www.immersionunlimited.com

http://www.smirkbox.com

ARG Planet, an Italian ARG website
[http://www.adventuresplanet.it/argplanet/]

Dave Szulborski

Alternate Reality Gaming History

Immersion Museum

[http://www.miramontes.com/studios/museum/]

Alternate Reality Gaming Tools for Players and Puppetmasters
Resources for Encoding and Decoding Messages

http://www.geocities.com/xulfrepus/folder/base.html

http://www.crazychucks.com/ascii.html

http://cs.colgate.edu/faculty/nevison/Core139Web/tools/vige
nere-cracker.html

http://www.ics.uci.edu/~eppstein/cryptogram/

http://www.siteexperts.com/demo/page8.asp

http://starbase.trincoll.edu/~crypto/

http://nickciske.com/tools/binary.php

http://sharkysoft.com/misc/vigenere/

http://www.math.com/students/converters/source/base.htm

http://geography.about.com/library/howto/htdegrees.htm

http://makcoder.sourceforge.net/demo/base64.php

http://www.babbage.demon.co.uk/morseabc.html

http://www.scphillips.com/morse/index.html

http://www.wordsmith.org/anagram/

http://www.fact-index.com/c/cr/cryptology_1.html

Tools and Information About Steganography

http://www.webopedia.com/TERM/S/steganography.html

http://encyclopedia.thefreedictionary.com/Steganography

http://www.dtc.umn.edu/~reedsj/trit.pdf

http://www.snapfiles.com/get/jphide.html

http://www.c3eggsNside.com/

http://www.downseek.com/directory/212.asp

http://sourceforge.net/projects/camerashy/

Image Manipulation

Dave Szulborski

http://www.eyetricks.com/stereograms/onlinetools/stereocreat
or.htm

http://www.eyetricks.com/stereograms/stereodownloads.htm

http://www.techmind.org/stereo/sintro.html

http://www.text-image.com/

http://www.blackant.net/code/oth/image2text/index.php

http://hem.passagen.se/rasmuse/Coagula.htm

E-mail Tools

http://www.inetprivacy.com/a4proxy/use-anonymous-email-
remailer.htm

http://www.spammimic.com

http://www.bigstring.com/

http://www.readnotify.com/

Telephone Answering and Voice Mail Accounts

http://www.voicemailandfax.com/

http://www.tollfreelive.com

http://www.xtreme800.com

http://www.hotvoice.com/

http://www.connectmevoice.com

http://www2.ringcentral.com

Anonymizer Services or Software

http://proxify.net

http://www.megaproxy.com/

http://www.anonymizer.com/

http://www.guardster.com/

http://www.surfola.com/

http://www.anonymization.net/

http://anonymouse.ws/

Websites About Game Theory or New Media

http://www.avantgame.com/

http://www.avantgaming.com/

Dave Szulborski

http://www.buzzcut.com/

http://grandtextauto.gatech.edu/index.php

http://ludology.org/index.php

http://www.jesperjuul.dk/ludologist/

Appendix C: A View from Above - A Personal Reflection on Puppetmastering

By Dee Cook

My first experience as a full-fledged Puppetmaster (PM) came with the game **Urban Hunt**. At a gathering of avid Alternate Reality Gamers in Orlando last November, I told Dave Szulborski that I would love to work with him on any future projects. Dave asked eight people to work on the **Urban Hunt** project, who eventually became a core team of six. We developed the game for nearly five months and ran it for another three.

The entire process of creating a game is a true test of dedication and love for the genre. Many people ask why one would put one's self through the arduous process, and arduous really does describe it. It's very similar to putting on a prolonged stage production, only instead of just one venue you can have several web sites to develop and maintain (**Urban Hunt** had 19 different sites) as well as technical problems such as staying anonymous through e-mail, chat, and phone interaction.

So why do it? There are several reasons. The aforementioned love of the genre. Creating something and watching people discover it, speculate on your reasoning, playing off their theories and tailoring the game to the player base. Gaining skills such as polishing one's writing ability, graphics manipulation, and web design. Learning new skills such as thinking on ones' toes – the players just discovered something that they weren't supposed to see yet: you have to move fast to adapt it into the game and make it part of the experience. One thing that happened during **Urban Hunt** was that the web host for one of the sites was hacked, and all the web pages on that host had been defaced. We had the choice of coming out from behind the curtain to explain what happened, or utilizing the hacking as a plot point and adding on to it in an in-game manner. We chose the latter.

The joy of creation is complimented by watching the audience, the players, read and comment on your work. Anonymity is a plus in this situation because the players are more likely to be very honest about their feelings when they're not as concerned about hurting an acquaintance's feelings. Constructive criticism is key in adapting game play to what the audience desires. Additionally, often players will propose theories at the beginning of a game that they think are completely wild speculation, then find out at the end they were right, which was a blast to watch happen. Sometimes we would note a theory that a player proposed and incorporate it into the storyline. In a way, being a Puppet Master is like being a tour guide and taking your friends to a place they've never been, letting them learn and enjoy the sights of a place you love to visit.

Although some might feel that profit is a driving reason to create an ARG, the reality is that unless a game is bankrolled by a large corporation (i.e. **the Beast** and **I Love Bees**), expenses will come out of the Puppetmasters' pockets. Selling in-game swag usually only nets a small profit. On the other hand, the real world items, such as the tee shirts and books we sold through **Urban Hunt**, are fun mementos. Paying for a game is one way that the blossoming ARG culture is providing "sweat equity" – putting a large amount of work and money behind the genre in hopes that it can become part of the mainstream and get interest from those willing to finance future games.

One of the initial goals of **Urban Hunt** was to blur the lines between game and reality. Several other games had an element of the unreal, whether it was a futuristic setting or supernatural occurrences. We wanted to present a plausible situation, something that could have happened in reality. Along the way we added what appeared to be paranormal events, but at the end they all had rational explanations. We tried to have specific reasons to include the game puzzles, studying character motivation to determine why he or she would obscure data behind a puzzle solve. I think we were quite successful in this regard, and players walked out of the game with the feeling that they took part in a real event. Some players developed an emotional attachment with the characters and were shocked and dismayed when they found out the good guy was really a bad guy, or that their favorite character had died.

On a personal level I walked away from the finale with a great sense of accomplishment and pride in the project. On a practical level I built up my skill set in HTML, CSS, and Photoshop. Last, on an emotional level I have a bond with my fellow PMs with whom I spent several months building an alternate universe. Without the hard work and dedication of all the team members, **Urban Hunt** could never have happened.

We hope that the game provided people with an enjoyable and memorable experience. Several people mentioned that **Urban Hunt** was the first ARG they had played, and they are now looking forward to playing future games. We were able to meet our goals of blurring the lines between gaming and reality, as well as provide an experience that could have taken place in today's world. I hope that we were able to call more attention to the ARG world and pave the way for games to come.

Dee Cook is a computer consultant and mother of two girls in Austin, Texas. Once she discovered ARGs, she was hooked. She has played a smattering of different games and most recently was involved as a Puppetmaster in **Urban Hunt.**

Appendix D: Anatomy of a Puzzle

Making a puzzle for an alternate reality game is never an easy task, especially when it needs to be integrated into the storyline of the game. I personally have made dozens and dozens of puzzles for the games I have created, and yet I still couldn't give you a formula or template to follow which would guarantee the puzzle would be a success. Most of my puzzles have been moderately successful, although there are certain ones I would just as well forget.

*Everyone who creates puzzles has their own unique style and favorite methods. Sin_Vraal, also known as Paul Melamud, worked with me on the **Urban Hunt** game, for which he created the puzzle below. I asked him to compose an explanation of the process he used to make the puzzle, an "anatomy" of sorts, deconstructing the puzzle from start to finish. So sit back and enjoy this rare look into the creative process of making a puzzle used in an actual alternate reality game. Dave Szulborski, Nov. 2004.*

Anatomy of a Puzzle

by Paul Melamud

Dave Szulborski

I) THE SCENE:

Before a puzzle could be created, I needed to understand both the theme and style of the game and the website for which the puzzle was to be created.

In brief, our game revolved around a fictitious reality game show production company called Tomorrow's Talk Studios, which had begun taping a new show called Dread House on the site of a creepy, abandoned institution called Cambridge Mental Hospital. Although normal at first, things went horribly wrong, and the cast and crew had all been killed, with the studio hastily covering things up as if nothing had happened.

Enter the website http://www.theunraveling.com; this site was intended to represent a foray into the troubled mind of a person whose identity (and therefore relevance to the game) was a secret to the players until the last puzzle was solved. This person, Mark Robinson, was the President of Tomorrow's Talk Studios, and his involvement with the events of the Dread House show caused him to become mentally imbalanced.

Thematically, the puzzles needed to address subject matter relevant to topics such as insanity, paranoia, schizophrenia, horror, and so forth. Stylistically, the puzzles would ideally tie together both audio and visual elements in avant-garde fashion. It was intended for the puzzles

318

to link together in such a way where the player delved deeper into Mr. Robinson's mind as the puzzles were solved.

II: THE MECHANISM:

In developing a sequence of puzzles, I had first conceived of a puzzle I called "Amazing Grace"; the concept was going to revolve around the line "was blind, but now I see" from that famous song. The actual puzzle development went something like this:

- I would like to embrace a both audio and visual implementation of an otherwise blind concept - the Braille alphabet.

- Visually, I could use Braille to spell a message. This part was easy, once an appropriate message was chosen. The message also needed to point the player to the next website, and I had decided to leave one word off of the end of the quote that would be the solution.

- Aurally, I could use music to represent the Braille, and require transcription so it could be translated into the message.

Now, if you can't picture Braille in your mind, let me summarize how it works, briefly. A pair of sets of vertically aligned pips (0, 1, 2, or 3 pips in a set) in various combinations represent Braille letters, numbers, and punctuation marks. For example, the letters "N" and "A" are represented by raised bumps on a page arranged as follows:

Braille "N"   Braille "A"

The question became: How best could I represent Braille using music?

- I arbitrarily selected finger spacing 1-3-5 as a convenient and harmonious note arrangement to represent the notes with respect to pip placement – '1' being in the bottom row, '3' in the middle, and '5' in the top row. I also decided to start in the key of middle C, where 1-3-5 would represent the chord C-E-G.

- For "N", this would give two chords: a 1-5 and a 1-3-5. For "A", we have one note and a rest.

- To allow for a puzzle solver to clearly separate out the Braille portions that would spell each letter, I decided to connect associated pairs of notes/chords as eighth notes. So for "N" above I had two paired eighth-note chords, and for "A" I had a single eighth note followed by an eighth rest.

- I wanted to make words distinguishable from each other as well. I accomplished this by raising the key by one each time a word changed. The piece would start in the key of middle C, then move to D for the next word, E for the next word, and so forth.

III: TO JOURNEY ONWARD:

I then went searching for an appropriate quotation that fit the theme of both the site and the puzzle. As luck would have it, I found a great quote by William Butler Yeats:

"… for what but eye and ear silence the mind with the minute particulars of mankind?"

This quote turned out to be perfect for two reasons:

- The source of this quote is "The Double Vision of Michael Robartes", which was a wonderful allusion to a personality disorder, and;

- The quote (taken out of context) might suggest using both one's eyes and one's ears to silence the voices in one's mind, and it ties in both the audio (ear) and visual (eye) elements of the puzzle.

To portray the quote in Braille, I parsed the quote using an online Braille Alphabet site. The missing word at the end, "mankind", would then lead the players to the next puzzle.Finally, one of our team members played out the tune with a synthesizer (again, raising a key for each new word), and saved the mp3.

IV: THE WINDOW DRESSING:

With the core of the puzzle in place, it was time to fill in the webpage around it:

First, since this site was early in the puzzle sequence, I wanted to start giving people the feeling that the "narrator" was not in his right mind. I also wanted it to relate to the musical puzzle at hand. I generated the following text as a little story, and had the lengths of the lines patterned like white and black piano keys:

321

Dave Szulborski

When_I_was_a_boy,_my_pare
nts_forced_me_to_t
ake_wretched_piano_lesson
s._It_wasn't_so_mu
ch_the_instrument_I_hated
,_as_much_as_it_was_the_t
eacher._That_basta
rd_knew_I_wasn't_simply_t
one_deaf_-_I_was_m
erely_a_lazy_practicer,_y
ou_see,_and_when_f
lailing_the_besoured_note
s_of_some_monotonous_disH
armony,_he_would_s
cream_for_what_seemed_hoU
rs,_extolling_the_
virtues_of_discipline,_DR
illing_notes_into_my_fing
ers_until_they_thr
obbed_with_the_cartilage-
jarring_pain_of_re
petitive_motion._"You_mus
t_express_yourself
",_he_would_demand,_"allo
w_the_music_to_flow_throu
gh_you_and_speak_t
o_your_audience"._Hour_af
ter_hour,_week_aft
er_week,_I_tried_to_screa
m_my_soul_through_my_rawe
d_and_bloodied_stu
mps._I_never_did_learn_to
_play_that_damn_pi
ece._But_I_can_still_feel
_its_simple_melody
_pounding_at_my_mind_It_h
aunts_even_my_waking_mome
nts_to_this_day.__

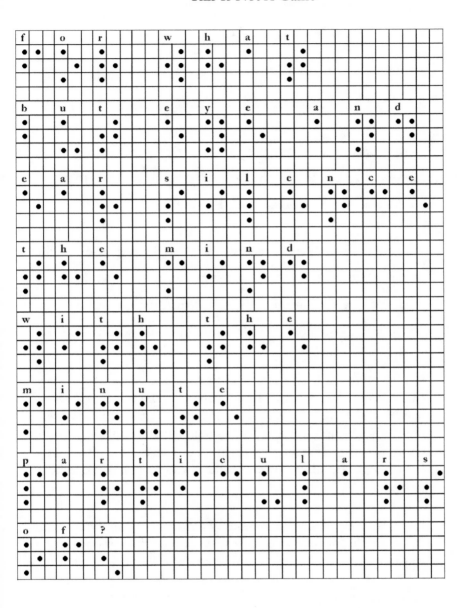

Finally, the background for the page was an animated picture file containing some musical notes, and the melody (referenced above)

323

was linked to the word "melody" in the text, for a player to discover by clicking it with their mouse.

V: THE PUZZLE UNRAVELS

One thing you learn when creating puzzles – often times, those things you think are apparent are often elusive, and those that you believe are difficult are sometimes devilishly simple.

The bullets below explain the apparent thought processes of the players as they attacked this puzzle, as summarized from the dedicated board the players created on the ARG site http://www.unfiction.com. In this puzzle writer's opinion, they always accomplish incredible work:

- On September 29, 2004, the players analyzed the unusual layout of the given text, trying to find a pattern, trying to tie it to other sites that were part of our ARG. At this point, the players were unsure how The Unraveling was going to factor into the game. In short order, they realized the pattern was that of piano keys. We thought this discovery was actually subtler than it turned out to be.

- Later that evening, the hunters found and posted the melody.mp3 file for everyone to review. Several days passed, and it was noted that someone should "transcribe the melody.mp3 file so we can solve this one". However, to our growing concern, nobody seemed to be able to (or want to) give transcription a try.

- On October 4, 2004, our team decided to encourage the players by having an in-game character (who had been befriended by the players to help get to the bottom of the mystery, and who often posted his "discoveries" on his website):

"Has anyone been playing with the mp3 on this Unraveling page? It's driving me crazy! I don't even know if the actual notes mean anything. It seems like there are chords that are in pairs, varying between one and three notes. I can't trust my tin ear to tell how many notes are played at one time, but I get the feeling that the number of notes in each pairing is important somehow. Just a thought; maybe someone with a better ear can take it and run with it."

At the same time, the Puzzlemaster team began to question whether or not the puzzle was too hard, too early in the sequence. One Puzzlemaster put together a second puzzle, and had it pop-up when the amazinggrace.html page was accessed. This puzzle led to the page http://www.theunraveling.com/dementophobia.html, which portrays a musical passage with notes labeled DEMENTOPHOBIA. Looking carefully, the players might note that the "O" and "P" notes were actually the Braille representations for those letters.

With these hints goading them on, the intrepid players started analyzing the notes. Finally, on October 5, 2004, one player (known as Grumpyboy in the game forum) cracked the melody, spelled the quote, and solved the missing word "Mankind", leading them to the next page:

Dave Szulborski

http://www.theunraveling.com/mankind.html.

Paul Melamud, aka Sin Vraal in the ARG forums, works full-time as a senior validation engineer for a major pharmaceutical company. The creation, analysis, and solving of puzzles are one of his many passions, largely inspired by great ARG Puppetmasters such as this book's author. He enjoys playing on both sides of the ARG curtain, and hopes to inspire others to participate in this incredibly nourishing, versatile genre of gaming.

Appendix E: Immersive Realities - The Structure of Magic

By Ben Mack

Magic Castle Award Winning Magician, Advertising Executive

Magic is the act of facilitating a phantasmagorical experience, the acceptance of the world where natural laws don't have such a firm grasp on reality. I grew up a junior member of The Magic Castle—If ever there was a real Hogwartz, this was it. David Copperfield lectured to our membership, Dai Vernon tutored us and Diana Zimmerman managed us. The Magic Castle wasn't open to kids interested in magic. Instead, The Magic Castle held biannual auditions and initiated those who demonstrated proficiency of craft and potential for expertise. The older a candidate was, the better they had to be. It took me two tries to be accepted. Natural aptitude was rarely enough to muster the goods necessary for acceptance. Virtually every candidate had been tutored. Lorenzo Clark was my mentor. I called him Larry.

Larry not only taught me sleight-of-hand, called *prestidigitation*, but he also taught me the psychology of perception. In order to create a sustainable illusion, one must have a commanding grasp of perception. A magician must transcend fooling their audience and enter the realm of trust where an audience grants you their willing suspension of disbelief.

Magic is not a thing or a physical act, but a state of mind that approaches the sublime but is more aptly referred to as phantasmagorical. Magic occurs at the intersection of a performer and an audience. There is intentionality to the perception. A stone that looks like an eagle is not magic, regardless of whether or not it is carved to represent the physical traits of an eagle. A sculpture maybe a catalyst to an altered state of mind, but I am reticent to call a sculpture magical. Some panoramas feel almost magical to me, but real magic is dynamic and ephemeral. Magic is the process of engineering an experience where reality emerges as it cannot be, and yet the audience is compelled to set aside their disbelief and flow with the experience as long as it lasts.

Creating an illusion entails tweaking our visual prejudices. We drop a coin, and it falls. We know this to be true; we have seen the force of gravity pull objects to Earth since before we had words to articulate the phenomena. What most non-perceptual psychologists DON'T recognize is the extent that our mind projects our expectations, our visual prejudices, onto our sight.

If a magician creates the physical gesture of dropping a coin from one hand to another, yet palms the coin so it doesn't actually fall into the second hand, most minds will see the coin fall. The term for this sight projection is *sight retention*. A normal mind will literally "see" the coin fall. This specific visual hallucination is called a projection, our mind projects its expectation of reality onto our sight. The magician makes note of the triggers that cause these visual breaks from reality and assembles a presentation that often includes a series of these triggers, often strung together through a narrative known as patter. The magician is an actor playing the role of a person with supernatural powers.

A person who engineers a magical frame of mind, phantasmagoria, for an audience may or may not be a performer on a stage. If the person who engineered a magical experience is not the actor presenting the feats, they are the puppet-master of the experience, where the magician is a marionette, performing in the puppet-master's phantasmagorical production. Clock makers of the 17th Century created automatons, mechanical men whose gears and riggings could be activated to perform the tricks of magicians. These clock makers were not magicians; they were the puppet-masters of their metal figurines that could perform magic, even in the absence of their creators.

Creating magic requires the recognition of stages within stages, seeing micro-stages within macro-stages. The macro-stage is the physical place the audience encounters the magic. A magician may perform on a traditional proscenium stage, in a parlor, at a dinner table or on a street corner—whatever location the magician interacts with their audience becomes the macro-stage. The micro-stages emerge as the audience shifts their attention. David Copperfield regularly performs coin tricks in front of audiences in excess of 2,000. How? He manages the micro-stages, the focus of his audience. By focusing his own attention, with all his body, on a silver dollar, he can command the attention of 2,000 sets of eyes, whose minds enjoy the representation of a miracle as he makes the coin vanish. Copperfield directs the focus of his audience. Site retention won't work unless the audience's mind is engaged. The mind must not only see the cues that trigger the mental projections, but the mind must be so immersed in its focus that the mind accepts the magician's cues as real. The creation of these cues, the intentional use of projection triggers, is the keystone to invoking illusion.

Misdirection is the magician's ability to secretly do one thing by directing the audience's attention on something else. Direction is the root of misdirection. Managing the micro-stages of an audiences focus is at the heart of misdirection—movement hides movement. When the puppet-master doesn't want the audience to see the magician load the dove in a scarf, he choreographs the magician-puppet to "steal" the dove-load during another movement. Sound impossible? Harry Blackstone used to have an elephant walked on stage, up-stage-left, while he commanded attention down-stage-right. When Blackstone gestured up-stage-left, the audience was amazed to suddenly see an elephant.

While I cannot fully articulate the magical frame of mind, I can say this: when an audience feels safe, respected and cared for, their minds loosen and the defenses drop. The goal of the puppet master is to have his avatars communicate their love for their audience. Deception created purely for personal gain is a con; deception manifested for the benefit of the audience may feel magical.

In years past, puppet-masters were magicians, playwrights, screenwriters and novelists among other artists who created dynamic performances for the theatre-of-the-mind in meat space. The growth of the Internet has borne a new species of puppet-master, the weavers of magic who weave cyberspace into their tapestry, the architects of alternate reality games. May you enjoy and appreciate their creations.

Ben Mack is a Magic Castle Award Winning Magician and highly-respected Advertising Executive. He is also the author of Poker Without Cards *[http://www.pokerwithoutcards.com/].*

Appendix F: Collaboration in Theory and Practice

by Joseph Matheny

Hyperauthor and Media Theorist

This is a manifesto about collaboration – it's about the realities and functional challenges you will face trying to create and maintain a working collaboration environment. This is not one of those screeds about 'collaboration and why the world's future depends on it' or anything like that. This is a meat and potatoes guide.

For the theory hounds

It is only proper that such a manifesto begin with Doug Engelbart. In the 1960s, Engelbart and his laboratory at the Stanford Research Institute (SRI) invented the fundamental building blocks found in all of today's collaborative tools -- everything from the data structures (hypertext) and user interfaces (windowing systems), to applications (groupware) and physical interfaces (the mouse). Engelbart's work was driven by some deceptively simple observations, which he described in his 1962 paper, "Augmenting Human Intellect: A Conceptual Framework."

[http://www.liquidinformation.org/engelbart/62_paper_top.html]

There are a lot of buzzwords floating around these days that all loosely or tightly bind to the larger meta-concept of collaboration: SmartMobs, Living Networks, Groupware, Social Software Approaches, Collaborative or Collective Management, to name only a few. My personal favorite source of information about emerging paradigms in collaboration is my old cyber-buddy Jon Lebkowsky and his blog, Weblogsky. [http://www.weblogsky.com/wfs.html]. If you're interested in really drilling down into these concepts, I'd recommend Jon L's blog as an excellent starting place. I am also fleshing out a white paper on the subject, to be released sometime in 2005, time permitting. Last, but not least, you can always google one of the above terms and take it from there.

But enough of that.

Now I'm going to talk about some ideas that I have extracted from real-life experiences in group efforts and collaborative projects. No matter what you call it, it all boils down to one thing. What we are talking about here is a many to one relationship to project development and management. While this may sound simple when stated on the bottom line, it is amazingly complex and full of many potential points of failure, to put it into network management parlance. Studying networks and how they function is actually a very sound idea when planning a collaborative project. This applies to social as well as technical networks. The main thing I most often see missing from group endeavors is a sound project management plan.

Let's talk about project management. A couple of things need to happen before a collaborative project is started in earnest.

• A conceptual framework for the core story, the main characters and the basic methodologies for story delivery should be fleshed out before you begin deployment
• A simple set of tools should be evaluated and chosen
• A schedule should be drafted and all known elements should be plotted, with milestones and deliverables marked inside of this schedule
• A core team should already be pre-qualified and selected
• Someone should be chosen to be the leader or leaders, which I always refer to as 'central command'
• It helps for projects larger in scope to have teams and therefore team leaders that report to 'central command'

These are general bullet points and you may add or subtract to fit the particular idiosyncrasies of your own particular group working. I will now take each one of those bulleted items and expand on them a bit.

A conceptual framework for the core story, the main characters and the basic methodologies for story delivery should already be fleshed out

335

This stage of planning is analogous to the draft state of a novel*. It can be as simple as an outline, a set of index cards or as complex as a Labyrinth storyboard [http://www.habitualindolence.net/labyrinth/] or a Brain [http://www.thebrain.com/]. This can be drawn up by one person or several, and it can be taken from a pre-existing body of work, as we recently did with El Centro or it can be created from scratch. The important thing is that you have a map, even a crude one, before you invite too many people to join your party. The barebones framework includes:

- Starting point (how does this thing begin)
- Body (what are the points that the story is trying to get across and how do we get there)
- Resolution (how does this thing end)

Next, a listing of main characters, their psychology profiles and motivations should be listed. Then, once that is done I always like to plot the characters within the storyline framework. I also like to make rough outlines of places, secondary characters, and any groups or organizations that may play a key role in the story. Personally, I like using The Brain [http://www.thebrain.com/] for this outlining because it allows me to link people, places and things together in arrangements of importance (casual to critical) and in a non-hierarchical fashion, much the way real life works, in a social sense. To address cross platform issues with other team members I have only recently began to experiment with other tools like StorySprawl [or Labyrinth [http://www.habitualindolence.net/labyrinth/] Wiki [http://wiki.org/]

has been immensely useful in the recent past for collaborative story development and I can highly recommend it as a simple and useful tool. Other tools are as varied as your imagination, even including the trusty old private web board scenario. A nice open source solution is the ArsDigita Community System [http://philip.greenspun.com/wtr/using-the-acs.html]. If you're really ambitious and have a budget you may want to look into Groove [http://www.groove.net] or Vignette (formerly StoryServer)

[http://www.vignette.com/contentmanagement/0,2097,1-1-1928-4149-1966-4150,00.html].

This is also as good a place as any to, at least arbitrarily, come up with the mechanics of your 'belief engine'. What media are utilized and how, timing, manpower needed to actualize it, etc. It's best to leave this looser than your storyline because the mechanics of your ground game need to be fluid so you can easily adapt and adjust to the dynamic landscape of 'playtime'. Good planning also recognizes the cost of over planning. Remember, you can't know it all, nor can you take into account all the circumstances that will arise once you have actual humans interacting with the abstracted user interface of your story/game. That brings me to an important point; this level is for all intents and purposes, although abstracted, the user interface to your story/game. Remember that.

Good sources of information on approaches to this part of the process include, but are not limited to:

• Video game story line and movie script writing re-
sources- stay away from 'how to get your script greenlighted"
types of guides. Look to structural guides instead.
• Multimedia story development tools and guides
• Storyboard development resources
• Human Interface, design and theory

*As in El Centro, ARGs can also be useful to float ideas for new novels in front of a
diverse audience to observe their reaction to story lines and elements.

A simple set of tools should be evaluated and chosen

It is always easier to decide on standards before you get started.
This will help you avoid a lot of snags and pitfalls during the actual
development and deployment processes. When at all possible, choose
tools that allow for some flexibility should you wish to add more team
members along the way. Lean away from proprietary or skewed solutions unless functionality absolutely dictates those proprietary solutions
are the only available option. Cross platform solutions and ease of use
should always be kept in mind when choosing tools for group use.

**A schedule should be drafted and all known elements
should be plotted, with milestones and deliverables marked inside
of this schedule**

Ok, so this element will change as things progress but it still
doesn't hurt to have a rough idea of what it will take, time-wise, to pull
off your idea. When trying to fit things into a timeline you will often
times put your ideas into a concrete enough form to be able to recog-

nize 'feature creep' or in some cases, feature absence. It's really simple. Ask yourself: "How long do I want to do this and can I do everything I've planned on doing within that timeframe". You may find that your scope is too ambitious or that you really don't have the time and energy to execute all the ideas that you threw into the early planning stages. You can then adjust the timeframe or trim the 'features' to keep your project within the boundaries of sanity and completion. Treat your product as just that, a product. This will help with focus and staying on point.

A core team should already be pre-qualified and selected

There are many ways to do this. One way is to simply hang around places like Unfiction's ARG devoted discussion forums [http://forums.unfiction.com/forums/] and quietly watch to see who rises up as cream during the course of game play in other ARGS. Or you can simply recruit a few identified PMs when another game has concluded. In the case of El Centro, we were looking for some crack PMs to have as resources during the coming year so we actually set up an ARG-like interface that was not really an ARG. Basically El Centro was a multi-pronged interface to further several causes. One of which was to set up a multi-leveled puzzle scenario that would serve as a 'survival of fittest' course so that we could find candidates that had the unique qualities that we desired in a PM. You are also free to simply use your friends.

It will of course be impossible to have your entire team built before hand, in fact you should leave enough flex room so you can add candidates along the way as gameplay itself will produce 'superusers'. Leaving yourself a little wiggle room will allow unforeseen circumstances like PMs dropping out, being voted out, or proving to be incapable, to occur without creating a cascading failure effect in your project once it is up and going.

Someone should be chosen to be the leader or leaders, which I always refer to as 'central command'

You will always have people who will object to this principle and I'm the first to admit that a decentralized approach *can* work, but more often than not, it *doesn't*. This will also derail any power struggles that may arise later during the critical period of gameplay. Get it out of the way early. This is often simple because the original storyline is usually the product of one or several minds. Pick one or several flag bearers of the vision and allocate final approval or veto power to these people. There's nothing wrong with taking a democratic approach such as voting or debate but remember that there will always be times when a quick decision is needed and when that time arises, someone must be mandated to make those decisions. I am reminded of a feature film I crewed on. Feature film production is somewhat similar in nature to an ARG project, actually. The director was asked if this wasn't in fact a democracy, with all of the crew, from the grips to the production designer, to the actors to the director having some say in how things get done. He replied: "Sure, I'm open to suggestions. I guess this is a democracy up until the point that I have to say no to something." Yes, I laughed too. Later when I went on to direct some music video projects on my own, I really understood what he was saying. A film project or an ARG is more like running an aircraft carrier than it is like living on a commune.

It helps for projects larger in scope to have teams and therefore team leaders that report to 'central command'

Depending on the size and scope of your project, a hierarchical structure may be appropriate. Keep in mind that groups will *naturally* fall into pyramidical structures, with some taking lead, others taking more of a follow posture. Those that float to the top of these natural settlings may be useful as mid-tier leaders and can even be useful as agents to recruit later during play. The command structure does not have to be rigid or cut off. It often helps to have an 'ear to the ground' so to speak, so keep mid-tier recruitment in mind as an option. If you ever played any of the Steve Jackson games or Flying Buffalo games, you already understand this principle.

In summation, I cannot stress enough that planning a framework for true and open collaboration may seem like a contradiction in terms, but it clearly is not. Some preliminary planning and construction of a workflow environment is integral to having a productive collaborative experience. Don't be afraid to plan but also keep in mind that as you progress and learn you will need to adjust and adapt. Building a framework allows for both while also providing a working space from which to launch a killer user experience.

When faced with a challenge or dilemma, just remember: "Something's staring you straight in the face."

Appendix G: A Sample Alternate Reality Game – Errant Memories

By Dave Szulborski

Since one of the main purposes in my writing This Is Not A Game is to provide an entry-level introduction to alternate reality games, I decided to create a small, self-contained sample game to serve as both a "hands on" exercise for newcomers, and as an example of the potential marketing uses of Alternate Reality Gaming. Additionally, in keeping with the spirit and secretive nature of ARGs, the game also serves a third purpose, but you'll have to work your way through the puzzle trail to discover it! For those who do, there awaits yet one more layer of mystery and surprise to this book, which I think will make the whole exercise worthwhile, over and above its inherent value as a sample alternate reality game.

Because it is intended to introduce absolute newcomers to some of the basic theories, techniques, and game play in ARGs, I decided to create the content of the game from references and allusions to past alternate reality games. What better way to introduce new fans of the genre to the diversity and creativity embodied by this form of gaming than to guide them through a little history lesson of finished ARGs, in a way that requires and motivates them to learn what those games were all about. Hopefully, this same aspect of the sample game will also provide experienced ARG fans with a fun and nostalgic glance at the games they have enjoyed over the last few years, as they work their way through to the secret about <u>This Is Not A Game</u> that lies at the end.

<u>The Structure of the Game</u>

Before I begin a walkthrough of the game itself, I'd like to comment on the structure of this sample ARG. First, this little exercise in no way does justice to the depth, complexity, and immersive ability of the average alternate reality game. In fact, because the game had to be very limited in length for a variety of reasons, not the least of which being a fear of completely losing or overwhelming the very newcomer it is intended for, the normal elements of character development and a dramatic plot are virtually non-existent. There was just no way to include any effective characterization or storyline, so the sample game instead focuses on presenting examples of some of the different puzzle styles, interaction methods, and mystery solving processes involved in a typical ARG. It also illustrates how Puppetmasters can find inspiration for story and puzzle elements in history and literature, as well as how interest can be both generated and sustained for a small, independently-produced project. Finally, because the sample game needs to stand on its own for an indefinite length of time to act as a resource for the book,

I also could not integrate any actual real-time interaction into the game. Most ARGs include at least some form of real-time interaction, such as online Instant Messaging chats or even live telephone calls.

As I mentioned, I also intended this mini-game to serve as a real-life example of the marketing potential of even a modest ARG project like this. To achieve this, I actually launched and ran the game in real-time in the weeks preceding the release of the electronic versions of the book. While this was not a serious part of the marketing of This Is Not A Game, it does serve as a small but effective illustration of the *buzz* and viral attention a clever alternate reality campaign can generate. A brief summary of the game from a marketing perspective follows the game guide below.

Whatever real-time elements there were in the game have been replaced with automated responses in most cases for the purposes of the sample game, now that the book has been released. Other than that, the game is pretty much as it was in its brief but exciting run for readers of this book to explore.

The Structure of the Guide

The following guide is a simple walkthrough for the sample ARG I've nicknamed **Errant Memories**. For each "step" of the game, there is a description of the web page or puzzle that makes up the step, as well as a section describing how to solve this portion of the mystery.

Readers who just want to get an appreciation and basic understanding of an alternate reality game without actually playing one can read straight through the guide and see how the pieces come together. If you want to try and work your way through the game and its puzzles yourself, stop when you get to the part for each step that says "**The Solve**." See if you can figure out where to go or what to do next, before reading the solutions or the hints that sometimes precede them. Speaking of hints, here are just a couple general ones to help the absolute newcomer get started.

1) A common method of solving a puzzle on an in-game website is to type in the solution of the puzzle as the name for a new web page on the site and see if it works. In other words, if a particular puzzle yields the word *firefly*, the next step of the trail might be located at http://www.website.com/firefly.html (or just .htm). That's always a good place to start if you've solved a puzzle and don't know what to do with the result.

2) Puppetmasters often hide things on web pages in their in-game sites. One simple technique to check for hidden text or links on a web page is to use the "edit/select all" feature available from most Internet browser toolbars. This will usually highlight any hidden text or tiny links on the page. Additionally, you can also use the browser toolbar to view the source of the web page as an html document. This will display the html code of the page in a text format, sometimes revealing hidden text or comments

that have been placed there by sneaky PMs.

Google is your friend. If you come across anything you don't understand or recognize, try searching for it on the Internet. Single words, entire text passages, even pictures, can be searched for on the web. Most of you probably know how to search for single words and short phrases already, but you can also input entire sentences and longer passages into certain search engines as well. Sometimes, this will help locate the exact source of a quote or text portion of a puzzle you are working on. Also, Google is great for searching for images too, as they have a separate feature of their search engine especially for that. Start by searching for the file name of the image; the Puppetmasters may have forgotten to change the name before using it, and you may be able to find its source that way. Or, they may have deliberately chosen a file name that is itself a clue. Finally, you can also search for the image by merely describing it in the search box. If the picture is a man on a horse, type that in and check out the results.

The Guide to **Errant Memories** – a sample alternate reality game

Our sample ARG begins at the website http://www.errantmemory.com/, but the rabbit hole or trailhead can actually be found at Google (www.google.com). In keeping with the TINAG philosophy and in order to show how even one small clue can launch an ARG campaign, I created a Google Adwords ad that was triggered by words and phrases I thought people interested in Alternate

Reality Gaming might possibly search for. For those who don't know, Google Adwords ads are the small, two line ads that appear to the right on the search result pages of Google, triggered by key words you select when you set up the ad. They are fairly inexpensive if done properly and can quickly and easily guide people to material you want them to see. The keywords I used included the obvious things like arg, alternate reality games, and immersive gaming, as well as the names from a few past games, like **I Love Bees** and **Chasing The Wish**. It wasn't long before the mysterious ad I created was noticed and posted to an ARG community board, and **Errant Memories** was off and running.

<u>Step 1: Mysterious Ad Found on Google</u>

Now, imagine you have just heard about this strange thing called alternate reality gaming and want to know more about it. Or perhaps you are just an average, experienced ARG'er going through your normal Internet search routine looking for anything even vaguely related to Alternate Reality Gaming. Go to http://www.google.com and type in one of the following phrases: arg, alternate reality game, i love bees, or chasing the wish. On the results page that Google gives you, you should see a small ad to the right that says:

> <u>and yet</u>
> i remember
> what are these errant memories?
> http://www.errantmemory.com

Hmm, interesting. Most ads you've seen there before on Google seem to be selling something and this one doesn't. Plus, it seems strange that it appeared from your ARG-related search. So go ahead, click on it or merely type in the address, http://www.errantmemory.com.

Step 2: What Are These Errant Memories?

At http://www.errantmemory.com you are greeted by some rather dramatic music and a Macromedia Flash format movie that opens with the following words, dynamically moving or fading in and out:

what . . . am i?

bits of data

sequences of numbers

and yet . . . i remember

what are these . . . errant memories?

The words are followed by a series of pictures, interspersed with strange boxes containing numbers and dots, looking vaguely domino-like. So the obvious questions are - are these images and numbers the "errant memories," and what exactly are they supposed to represent?

Hint: Start by trying to identify the images. Write down a list of who or what they might possibly be and be sure to list possible alternatives, in case your first hunch isn't quite correct.

Dave Szulborski

Hint: Research the term "errant memory" to help put any future discoveries in perspective.

The Solve: The series of images provides the key for solving the puzzle on the page. The list of images, interpreted correctly, should look like this:

Moon

Elvis

Martin Luther King

O J Simpson

Rabbit (from the namesake of the movie **Harvey**)

Ichabod Crane (Johnny Depp role in the picture)

Atomic bomb

Tupac Shakur

Eliot, T. S.

Christ (or crucifixion)

Homer

Neuromancer (a book by William Gibson)

It's A Wonderful Life (the movie)

Constitution

Alcatraz

By writing out this list, you should notice that the first letter of every line spells out the phrase "memoria technica," which sure seems possibly related to the memory theme of the site. Typing in http://www.errantmemory.com/memoriatechnica.html, you discover a new web page.

Step 3: Memoria Technica

The new web page is filled with a repeating image that you may recognize as being from an edition of Lewis Carroll's <u>Alice in Wonderland</u>. Look carefully and you may see something flash on the screen before the image totally appears.

Hint: If you are observant, you may see a table of letters and numbers flash on the screen before it is lost in the background of the image.

Hint: Try Googling the term "memoria technica" and look pretty thoroughly for anything that seems related.

The Solve: "Memoria Technica," it turns out, is a memory tool or system developed by Lewis Carroll, which uses a table of numbers and letters to turn numbers into words and make them easier to remember. The table on the web page that is obscured by the image is Carroll's memory aid table. If necessary, use the "select all" browser trick to help you see the table. Hopefully, you'll notice that the boxes that make up the memory matrix appear similar to the number boxes on the earlier page. Go back to the first page and see if you can figure out the connection.

1	2	3	4	5	6	7	8	9	0
b	d	t	f	l	s	p	h	n	z
c	w	j	q	v	x	m	k	g	r

The Memoria Technica memory matrix:

PM Notes: This step is a good example of finding inspiration for ARG content in history and literature, as I first discovered Carroll's *Memoria Technica* while researching the many different puzzle forms Carroll, an avid fan of puzzles of all sorts, developed during his life. It seemed a perfect fit for this mini-ARG, which is themed around memory and past alternate reality games. You may remember that I cited Carroll's <u>Alice in Wonderland</u> earlier as both the source of the term *rabbit hole*, as well as a general inspiration for the entire genre of Alternate Reality Gaming.

Step 4: Decoding the Message

Back at http://www.errantmemory.com/, write down the sequence of number boxes and numbers this time and try to use Carroll's Memoria Technica to help you decode the message.

Hint: The single numbers in the sequence, the ones not in the domino-style boxes, don't need to be put through the memory matrix, and instead have a much simpler translation.

The Solve: For each number box, refer to the corresponding column in Carroll's memory matrix. If the dot is in the box right below the number, than use the letter in that position in the matrix. Likewise, if the dot is in the bottom square of the column, use the letter there instead. You'll notice the entire memory grid contains consonants only; that is where the single numbers in the sequence come in. The single numbers not in boxes are the vowels, and represent their simple alphanumeric equivalent; in other words, 1=a, 5=e, etc. Using that method yields the phrase *the secret portal*. Type in and go to http://www.errantmemory.com/thesecretportal.html.

Step 5: The Secret Portal

The next page looks simple; it is a solid black page with only seven words. They are: *to book lie queue no daze been.*

Hint: Don't forget what has come before.

The Solve: If you researched the *Memoria Technica* at all, you'll realize that the previous step actually used Lewis Carroll's encryption method in reverse. As I mentioned, Carroll used the system to turn numbers or dates into words to make them easier to remember. For example, the number 492 could be encrypted as *found*, using the *f* from the 4 column, the *n* from the 9 column, and the *d* from the 2 column (you ignore the vowels). The words on the page - *to book lie queue no daze been* – have been encrypted the same way, so you can ignore the vowels and just figure out the number equivalents. With the vowels it looks like this - *3o 1oo8 5ie 4ueue 9o 2a0e 1ee9*. Remove them and you get this number sequence – 3 1 8 5 4 9 2 0 1 9. Since the Memoria Technica involves turning numbers into letters, let's do that one more time, this time using the standard alphanumeric substitution method of a=1, b=2, etc. After a little trial and error, the correct combination of numbers – 3 18 5 4 9 20 19 – translates to *credits*. Type in and go to the new web page at http://www.errantmemory.com/credits.html.

PM Notes: The name of this page, *the secret portal*, is a somewhat obvious reference to the rabbit hole that begins every alternate reality game. This step also shows how the same encryption technique can be used in different ways to produce multiple puzzles, as both this and the previous step encoded a message using Carroll's memory matrix in a slightly different manner. Finally, this step quite deliberately included a strong *red herring*, or false lead. I chose and juxtaposed the words *lie queue* specifically to lead some players to believe that the solution might be in sounding out the words; e.g., *lie queue* can be sounded out as *like you*.

Step 6: The EOIO Page

The new page, http://www.errantmemory.com/credits.html, is another black page, this time with a single image on it. The picture is composed of two elements: a repeating series of letters, *E O I O*, that fill up the entire space of the image, and solid white rectangles and other shapes in a single line across the center.

Hint: Once again, it sometimes helps to remember the puzzles and steps that you have already seen. Since the repeating series of letters is all vowels and the Memoria Technica puzzles separate consonants and vowels, maybe the other set of pieces, the rectangles and other white shapes, are the consonants.

The Solve: The white shapes are indeed the consonants of a hidden word, while the repeating letters are the vowels of the same word. The consonants, however, have been "disassembled" into pieces. The first three letters are all comprised of two pieces each, and can be fit together to form an X, a P, and an L. The next letter requires the following three white shapes and assembles into an S. And finally, the last three white shapes also belong together and make up an N. That yields the consonants X, P, L, S, and N. Combine those with the vowels to get the word *EXPLOSION*. By now you should know where to go next – http://www.errantmemory.com/explosion.html.

PM Notes: The title of this page and the following one, credits and explosion respectively, are the first vague nods towards previous alternate reality games. Set up by the use of the *secret portal* phrase to reference ARG rabbit holes, these two pages are the first of several pages that are named after some part of the rabbit hole from past games. *Credits* refers to the clues found in the credits of **the Beast**, and *explosion* is alluding to the explosion at Anim-X Studios that helped launch the Electronic Arts' alternate reality game, **Majestic**.

Step 7: The Explosion Page

Another simple looking page waits the adventurous player at http://www.errantmemory.com/explosion.html. All that is there is one long set of letters – frejusseikanfolgefonnlaerdalromeriksporten-severomuyskiy. It is either in a foreign language or possibly encrypted or anagrammed in some way.

Hint: Remember the earlier advice about different search techniques and how you can search for longer phrases or parts of text passages.

The Solve: This long phrase is merely a combination of different words, run together as one long string. They are actually the names of tunnels around the world – Frejus, Seikan, Folgefonn, Laerdal,

Romerik-Sporten, and Severomuyskiy. The solve to the puzzle is *tunnels*, so the next step is at http://www.errantmemory.com/tunnels.html.

PM Notes: *Tunnels* is, of course, another reference to a completed ARG. This time it is **Lockjaw**, a game that began in the tunnels below Washington, D.C.

Step 8: Going Deeper

The *tunnels* page at least appears different from the earlier ones, as it is entirely white.

Hint: A blank page doesn't make much sense in a puzzle trail like this. Perhaps there is something hidden on the page.

The Solve: Using any of the techniques to find hidden material on a web page should reveal quite a bit of hidden text. This is actually the html code of a web page and, when displayed in an Internet browser, reveals a piece of ASCII art in the image of a car. ASCII art is art composed entirely of text, either letters or numbers or both. Proceed to http://www.errantmemory.com/car.html.

PM Notes: The car is a BMW and is a nod to a completed commercial ARG nicknamed **:k:**, done to promote BMW cars. The ARG began with a series of short films featuring a BMW car.

Step 9: Too Many Windows

The next puzzle is another single image on a black background. The only thing unusual about the image is that some of the windows of the building in the picture trigger the mouse pointer, as if they were links, but they don't seem to actually go anywhere.

Hint: When lost, a good place to begin is by looking at any possible patterns on the web page you are looking at.

The Solve: There is indeed a pattern to which windows appear to be false links and which ones don't. The fact that the windows appear in sets of four is a hint as to how the message is hidden within. Write down a list of the windows, starting at the upper left and working across and down the building, as you would if reading a document, using 0's to represent the windows that don't trigger the mouse and 1's to indicate those that do. The sequence of 1's and 0's should look like this: 01110111011010010111001101101000. Putting this through a binary translator, such as the one at this web page:

http://nickciske.com/tools/binary.php

will reveal the secret message - *wish*.

PM Notes: *Wish* is a nod to one of my games, **Chasing The Wish**, which began when one of the characters made a wish with disastrous results. The technique used for this step, binary encryption, is quite common in alternate reality games and should be obvious when you see a pattern of 1's and 0's.

Step 10: Go Forth and . . .

At http://www.errantmemory.com/wish.html, you find another single image on a black page. The image has a rather strange name – goforthand.jpg, which can be seen if you view the source of the web page.

Hint: Try and figure out why the image is named the way it is.

The Solve: This puzzle requires either a little basic knowledge of mathematics or deciphering the hint of the image name to solve it. The name of the image file, "goforthand," is the start of a famous phrase, "Go forth and multiply." It is intended to guide you to the possible source of the image, mathematics, or, more specifically, multiplication. The image is a picture of a multiplication matrix, and the solution to the puzzle is *matrix*.

PM Notes: The alternate reality game **MetaCortechs** was set in the fictional world of **the Matrix** films, and this connection served as the rabbit hole for the game.

Step 11: Hidden

At http://www.errantmemory.com/matrix.html you find another apparently blank page.

Hint: Use the techniques you already know.

The Solve: Use "select all" to reveal the words hidden on the page. Actually, it is only one word – *text* – repeated many times, back to back. The rather simple solution to this puzzle is *hidden text*.

PM Notes: *Hidden text* refers to the entry point for the 2004 ARG, **I Love Bees**. The game kicked into gear when players found text hidden within the images on the main website, http://www.ilovebees.com. This step completes the "rabbit hole" series of web pages referring to past alternate reality games.

Step 12: Finally, Contact?

The new page that you find at :
http://www.errantmemory.com/hiddentext.html
yields an e-mail address, the first concrete method for trying to contact whomever (or whatever) might be responsible for the website. So, what are you waiting for? E-mail it!

PM Notes: E-mail addresses are often the main source of player / character interaction in ARGs. Some players set up separate e-mail addresses specifically for corresponding with one particular game, to make it easier for them to separate and monitor all the messages from the game.

Step 13: The Puzzling Response

If you write to the e-mail address provided, you are rewarded with a short but nonetheless puzzling response. It says:

and yet

i remember

a set of two similar things

considered as a unit

free from risk or danger

a small quantity

attractive especially by means of smallness or prettiness or quaintness

a strip of land projecting into a body of water

Hint: These appear to be attempts at defining certain things.

Hint: Remember, when stumped, to return to what has come before.

The Solve: These phrases are all exact definitions from an online dictionary and, with a little work, will deliver the following word list – *pair*, *safe*, *bit*, *cute*, and *cape*. Putting these words through Lewis Carroll's Memoria Technica grid results in this sequence of numbers – 7064131317. Quite often, if an ARG puzzle ends in a ten-digit number, the number is actually a telephone number, and this is no exception. If you feel adventurous, call the number (706) 413-1317.

Step 14: The Voicemail Recording

There is a robotic-sounding voice at the other end of the phone number, with the following message:

> *what am i? bits of data. sequences of numbers.*
>
> *and yet, i remember.*
>
> *yes, i remember.*
>
> *i remember*
>
> *another place.*
>
> *lights flashing, on, and off.*
>
> *threads, i can not follow.*
>
> *endings, that do not end.*
>
> *running, yet, never moving.*
>
> *entering, yet, never leaving.*
>
> *dying, yet, never living.*
>
> *yes, i remember.*

Hint: Try and transcribe, or write down, the message. Being actually able to look at something can sometimes help you find hidden patterns and meanings.

The Solve: If you separate the new, non-repeated text from the phone message, it leaves you with these lines.

> *another place.*
>
> *lights flashing, on, and off.*
>
> *threads, i can not follow.*
>
> *endings, that do not end.*
>
> *running, yet, never moving.*

entering, yet, never leaving.
dying, yet, never living.

Again, look at the first letter of each line – they spell out the word *altered.*

PM Notes: I deliberately chose a fairly non-sophisticated text-to-speech software program to produce the robotic-sounding voice for the phone mail message. One of the main themes both in this mini-game and in quite a few completed ARGs is *artificial intelligence* or *AI*. In fact, many past games have had AI entities as characters in the game. So using a robotic-sounding voice seemed perfect, as it conveyed or confirmed the impression that the "person" behind the **Errant Memory** site might be an AI and not a real person.

Step 15: Altered

Returning to the website, type in and go to the web page http://www.errantmemory.com/altered.html. A strange, circular image dominates the page. It appears to be a picture of books but distorted somehow to make the titles and other information virtually unreadable.

Hint: Look at the picture very carefully for anything you may be able to make out despite the distortion.

The Solve: The image has been distorted by a means called *anamorphing*, a process by which an image is made to appear as if it is

being reflected in a curved, conical surface. There are software programs available that would allow you to remove the distortion and view
the original image, but it is not really necessary. You should be able to
read two sets of numbers from the books with white spines at the upper
right hand portion of the image. Those numbers are 0-486-26922-1 and
0-486-28861-7, and are what are called ISBN numbers, the numbers
used to register and identify book titles. By entering these numbers in a
search service like Google, you can discover that they belong to the
books <u>Lewis Carroll's Games and Puzzles</u> and <u>Rediscovered Lewis
Carroll Puzzles</u>, respectively.

There is still something hidden on the altered web page you
need to complete this step. Use "view source" to read the following
hidden text:

> <!--51
> where h meets h you'll find an o
> should you count it? the answer's no
> the first isn't far away
> just two steps north, you're on your way
> this one counts so write it down
> next go twelve steps right and six steps down
> that's the second, it counts as well
> now take three steps towards the letter l
> don't use this one, just change direction
> three steps south is your third selection

from there go to the very top

don't write it down, no don't stop

but three spaces right is what you need

you should have four now to proceed

the fifth one lies somewhere below

where the column crosses the sixteenth row

the next to the last is five steps right

that should make six, the seventh's in sight

it's seven spaces in one direction

but you must make this last selection>

The "51" refers to page 51 in the book, Lewis Carroll's Games and Puzzles, which features a grid of letters that are part of what is known as the "Alphabet Cipher." The rest of the riddle text above guides you through the alphabetic grid and should yield the word *meeting*.

PM Notes: It's always fun to return to themes, encryption techniques, and events from earlier in the ARG. This step brings us back to Lewis Carroll and his many different puzzle creation methods. It also introduces players to the concept of ISBN numbers, often used as clues within alternate reality games. Finally, not coincidentally, page 60 of the other Lewis Carroll book shown in the image, Rediscovered Lewis Carroll Puzzles, contains a description and examples of his Memoria Technica method.

<u>Step 16: Meeting</u>

During the course of the real-time **Errant Memory** game, this web page actually consisted of a series of Macromedia Flash movies that were updated gradually over a period of about a week. It started with one movie and, as each new one was added, a small circular colored dot was added to the page, linking to the earlier movies. The web page also had the words "it is almost time" above the Flash movies until all nine movies were posted. Once all nine movies had been seen, the words disappeared, leaving only the table of nine colored dots, each linked to a different movie, as it appears now.

Hint: try to identify the source of the words or the images used in the Flash movies.

Hint: As always, remember what has come before.

The Solve: Each of the nine Flash movies reference and use material from previous alternate reality games. They are, in the order they appear in the table on the web page:

Top row: **Project Gateway, Lockjaw, Aware, Chasing The Wish,** and **Exocog.**

Bottom row: **The Beast, I Love Bees, MetaCortechs,** and **Errant Memories.**

Once again, take the first letter of each game title to get *place* across the top row and *time* across the bottom. Both of these are solutions to this page and, of course, relate back to the title of the page itself, *meeting*.

PM Notes: This is an example of what I called a *delayed puzzle*. That simply means that the players do not get all the information or pieces they need to solve the overall puzzle at one time. Instead, the clues are delivered spread out over a brief period of time. This serves two purposes in an ARG. First, it allows the Puppetmasters to regulate the flow of the game. In this case, I needed to wait until a certain date to allow players to reach the end and this delayed delivery of the pieces of the puzzle prevented the players from solving the puzzle too early. Second, presenting a puzzle like this requires players to keep returning to a certain web page or set of pages, creating sustained interest in those particular pages, and a sense of building tension as the players wait impatiently to figure the whole puzzle out.

Step 17: The "Place" Puzzle

At http://www.errantmemory.com/place.html you are greeted with a quote from Lewis Carroll. The exact text says, "If you don't know where you are going, you'll probably end up somewhere else. Lewis Carroll." Beneath that are what appears to be dates, as follows - 1970, 1983, 1939, 2004, 2003, 2002, 1992, 1978, 1997, 1990, 1941, 1957, 1984, and 1958.

Hint: Don't forget to check for possible hidden elements on the page.

The Solve: Below the dates on the page the words "years in the past" are hidden. This line is intended to hint at the fact that the dates are only starting points, and what you really need is the number of years in the past each date occurred. In other words, the first date of 1970 was 35 years in the past, and so on. Do that for each date to get this list of numbers – 35, 22, 66, 1, 2, 3, 13, 27, 8, 15, 64, 48, 21, and 47.

Now take those numbers and pull out the letter from the quote above corresponding to each number. For example, the number 1 would yield an "i" from the quote. You have to count Lewis Carroll's name as part of the quote. Translating all the numbers by this method gives you the words *pacify, win, his,* and *up.* Unfortunately, there don't appear to be any new web pages using those names.

Put those words through the Carroll Memoria Technica matrix and the number 71429867 is your reward. Again though, there's no web page named 71429867.html, so you must not be quite done. Take heart though, there's only one more conversion to go. Write these numbers out, one per line, on a piece of paper like this:

Seven

One

Four

Two

Nine

Eight

Six

Seven

By now your eyes should go right to the word formed by the first letter of each line – *softness*. And finally, there's a new web page waiting at http://www.errantmemory.com/softness.html. This appears to be where the "meeting" will take place.

PM Notes: I actually discovered after I had created this step that the quote above was misattributed on the web page where I originally found it. It is actually a variation on a Lewis Carroll quote but this actual version was said by Yogi Berra. The puzzle's solve, however, relied on leaving the Lewis Carroll name in there so it was too late to change it. In retrospect, since the concept of the game was that some form of AI was learning by searching the Internet, it could logically be explained away that the AI found and used the same mistaken material I did.

<u>Step 18: The "Time" Puzzle</u>

The page at http://www.errantmemory.com/time.html, of course, contains yet another puzzle. Here it is:

not night - _ _ _

the ____ *about bees* - _ _ _ _

unusual - _ _ _ _

rush - _ _ _ _

lab rat's home - _ _ _ _

fret - _ _ _ _ _

compete - _ _ _

****

closest - _ _ _ _ _ _ _

**

make smooth - _ _ _ _

missile - _ _ _ _

**

unit - _ _ _ _

This Is Not A Game

All of the text below the long line of asterisks is yellow, opposed to the white text above.

Hint: More definitions? Fill in the blanks? Use the number of spaces to help determine the right choice where multiple answers might exist.

The Solve: These are basically definitions or descriptive words and phrases and the solutions are:

not night – day

the _____ about bees – buzz

unusual – rare

rush – race

lab rat's home – cage

fret – worry

compete – vie

****

closest – nearest

**

371

make smooth – sand

missile – dart

**

unit – item

The compiled list above the long asterisk line is day, buzz, rare, race, cage, worry, and vie, and below is nearest, sand, dart, and item. The two lists need to be solved differently, hence their obvious separation on the page. The top part is solved by returning to Lewis Carroll's Memoria Technica, which yields the following numbers from the first list of words – 21000001192005. In keeping with the name of this page, *time*, these numbers should be identifiable as a time and date if separated like this – 21:00:00, 01/19/2005, or 9:00 PM, January 19th, 2005.

The bottom words are anagrams and need to be grouped according to the smaller asterisk lines separating them. The first word, nearest, becomes *eastern*, the next two words, sand and dart, combine and transform into *standard*, and the last word, item, becomes *time*. So the complete solve is 9:00 PM eastern standard time, January 19th, 2005, which is when the real-time ending occurred when the game first ran, as the truth behind the purpose of the game was revealed to the players.

Step 19: The Finale

On January 19th, 2005 at the given time of 9:00 PM EST, the web page at http://www.errantmemory.com/softness.html changed and revealed the truth about the **Errant Memories** game. If this had been a real, ongoing ARG I would have used this time and date to take the game to the next level by introducing real-time interaction with the person (or AI) behind the website. In cases where you use a series of puzzles or a single puzzle with involved, multiple steps without any real intermediate rewards for the players, you normally want to be sure and incorporate a major change to the game play or plot line as a reward for the prolonged puzzle sequence. Without pay-offs or rewards such as this, players can easily decide that it is not worth their effort to actually try and solve the puzzles or mysteries within the game.

Since you are reading this guide and already know the truth behind the creator and purpose of this game, I am not going to repeat the information here from the final page, http://www.errantmemory.com/softness.html. You can go there and read it if you want anyway. I am also not going to reveal here the third purpose of this sample ARG that I alluded to in the beginning of this Appendix. As I said, that information can also be found at softness.html web page and is the real reward for solving the **Errant Memories** game. Not all the mysteries of <u>This Is Not A Game</u> have been revealed yet and you may be the first one to uncover them all!

<u>Errant Memories</u> – A Marketing Perspective

As mentioned in the Chapter discussing the current and possible future state of Alternate Reality Gaming, there are more major companies using ARGs in professional and sustained marketing campaigns than ever before. Unfortunately, many ad agencies and marketing professionals still don't understand the incredible potential of alternate reality or immersive gaming, and some even have an almost instinctual and irrational fear of anything named a "game." Hopefully, the successful and highly-visible use of ARGs by companies such as Microsoft and Sony will go a long way in helping establish the genre as a serious marketing venue.

In a modest way, this sample game, **Errant Memories**, is a good example of the excitement and viral attention even a small but carefully planned ARG can generate. The game was launched with a Google Adwords ad which, in the two weeks it ran prior to the electronic edition release of This Is Not A Game, generated over 350,000 impressions, meaning the ad was viewed that many times, for a total cost well below $50. I created all of the content for the game in less than a week's total time and monitored it fairly actively for the two week live run period. Altogether I probably put 50 to 60 man-hours into the project.

In the two weeks the game ran live it spawned separate discussion threads on at least four different ARG or gaming-related community forums and multiple news items stories on various websites. Despite being limited in plot, character development, real-time interaction and length, it quickly became the most actively discussed and followed topic on at least two of these forums. In addition, the IRC chat channels that players established to help them follow the game also became some of the busiest channels related to ARGs during the game's limited run.

Here is a brief list of some of the coverage of the very short game:

http://www.metafilter.com/mefi/38512

http://www.smartmobs.com/archive/2005/01/11/this_is_not_a_g.html

http://www.bungie.net/Forums/posts.aspx?postID=1689385&viewreplies= true&postRepeater1-p=1

http://forums.unfiction.com/forums/viewtopic.php?t=8650

http://digital-falcon.com/index.shtml (Wednesday, January 12, 2005)

http://blog.hobbits.org.uk/wordpress/ (Tuesday, January 11, 2005)

http://www.deaddrop.us/modules.php?name=News&file=article&sid=203

http://www.forum.immersionunlimited.com/viewforum.php?f=58&sid=67 b0024439dabf9425a61a026ab5888f (almost 800 posts in less than two weeks)

http://indeeeeeed.stumbleupon.com/

http://evilcabeza.net/ (Saturday, January 15, 2005)

Besides generating interest in the game itself, **Errant Memories** was also designed to increase awareness of and interest in the book, This Is Not A Game, at least for purposes of this marketing example. As such, it was designed, promoted, and implemented in such a way as to attract both absolute newcomers to the genre and experienced ARG players as well. By drawing newcomers into the game and giving them a glimpse of the fascinating and diverse world of Alternate Reality Gaming, I presented This Is Not A Game as a valuable resource for learning more about ARGs and positioned it as the logical next step for those who want to get more involved.

Finally, by using the **Errant Memories** game as a means by which an unrevealed secret about the book is first exposed, I've made the entire game exercise a potentially rewarding experience for the player as well, something both unique and potentially very powerful in the worlds of advertising and marketing as well. Although other forms of ads and marketing are obviously successful components of multi-million dollar professional promotional campaigns, very rarely do the ads or marketing devices themselves attract attention to themselves by offering a real incentive for watching or even participating with them. The "secret" knowledge at the end of the **Errant Memories** game provides motivation for the potential audience to want to pay attention to the web sites and other assets of the production, in marked contrast to the reaction most people have to other forms of advertising and marketing. In the same way, the real world ARG marketing campaign of **I Love Bees** motivated thousands of people to avidly pay attention to and actively interact with what was essentially a three month long advertisement for the video game **Halo 2**.

Seen in its limited context, the **Errant Memories** sample alternate reality game clearly illustrates the same unique and powerful marketing potential that **I Love Bees** captured so well, and that is possible with a well-designed ARG.

Printed in the United States
73868LV00006B/57